CITY OF NIGHT BIRDS

ALSO BY JUHEA KIM

Beasts of a Little Land

CITY OF NIGHT BIRDS

A NOVEL

JUHEA KIM

ecco
An Imprint of HarperCollins*Publishers*

HarperCollins books may be purchased for educational, business, or sales promotional use. For information, please email the Special Markets Department at SPsales@harpercollins.com.

FIRST EDITION

Designed by Alison Bloomer

Library of Congress Cataloging-in-Publication Data has been applied for.

ISBN 978-0-06-339475-9

24 25 26 27 28 LBC 5 4 3 2 1

To my readers

And in loving memory of my grandfather

Kim SuKyung (1925–1994)

CITY OF NIGHT BIRDS

OVERTURE

Call me a sinner,
Mock me maliciously:
I was your insomnia,
I was your grief.
—ANNA AKHMATOVA,
"I HAVEN'T COVERED THE LITTLE WINDOW" (1916)

And it seemed to me those fires
Were about me till dawn.
And I never learnt—
The colour of those eyes.
Everything was trembling, singing;
Were you my friend or enemy,
And winter was it, or summer?
—ANNA AKHMATOVA, "FRAGMENT" (1959)

I FILL MY CUP WITH VODKA. IT TASTES OF THE STRANGE LONGING PECUliar to flying into one's old city at midnight.

Outside the rounded window of the plane, the lights of St. Petersburg glimmer through the clouds. I remember then that it is the White Nights. Descending from the gray heights, the earth looks more like the night sky than the sky itself, and I have the brief sensation of falling toward a star field. I close my eyes, breathe, and reopen them slowly. The city is utterly familiar and unknown at the same time, like the face of someone you used to love.

Say you run into this person by chance, at a park or on the lobby staircase between the orchestra and the parterre, with a glass of champagne you bought in a hurry during intermission. You're going up; your lover is going down. You recognize him not by his features, which have changed, but by his expression. You're splintered by doubt that this couldn't be him, yet in the next moment you accept that this could be no one else. You take measure of his body, while wondering how you look—your makeup, hair, heavy rings and earrings that you remembered at the last minute of getting dressed, and for which you're now grateful. You still haven't made up your mind whether to meet his eyes, to be coldly indifferent, to smile, or to say something, when you pass by each other on the worn marble staircase and the bell rings to announce the end of intermission. It's already over in less time than it takes for the champagne to lose its effervescence.

"Your seat belt."

A flight attendant stands in the aisle and glares at me until I buckle up, gather the empty mini bottles of vodka, and drop them into her plastic bag. Earlier, one of the other attendants had asked for my autograph, and I'd declined. "You're really not Natalia Leonova?" She'd questioned once more before going back to the clutch of her colleagues standing near the kitchen area. After that, all the attendants pointedly ignored me, as if slighting one of them meant slighting the entire crew. I close my eyes to their sidelong glances and see the faces of those I left in this city.

When the plane lands, my reveries cease. All I can think of is hiding where no one—other than myself—thinks I'm a horrible person.

I check into the Grand Korsakov, my usual hotel off Nevsky Prospekt. Although the view from the balcony is the best in Piter, I pull my curtains shut against the White Night. On the coffee table, there is a bottle of Veuve Clicquot, a vase filled with twenty-five cream-colored roses, and a card that says, WELCOME BACK, MLLE NATALIA. For a brief moment I wonder about the sender, but the hotel logo on the card lets me know the manager, Igor Petrenko, must have been more than usually excited to see my name in the reservations. No one else knows I'm here. I take off my clothes, open the champagne, and bring it to bed with my pills. I've always enjoyed the sensation of sliding my legs into fresh sheets, and it is the one comfort I relish even now; but that solace turns quickly to disgust that not much else is left. To forget this fact, I put a Xanax on my tongue and drink from the bottle. When the fizziness floods my mouth, my nerves dull and I feel everything less—my stupidity, my heart, my ankles held together by threadbare tendons.

The sky glows all night like candlelight. Curtains do little to shield the restless violet. After tossing and turning, my eyes open when the room fully brightens. Evidently I've slept in—it is four in the afternoon. An involuntary groan escapes my mouth as I slowly swing my legs out of bed. Although I haven't danced in almost two years, my feet ache like an old woman's when they first land on the floor after waking up. I limp to the shower, leave the light off, and stand still under the hot water. It restores my energy enough that I decide to venture outside. But not enough that I can face Mama.

I slip out of the marble lobby without running into the manager. Summer air in Piter is thicker and sweeter than that in winter—like ice cream compared to iced coffee. It is filled with the scent of flowers, the molecules of water evaporating from the canals, and the orbs of pearly light between the Neva and the sky. People are walking in groups, taking photos and laughing, all their movements slackened as in a slow-motion video, which happens on sun-dappled days in cold countries.

I stop by a café and order a cappuccino to go. Then I walk west along Nevsky Prospekt until it reaches the Neva, flowing lapis blue like the robes of the Virgin in an icon. To the river's right, the lilacs are in full bloom in the Field of Mars. I once spent one of the most beautiful days of my life here, and without closing my eyes I can almost see the shadows of our bodies on the grass.

Not far from where we'd lain, a string quartet is playing Vivaldi's "Stabat Mater." They are probably students at the conservatory, judging by their slightly different variations of white shirt and black pants.

A contratenor begins to sing, "*Stabat Mater dolorosa, juxta crucem lacrimosa, lacrimosa* . . ." The lyrics call to my mind Mama's round face and hands, reddened from rosacea and labor. Her dull espresso hair that turned both limp and airy with age, resembling winter grass. I dwell on her image, willing it to give me peace. Yet the moment I realize I can't remember her voice, my mouth tastes of ashes. After everything I've done to return for Mama, I am not ready to see her.

The singer's voice stills me, keeps me rooted on my achy feet until they finish that song and another piece that I don't recognize. A small crowd gives them a hearty applause that bursts like flowers in the atmosphere. The musicians stand, glowing in the praise, then loosen the hair of their bows, lock up their instruments, and meander away together, hunching under the weight of their hard cases and music stands. Probably on the way to dinner. I realize then that I haven't eaten anything all day. I'm not hungry, but because of the music and the hopefulness from being around happy people, I pull out my phone and text Nina. Because we're now physically close, I feel that my overture after so many years of silence is permitted.

I just flew in last night. If you're free, would you like to get dinner?

I am taken aback and then excited by the three dots that appear, showing she has seen my message and is writing a response.

Natasha! You should've let me know earlier! But I can't—Swan Lake tonight.

Of course, I write back, disappointed as well as relieved. I hadn't checked the Mariinsky schedule—in fact, nothing could convince me to go back to that place or even look up their calendar.

Can you wait until after the show? I'll be done by eleven. Where are you right now?

I hesitate, thinking of all those times we had vodka and vareniki after performances, our faces adorned by half-erased makeup and youth.

I'm around the Field of Mars.

Just hang out there and come meet me at the theater. Please?

I think I should go to bed early. Jet lag, I type and press send. Nina doesn't say anything, and I realize with a pang of regret that I didn't even tell her *toi toi toi*.

My feet ache painfully, but I don't want to go back to the hotel just yet. I wander off to the Summer Garden and walk under the linden trees in bloom, their nectar so intoxicating that with one sip, bees drop to the ground.

I stop when I reach a gallery of Greek sculptures. I sit on one of the green benches between the statues and watch the sky turn from cobalt to violet and rose-gold. The twilight will last until sunrise. There is no place other than St. Petersburg in the summer where I've felt this slowing of time. Instead of the past, present, and future all flowing in order like train cars, they fold translucently into one another; and many years ago feels as close and real as yesterday, tomorrow as distant as years from now.

As if my thoughts have opened a portal, I see him between the white statues. Perhaps a phantom, or a piece of my imagination that has escaped like a moth into the night air. I grip the armrest of the green bench. But he begins walking toward me, and his quality of movement lets me know he is real. By god, there have been only a few humans who could look so alive. He darkens, lightens, darkens, lightens as he passes through the shadows of the statues. Darkens. Lightens again—revealing his arched eyebrows, black hair. Flashing green eyes that can rage or laugh without saying anything. The great Dmitri Ostrovsky to his fans, Dima to his friends, Dmitri Anatolievich to his company members. But to me, he is Janus. My two-faced downfall, and the only person in the world I would not hesitate to call my enemy. We maintain eye contact until he stops abruptly in front of my bench.

"Natasha," he says with a nod, as if it were the most natural thing that we have run into each other.

"Dmitri." I level my voice so as not to give him the satisfaction of unnerving me. "What are you doing here?"

"What a way to greet an old—" He laughs. "Whatever you want to call me. May I?" He gestures at the spot next to me and sits down without waiting for my answer.

"Welcome back to Piter," he says, stretching his legs out before him and crossing them at the ankles.

"Let us dispense with the niceties," I say, and he smiles.

"I could never understand why you hate me so." Dmitri looks out at the statues, shaking his head in an exaggerated show of regret. The frown disappears in a moment, restoring the smooth planes of his face. He hasn't changed much since our last meeting. I remember the light filtering through the flute of champagne in his hand at our bar off Place des Vosges. I can hear the moonlight rushing through the four fountains and dropping like silver spoons into the basin. Our friends murmur toasts in French and Russian—*Santé! Budem!*

That night was just before my accident—and then I realize with a start that Dmitri might be the same, but I've lost everything since then.

"I have nothing to say to you, except that we are two people who should never have met," I say, managing to keep my voice slow and steady. The air glows violet and warm between us. He cups his chin in one hand and turns to face me.

"Natasha, for my part I have always been truthful. Whatever I believe is what I do and what I say. You see how strange this is to most people, who live by deceiving everyone and, above all, themselves," he says, smirking. "Were *you* always truthful?"

"Why are you here? How did you know where to find me?" I hiss, nearly standing up. He reaches his hand out and stops me by the elbow. The touch is surprisingly gentle, and my body remembers it in an instant. *Swan Lake.* The smell of sweat, crushed rosin, and damp wooden floors.

"Fine. I came to talk to you," he says, withdrawing his fingertips and leaving only memories like bruises. "In fact, I came to offer you a job. I want you to dance Giselle at the Mariinsky in the fall season."

I stare at him in disbelief, and he calmly holds my gaze. I can't help but ask, "Why would you want me?" A smile ripples across his face; he loses the seriousness and becomes mocking again.

"As the director, my job is to give people what they want to see. And there's no one else who sells tickets like you do, Natalia Nikolaevna."

"They won't buy tickets when they realize I haven't performed in two years." I roll my ankles as I speak, testing out the edges of the pain. When it returns, my eyes sting and my tongue becomes hot and heavy inside my mouth. What Dmitri doesn't know is that I haven't even gone back to the studio, let alone the stage, since the accident.

"Hold yourself together, Natasha. I'm offering opening night, with our newest premier as Albrecht. I'm not going to repeat myself." He rises, smoothing down his pant legs over his thighs. Just before vanishing between the rows of statues, he turns around and says, "The class still starts at eleven. See you tomorrow."

AT TEN IN THE MORNING, I go downstairs to the dining room. The sun is filtering in through the green stained-glass wall, and young waiters in white waistcoats circle self-importantly around the tables in a grand allegro. I take a seat and order a cappuccino and a croissant. It's a habit I acquired in Paris, and the heady smell of butter wraps me in comfort like a shawl. For a moment I forget that I'm in Petersburg; it's as though I'm sitting back at our favorite café in Le Marais on a Saturday morning. But the sense of calm was premature; at my slightest touch, the croissant defiantly shakes off a hundred golden shards on the clean tablecloth. As I'm brooming the fallen flakes with my hand, I hear the sonorous bass of Igor Petrenko addressing me.

"Natalia Nikolaevna, it is a splendor to see you again."

The hotel manager then comes into view, wearing a navy pinstripe suit with signet cuff links and a fat tie struggling against a little diamond pin. A shopping bag is dangling from the crook of his left wrist, just below an enormous gold-faced watch. I have always held a secret place of scorn in my heart for men whose personal style tends toward "lavish." Yet Igor Petrenko has never been anything but perfectly courteous, which leads me to conclude that he is simply what's called an old-fashioned gentleman.

"Igor Vladimirovich, great to see you. And thank you for the flowers and the champagne."

"Oh, I cannot take the credit!" The hotel manager gasps. "It was from a gentleman—" Before I have a chance to ask "Who?" Igor Petrenko presents me with the shopping bag.

"The same gentleman who messengered this over, early this morning. Dmitri Anatolievich Ostrovsky."

The taste of cappuccino turns black like petroleum in my mouth. Noticing my changed expression, the manager tactfully lays the bag on the table instead of handing it directly to me. "I hope you have a wonderful day. If there's anything I can do, please don't hesitate to ask." The manager smiles and takes his leave.

Once Igor Petrenko vanishes, I take out the contents of the shopping bag. A pair of new ballet slippers. New pointe shoes, the same size and make as my last ones at Mariinsky. Elastic and ribbons. A small sewing kit. Three pairs of tights, one in pink and two in black. Three leotards—forest green, white, and mauve. A black knit warm-up overall.

A glance at my phone tells me that it's 10:40 a.m. now. I stare at the shoes, raking my loose hair away from my face. I find it hard to breathe—how did he know I was staying here? And why won't he leave me alone? What I find most deeply disturbing and impossible to understand in the world is people who cling. All my life I have been a leaver.

When I gather up the shoes and clothes to put them away, I find a piece of paper in the bottom of the bag. It's a printout of the fall casting list. I see several names of my generation and some younger ones I don't recognize. And under *Giselle*, I find TaeHyung Kim (Albrecht), and next to it—written in by hand—Natalia Leonova (Giselle). I can't help but chortle at this bait. Dmitri always knows what gets me worked up: my competitiveness, the stage, and an exceptional partner. I saw Tae at a gala concert in Tokyo a few years ago, when he was a twenty-four-year-old, newly minted Mariinsky premier. The stage was big, almost as big as the Bolshoi's, and Tae ate it up with his coupé-jeté. The others watching from the wings—principals from La Scala, La Colón, ABT, the Royal, Stuttgart—took a collective gasp when he ended his variation with a triple tour double tour, a feat I've never seen anyone else perform live, before or since. Someone said "Fuck me now!" which surely reflected, in some weird way, how we all felt. When he came back to the wings, these leading dancers—

every one an international star—floated over to him like swooning corps members. He patiently took pictures with them and spoke with humility, which is not a quality usually seen in a stupendously gifted young male principal. I saw that humility in his dancing, too. With true artists, it is not their dancing that you see and admire onstage, but who they are as people.

It is ten forty-five. I grab the bag full of shoes and hail a cab for Mariinsky. When I get in the car, the sky is milky and overcast so that the city feels like it's inside a pearl. By the time I'm crossing the plaza, the enormous pistachio-hued theater is glowing in a column of sunlight, which has just begun to break through the clouds. Seeing it, my stomach churns; I feel breathless and almost stop walking. Muscle memory.

Yet there is a part of me that wants to know: How much of what I remember is real?

ACT I

There is nothing better than Nevsky Prospekt, at least not in Petersburg; for there it is everything . . .

Oh, do not believe this Nevsky Prospekt! . . .
Everything is deception, everything is a dream,
everything is not what it seems to be!

—Nikolai Gogol, "Nevsky Prospekt" (1935)

i

I WASN'T MEANT TO BE A DANCER. IT HAPPENED ONLY BECAUSE OUR north-facing window looked across the courtyard and into the apartment of a Ukrainian couple: a slender, soft-spoken mailman named Sergei Kostiuk and his cheerful and dark-haired wife. That family's apartment was a diorama for my curious and bored eyes, as is often the case in compressed quarters of poor neighborhoods—although I didn't yet think of myself as poor.

The Kostiuks had a son my age called Seryozha, whose padding around the rooms in a white sleeveless top and underwear is one of the earliest images I can recollect. Seryozha's arms were all one thickness from shoulder to wrist, and he was pale, thin, and soft in a way that reminded me of a Q-tip. Like the other boys in our class, he filled me with disdain. I hated how they spoke in short, overlapping shouts that only they could understand, how they pulled on girls' ponytails, the dirt caked under their nails, their damp smell like earthworms. Out of them, Seryozha was the worst because he constantly ran into me outside of school. When we crossed paths in the stairway I looked coldly away, although Mama said I should be nice to him because he was nice to me. I was sure Seryozha was only nice to me because his mama was saying behind our backs that I was nice to him. And so, on and on it went, the chain of mothers who forced their children to be nice to their neighbors' children.

It was a cold and raw Sunday morning. A sense of resignation coursed through the dead leaves and fallen apples strewn in the courtyard. The crows on the electric lines started cawing and Seryozha turned to his window—he caught me staring, turned red, and disappeared. A little later the yellow curtains of his room were drawn hastily shut. The birds cried louder, then lifted off as Sveta entered the courtyard below. Something that I learned from her is that some women are beautiful even from above. I called out to Mama, "Sveta is here!"

She opened our door before Mama had a chance to do a quick sweep around the apartment. Sveta—as I called her instead of Aunt Svetlana, at her insistence—had been visiting us as long as I could remember. Even as I grew older and Mama went to the theater more, Sveta enjoyed the tea, gossip, and bespoke adjustments Mama made for her at our home. She kissed Mama's cheeks and the top of my head while pulling off her tight-fitting leather gloves, one finger at a time. Then she stood in front of Mama's sewing table, exuding glamour at ten in the morning on a Sunday. It was the small details that proved fatal in ballet, Sveta said. Her Lilac Fairy costume was too tight in the bodice; the shoulder straps restricted the movement of her arms as she leaped onto the stage for her variation, so she couldn't get any ballon. Sveta had asked the chief seamstress of the women's costume department to loosen the straps so they could fall slightly off-shoulder, but the answer was a firm no. This was the costume design from the original 1890 production of *The Sleeping Beauty*, and changing something at the whim of a mere second soloist went against everything that the Mariinsky stood for, which was tradition—the very fabric of ballet passed down from feet to feet for two centuries. As Sveta said this, I imagined pointe shoes trampling all over the theater's pale blue velvet curtains fringed with gold tassels.

Mama told Sveta not to worry and then ordered me to go play in the living room. I turned on the TV and sat on the floor, where Mama had laid out the finished costumes to be steamed. The news program ended, and a black-and-white figure of a ballerina appeared on the screen. She looked like Sveta, with long thin legs ending in pinpricks of pointe shoes—and she bounded off those sharp feet with one leg reaching high behind her so that it almost grazed her marvelous backbend. Her every movement was quick and spry like a sparrow's, as if she barely needed to touch the ground. But what I really couldn't resist was the music. I ran to our room to get my tutu that Mama sewed out of scrap tulle. I pulled it over my hips and started mimicking the dancer on the screen, shouting, "Mama, Sveta, look at me!" I turned up the volume of the TV, knowing that would annoy them. But I'd miscalculated how much I could push my luck, and a fatal back-bending jump sent me landing right on top of Mama's piles of costumes.

Before my foot slid out from underneath me and my bottom crashed to the floor, Mama rushed over screaming. "I didn't mean to," I began to say, curled up on the floor. I could feel the beginnings of a massive bruise on my bottom, but I didn't dare cry in front of Mama. She shushed me and examined the pieces one by one. There was a finger-length tear on a soft white tulle tutu, and she ran to the fabric closet in our room, swallowing curse words. When I made trouble like this, Mama whipped me with her belt. I wondered if she'd do that then—and suddenly I didn't want to dance or wear a tutu or do anything, I didn't want to live. I reached over and grabbed Sveta's hand, and she folded me into her stomach.

"Sveta," I closed my eyes and whispered. "Please take me with you."

She stroked my hair and patted my back, the way I wished Mama would do more often. She then crouched down to kiss my cheeks, and said, "Natashka, I can't."

I stepped back from her in disappointment, but she held on to my shoulders and smiled. "I saw you dancing. Do you know what ballet that was?"

I shook my head.

"That was a solo from a ballet called *Don Quixote*. What you did is called a Kitri jump. How old are you, Natashka?"

"Seven," I said, rolling my eyes to the ceiling while recalling the few significant dates in my short life. It was 1992 and I was actually seven and three months old. Less than a year ago, all the flags had been changed from red and yellow to white, blue, and red.

"Well. I'm going to tell your mama that you should start taking ballet, as soon as possible. You're the rarest thing for a woman dancer, and by that, I mean you're a jumper, Natalia Leonova."

Sveta left early, promising to return soon for more gossip and fittings. The minute she walked out, Mama called me to her and boxed my ear hard. Just once, so I would know she meant only to set me in my place, to make me behave and not act so wild. It was not because she hated me—in fact it was because she loved me, she told me later while snuggling me tightly in her arms. I believed her words, the warmth of our creaky bed, her gentle hand caressing my head, which she kept reassuringly moving like an oar dipping into a lake, even though she was so tired. She was so tired that she sometimes fell asleep with her eyes open, but she would keep stroking my head for hours until I forgot that she'd struck me with that same hand. This was what love was, I thought—being able to forgive. But it was not happiness.

I KNEW THAT MAMA COULDN'T teach me happiness because she'd never been happy. At least not since Nikolai—a name that was within my name, yet so unfamiliar to me. Mama never talked about him with me; everything I know, I heard through whispered conversations between Mama and Sveta when they thought I was asleep. Mama met Nikolai while working as an alterations seamstress at a department store. Two men, rather shabbily dressed, walked in one day wanting to buy winter suits and coats and tailor them on the spot. They were friends who lumbered out in Sakhalin in the Far East; they had just come out for a monthlong vacation after an eighteen-month run. The short, skinny, polite, clean-shaven one was Pavel, and the tall, blond, bearded, silent, and somewhat wild-eyed one was Nikolai. They were both flush with their wages that they hadn't had the chance to spend for a year and a half. During that time, they had caught a glimpse of fewer than five women on the entire island of Sakhalin. Both were eager to do something with their money and to hold a woman close. And it so happened that Nikolai was the one who spoke to Mama first, which set the tone for all the rest that followed. If Pavel had been the one to approach her, Nikolai would have fallen respectfully behind his friend, and Mama would have gone along for the ride just the same, only her entire life would have been different.

Mama hemmed the coats for the two friends and they asked her to join them for dinner after her shift. After a few days of meeting like that, Pavel naturally fell away and Nikolai and Mama spent time together alone. Mama had not been courted until then. No one had bought her boxes of chocolates or walked the scenic way along the canals instead of taking the Metro. Nikolai quoted from the poets and asked Mama about her girlhood; and when she explained how lonely she'd felt her entire life, he wrapped her tightly in his arms and squeezed all the breath—and sadness—out of her. Nikolai, whose father had downed a bottle of vodka a day, ran away from home when he was fourteen and had been making his own way ever since. The only friends and family he had in the world were books and trees; he stared into loneliness every time his eyes opened in the morning. But not anymore—he told her, interlacing his hand with hers. His every word, glance, and kiss burned her like hot coal. In short, Mama fell in love with Nikolai.

At the end of the month, Nikolai flew back to Sakhalin, promising to call and write as often as he could. He did call every week for a number of months—even after Mama told him she was pregnant. Later she gave birth and had to stop working at the department store, and Nikolai started sending her money, too. I was already nine months old when he came to visit on leave. He spent hours playing with me, reading out loud from Pushkin and rocking me to sleep. Only on a few occasions, he disappeared and came back the next morning, saying he went out with his logging buddies and lost track of time. Mama was so relieved to see him, and the time she could spend with him was so short anyway, that she immediately forgave him.

Some months after Nikolai returned to the lumberyard, Mama couldn't get ahold of him. He didn't pick up, so she would leave messages. Did he miss her and Natasha? Did he still love her? He called her back, and they talked briefly about her concerns until he went back to work. This happened several more times—anywhere between four to a dozen times, her memory falters—but what Mama does remember is that, during what was to become their last phone call, he quoted to her these lines from Dante: "Take heart. Nothing can take our passage from us / When such a power has given warrant for it."

By this time, his designated monthlong vacation was drawing near. Mama believed that he would show up one day bearing a box of chocolates and toys for me. Incredibly, she never lost this faith until the last day of what was supposed to be his leave. When even that day passed without any sign of Nikolai, Mama would have gone mad if only she hadn't had a toddler to feed and raise. Nikolai hadn't sent money in months, and she had no idea how she could work. One winter day, when she had mustered enough energy to take a walk with me in a stroller, a gentleman in a familiar coat called out to her on the street. It was Pavel, wearing the same dark green wool gabardine coat she had sold to him, a lifetime ago it seemed. Nikolai had one exactly like it, she couldn't help but recall at the same time. A thought crossed rapidly in her mind that she'd much rather have seen Nikolai in that coat instead, and this weakness shamed her as Pavel reached out his two gloved hands and wrapped them around her own. Pavel had gotten out of lumbering in the past year—he'd made enough to buy a co-op apartment for him and his new wife. After listening to him for a while, heart pounding from impatience, Mama finally asked in a shaky voice if he'd had any news of Nikolai—she was afraid he had been killed in a logging accident. Pavel looked at a loss for words, studying the face of the toddler in the stroller. Finally he said, very sadly, "I respect you so much, Anna Ivanovna; it hurts me that neither truth nor lie can bring you any comfort. In that case I think you might prefer hearing the truth. Nikolai is well. He found a better-paying post in Vladivostok, which isn't so wild as Sakhalin. I didn't know he stopped calling you."

To Mama's credit, she did not break down in tears out there on the plaza. She thanked Pavel for giving her this news with integrity and compassion. To Pavel's credit, he did everything he could to help this woman whom, after all, he'd only met for a few days, several years ago at this point. His wife knew a makeup artist at Mariinsky, and through her he got Mama some sewing work that she could do at home.

So I learned early on that the most painful thing in the world is uncertainty. Not knowing whom to trust. Not knowing who will stay. The only way to ensure that you don't get left behind is for you to be the one to leave.

When I lay in bed at night, I didn't fantasize about getting married in a white wedding dress as did other girls, I fantasized about leaving.

But instead of disappearing like Nikolai, I dreamed of becoming so famous that the only way the ones I left behind could see my face would be in photographs, in newspapers.

AT THE ARTIST ENTRANCE, AN unfamiliar porter is listening to Puccini on the radio. When I walk in, he stops humming, uncrosses his legs, and gets up from his swivel stool so abruptly that it skids to the back wall.

"Natash—Natalia Nikolaevna," he stammers. "I am so— It is wonderful to see you again."

I am ashamed to admit that I don't remember him at all. "Please, just Natasha," I say. "I'm here to take class."

"Yes, of course." The porter smiles nervously, smoothing down his dwindling hair with one hand and gesturing toward the hallway with the other. When I'm about to turn away, he stops me by my elbow.

"Natasha," he reaches and clasps my hand, which costs me a great deal of effort not to flinch.

"Welcome back to Mariinsky," he intones rather formally, and when I smile and thank him, he releases me with an expression of terrified joy.

The dressing room is empty, and so quiet that the second hand of the yellow-faced wall clock can be heard. It's three minutes past eleven; the company class has already begun. I change into one of the brand-new leotards and tights. Without looking at a mirror, I rake my hair up into a bun. Inside ballet slippers, my feet begin to feel more alive and alert, connecting to the floor, lifting my kneecaps, turning out my hips. My shoulder blades pull down and back, my neck lengthens upright. A shocked relief courses through my body. I recognize myself again for a moment, like a candle flame enlarging and then coming into focus.

A trickle of music seeps into the dressing room, and I follow it out the hallway. The studio door has been left open. They are doing pliés, and as I slip inside to find a spot at the barre, all eyes turn to me—the ones facing me and even the ones facing away, who are staring at me in the mirror. They are expressionless. I cannot tell whether they are happy to see me or hostile—except Nina, who flashes me the briefest, kindest smile from her perch. Out of habit, I scan the room in vain for Seryozha. Not seeing him here gives my heart a brief, sharp sensation like a pinprick under your nail. The only person resolutely not looking at me is Katia Reznikova, who at forty-one is still ravishingly beautiful and commanding as only true primas can be. All this transpires before the pliés finish and Dmitri stands before the company with a hand on his hip, announcing, "Natasha will be guesting in the fall season, dancing *Giselle* with TaeHyung. Please welcome her back."

A scattered round of applause, led mostly by Nina. I find a space at the barre and do a few pliés on my own before jumping into battement tendus with the others. Without any conscious thought, my toes activate against the floor like they're plucking harp strings. That simple and ingrained movement floods me with an exquisite consciousness of my body; and it shocks me to realize that for the very first time since the accident, I am hopeful. But during frappés, the pain returns to my feet, traveling up to my ankles, then calves. A short center combination makes both my ankle and arch collapse, and I'm hopping out of a single pirouette. When Dmitri gives a basic coda ending in a fouetté, I have no choice but to leave the studio rather than expose my complete inability to execute what was once my signature.

In the dressing room, I slump down on the bench with elbows on my knees, cradling the weight of my head in my palms. When the faint trickling of the piano stops, I pick up my things and walk out.

Dmitri is waiting outside the door, leaning against the wall like an adolescent.

"Let's talk in my office," he says in a neutral voice, devoid of his usual mocking tone.

"It's really not necessary," I reply, sounding colder than I intend or feel. "Look, Dmitri. Aside from all the things in our past—I appreciate the confidence you've shown me. It was tempting, I admit. But as you can see yourself, I can't do this." For a second, I worry that I might break down while saying this. But my eyes remain dry—there are no more emotions I have left for this situation.

"We don't have to go up. Let's just talk in here." Dmitri walks inside an empty studio and motions for me to follow. Since I have come to take his class, I at least owe him a conversation. Dmitri sits down on a chair in front of the mirrors, and I take a seat next to him. He smoothes his hair away from his face and exhales, and says something I didn't expect.

"Tell me about your injury."

After so many years of knowing Dmitri, he remains an enigma—not just to me, but to most of the world—which is probably why my eyes pool with moistness at the hint of something that, in anyone else's voice, could be construed as compassion. His sudden openness catches me off guard and compels me to speak.

"Arches. Achilles. Calves also—but mostly down in feet and ankles."

"Which side? Both?"

"Both."

We are silent for a while. In the next room, the accompanist has begun playing the Act III pas de deux in *La Bayadère*, a sound as calm and luminous as spun moonlight. Moonlight, fountains, clinking of glasses, Dmitri's laughter with my friends as I hid in a corner in pain. The memory comes alive as the swelling, throbbing pain in my feet—and then as fresh anger.

"My injury is because of you."

Dmitri snaps his gaze onto me. "Natasha, I know you're not my fan. But let's be fair. I didn't cause you to get hurt."

"If it weren't for you—" I struggle to string my words. "No accident."

All traces of what I thought was compassion disappear from his face. "I wasn't even there, Natasha. I—" He raises his eyebrows and emits a short laugh of disgust.

"You used to be someone who took responsibility for her own life. At the very least, I liked that about you."

More silence. The pair in the next studio must be talking, working through the difficult lifts and transitions. After a minute, the piano restarts fitfully.

"Here's what I think," Dmitri begins again. "It wasn't right to jump straight into company class. Let's get you working slowly back up with your own pedagogue. And we'll get you started on physiotherapy. I know you can do it."

"It's not possible," I say weakly. Dmitri becomes impatient again.

"Natasha, I was watching you during class. Do you really want to know my opinion?" He fixes his grass-colored eyes on me, and I shrug.

"Your injury," he says, tapping the side of his temple. "It's mostly, if not all, in your head."

ON THE WAY OUT, I pass by the next room rehearsing *La Bayadère* and see Nina working with her partner. She breaks protocol by stopping midsequence, causing the piano to peter off; and then she comes over to lock me in a tight embrace.

"I have a break in thirty minutes. Let's get tea," Nina says, standing close so I can see a cropping of lines on her forehead and the lovely flush of her cheeks. There is a new slackness to her skin over her neck, collarbones, and knees, which would not be discernible onstage. It is unexpectedly attractive off stage, in the way a white shirt feels more elegant after a few hours' wear, when it's not so pristinely pressed. Also new: shooting stars threading across the midnight black of her center-parted hair. Nina makes aging look like an adornment. I find myself mesmerized by her appearance, as if meeting an actress in real life—because so much of her now lives only in my memories.

"I'm so sorry, Nina," I implore. "We have to catch up, but I'm exhausted right now. You saw me earlier, so you know why. I'll be back tomorrow."

"You really are coming back?" she asks doubtfully, and I nod. Her face softens with relief because the Natasha she knew would stop at nothing to fulfill what she said she'd do. Nina doesn't know that this Natasha is gone. All I can think of now, standing with a parched throat and inflamed feet, is the Xanax on my bedside table. The pills are rattling like white bees in their bottle—soon they will take me to a room covered in down pillows, floor to wall to ceiling. I so look forward to the feeling that a tear forms at the corner of my eye. Nina sees this, mistakes it for the normal disappointment of a bad class, and pats me soothingly on my arm.

"It will get better. See you tomorrow, Natasha."

Before I met Nina, I'd never had a real friend. I was always alone at school. It's not that I didn't want to make friends; but the other girls instinctively sensed that I was different. They were lambs—soft, pretty, playful, easily satisfied, happy in flocks. I didn't have such endearing qualities. I was not good-looking, rich, pleasant, or noticeably bright. I was already serious and brooding, and my obsessive nature grated and exhausted me without a proper focus. What helped me later didn't make me an ideal lunch companion in primary school. I dimmed the light behind my eyes, laughed at their jokes, and hid that thing that burned inside me, sometimes like ember and other times like molten rock. A secret power that others couldn't fathom. I concealed this part of me at home, too, so that Mama wouldn't have one more thing to upset her. It was when I was alone that I didn't have to act like what I was not—and only then did I not feel as if bursting into flames from the roots of my hair to my toes.

One day after school, I was walking home alone through the snow-packed streets. This was my favorite time of day, when I could be free to regard the world—even if that world was just bare black trees, brick buildings, and white fumes rising from smokestacks and pouring into the sun-blushed sky. In the summertime, the burning smell stung my nose and I ran as fast as I could. But now the iciness sealed everything cleanly and I breathed in only the pure scent of snow. As the wind blew and the evening chill set in, the crows began cawing from electric lines, tops of buildings, even the thin air where you couldn't see but still hear them. Then above their cacophony, a sound of rapid footsteps was layered over my own, and momentarily my blood froze. Before I panicked, he caught up to me.

"Natasha." It was Seryozha, with bright red cheeks. Like a couple of baby turtles on the sand, we used to clumsily overtake each other in height so that he was taller one year and I taller the next. This was evidently Seryozha's year: he'd grown since I last stood so close to him, and I could see that he was now the exact height of a standing piano—which made me look up at him by a few centimeters. A little breathless, his blond hair swept up from the run, he asked if I would come with him to a party. It turned out that a certain Reznikov, his father's boss's boss, not just a postmaster but someone at the Ministry of Communications, was hosting a New Year's party. Despite their difference in rank, the Reznikovs met the Kostiuks because their daughter used to train at Seryozha's ballet school. I hadn't known that he had been taking ballet lessons since he was three, and stared at him until his cheeks looked smeared with beet juice. I had never been to a party before. I said yes and Seryozha's eyes brightened so that I could clearly see the starbursts of his blue irises. Somehow they reminded me, briefly, of snowflakes.

On the night of the party, which was very cold, the Kostiuks and I took the Metro to the Reznikovs' apartment. After getting out of the station, we still had to walk many blocks to the Fontanka Embankment. Seryozha's mother occasionally turned around to ask us if we were okay. Seryozha and I both shrugged, although I could feel my two pairs of thick tights had already become wet inside my boots. Soon, Seryozha's father walked ahead to the ornate facade of a building, and motioned at us to catch up. On either side of the entrance, a pair of lanterns held the dancing light of real flames. The canal shimmered white in the moonlight except where people's footsteps had dented the snow, revealing the hard, black ice beneath.

When we arrived, the door was opened by an elegant woman, older and more beautiful than either my mama or Seryozha's. Her rust-red hair was swept up into a low bun, a style that usually suited young women better but looked perfectly becoming on her. She kissed Uncle Sergei on both cheeks, then moved on to his wife and son. Finally, Uncle Sergei pointed at me and said awkwardly, "And here is Natasha, a friend of Seryozha's." She barely glanced at me, but the way she smiled at Seryozha made me realize that they knew each other already—and that she thought highly of him. It struck me then that the Reznikovs invited the Kostiuks because of Seryozha, not Uncle Sergei.

"Have you been practicing hard for the Vaganova auditions? How are you getting on with your double tours?" she asked Seryozha, leading us through a hallway lined with paintings.

"I've been improving, thank you," Seryozha said as we entered a large room. It was suffused in a smooth golden light that blurred the edges of everything. Guests were gathered in groups of twos and threes, never alone and never more than four; they were well-dressed, well-coiffed, and appropriately funny, like actors in commercials. The women were slender, polished, and lovely in a way that made me feel self-conscious for Seryozha's mother. Madame Reznikova gestured in the direction of a striking girl, whose fiery hair immediately called to mind her own, and said, "There's Katia. Why don't you go say hello, Seryozha," before being seamlessly pulled away to a sphere of guests.

Seryozha surprised me by walking up to Katia and greeting her. She was so much taller than him—she looked about sixteen or seventeen—but she smiled at him without impatience, much like her mother. Seryozha introduced me, standing a bit behind him, and she smiled at me, too. I was bewildered—why did this beautiful older girl act as though she was friends with Seryozha? He spoke rarely in class and never made any lasting impression; our teacher hardly paid more attention to him than to me. But here, Seryozha was at ease. They talked of his upcoming audition for Vaganova, where Katia was a star student in her final year. I gathered that this was the best and oldest ballet school in Russia, where the most talented children trained all day to become professionals.

As night deepened, guests grazed on the aspic, deviled eggs, and tiny buttered toasts topped with caviar. I was hungry but resisted going to the buffet table and drawing attention to myself. No one noticed that I was not eating or talking to anyone—not Seryozha, nor his parents, who were quietly milling around the room as if terrified.

The clock struck eleven. Everyone downed glasses of vodka until their careful mannerisms unraveled and they became messy; the men got red in the face and sweaty, and the women's makeup wore off and looked dry on their skin. Then a tall man with tin-colored hair, who had been shaking hands with guests all night, raised his glass and called the room to attention. A hush spread around him.

"Thank you everyone for coming to our home and blessing us with your friendship," Reznikov began, then proceeded to salute a long list of guests, no doubt in the order of importance at the Ministry. The air became slightly tense as this went on for a while; some guests had thought they ranked higher in Reznikov's esteem, and when they lay down in bed later, they would toss and turn over this snub.

Then, most extraordinarily, Reznikov turned his attention to Seryozha.

"And I want to point out this brilliant young man, a gifted dancer, whom I met while my daughter Katia was still dancing at her old studio. I must say, I used to think ballet was for girls—I was happy for Katia to learn it, but took no interest in it myself. It was when I saw Seryozha dancing that I came to truly appreciate the art form."

I thought that Seryozha would turn beet red and stare at his feet, but he didn't. He stood tall and glowed as the elegant adults around him cast admiring glances.

"Speaking of ballet." Reznikov now gestured at Katia, who had been allowed to drink a little bit of vodka for toasts. "Katia has just been offered the title role in *Cinderella* at the Mariinsky—*six months* before her graduation!"

Reznikov started clapping, and the guests followed suit, murmuring with astonishment; Madame Reznikova wrapped her arm around her daughter's shoulder and embraced tightly. After the applause died down, Reznikov changed the music and asked Seryozha to dance. This surprised me less than the fact that Seryozha, the shy boy across the courtyard, showed no hesitation at the host's request.

Seryozha's eyes were glittering—not in the dreamy, soft, snowy way they usually did, but hard like diamonds. He walked to the middle of the salon's wooden floor, gently nodding his head to the beat of the strings. The guests fell into an attentive silence. Without any preparation or forewarning, Seryozha took his right foot to the side and then pushed off onto his left tip-toe, putting his right toes to his left knee. Then he turned. And turned. And turned.

I understood then the reason the Reznikovs took an interest in him—he was marked by talent, as young as he was. And if you were talented enough, it didn't matter if your papa was a postman or if your mama was heavyset and unfashionably dressed, even the rich adored you. They remembered your name and noticed if you haven't eaten or drunk anything. But these things, I did not envy. It was the expression on Seryozha's face as he spun that made me burn with longing—and in that moment I realized that my inner fire, of which I was so proud, was not talent like Seryozha's: it was merely desire.

MAMA WAS WAITING UP FOR me to come home, wrapped in a blanket and drinking tea at the kitchen table. The TV in the living room was softly playing the rerun of the president's New Year's address, the only sign of the holiday in our family. I sat next to Mama and asked if I could audition for Vaganova. I guessed she would tell me no, because she mostly disapproved of new things or "nonsense." But she took a long sip of her tea and told me I could, if I really wanted. She herself thought it was a bad idea. They auditioned thousands of girls each year and took thirty. And half of that number didn't make it to their final year. Out of the remaining, just a few of the best graduates would enter Mariinsky as corps de ballet, mostly to be a prop in the background. If you were lucky, you could dance Queen of the Dryads some year or Myrtha in *Giselle*. Then your body would break down, a new crop of hungry graduates would fill your shoes while you languished in the rank and file. So you were finished with your career at thirty-eight, with no education or experience anywhere else outside the theater. It would be better to choose something more sensible. They always needed nurses and teachers.

"Mama, I know I can do it. Dance Odette—dance all of it," I said quietly, and she shook her head.

"There's something that they told me, Natashka. Prima ballerinas are born once in a decade." As she said this she stirred another spoonful of jam into her cup of tea, as if to neutralize the bitterness of her words. But it wasn't just her words. It was her thoughts about the world, about me.

That was the first time I realized something very important. Everyone—the girls at school, my teachers, even Mama—thought I was nothing. No, *nothing* would be infinite and consequential, like the vast black emptiness of space; I reminded them of something so little and ordinary, like a cat or a comb or a kettle, that it would be ridiculous to think of it trying to become anything else. Tears rained down my face and dropped on my lap. "I don't want you to suffer, Natashka," she said, patting my back.

But later that night, Mama called Svetlana, who had taken a teaching position at Vaganova. She was encouraging of the idea of auditioning and promised to register me herself for the August cycle. "I don't know why she has to overreach," Mama said to the receiver, not even bothering to lower her voice. "But I guess she was always bound to try something like this." Hearing this, I jumped up and down in silence, pumping my arms in the air. From then on, I practiced copying the movements I saw on TV, leaping on my way to school and stretching my legs at night.

In June, Seryozha auditioned and was accepted, as his mama proudly told us at the stairwell. Mama smiled and agreed with her that indeed, Seryozha was exceptionally talented. She didn't mention that I was auditioning, too. After we came back to our apartment, Mama opened the pantry door and said quietly to the jars of pickles, "Let's not get our hopes up and just show up, Natashka."

On audition day, Mama and I left together for Vaganova Academy on Rossi Street. Painted in cake-batter yellow and lined with white columns, it stretched an entire block toward the Alexandrinsky Theatre. There were dozens of children and their parents crowding around the entrance, and we took our places on one side of the stone stoop. A bronze-faced man with high cheekbones turned to Mama and asked, "Your girl is auditioning?"

"Yes, her name is Natasha," Mama said, stroking my head.

"She has a nice form," the man complimented me offhandedly before continuing. "My boy Farkhad is trying out, too," he said, clasping a scrawny boy a few times on the shoulder. The son was his father's miniature with dark almond-shaped eyes and sharp cheeks.

"Has your girl been doing ballet for a long time?" the man pressed, although Mama pursed her lips to show she wasn't inviting further conversation.

"No, she hasn't taken any classes. But she dances wonderfully."

"Farkhad has been training and performing since he was five." The man cast loving glances at his son, who reminded me of Seryozha with his mild discomfort around hovering parents. "But do not worry—I'm sure your girl—Natasha?—will do fine. You see, when I was admitted to Vaganova, I had no training, either. They look for ability, not experience."

"You were a student here?" Mama asked, forgetting to be annoyed at the man's talkativeness, and he responded with enthusiasm.

"Yes! I started in 1960, right before Nureyev defected. It took my father and me three days to take the train from Nur-Sultan to St. Petersburg when I was ten. We packed all of our food for the journey, and I got so sick of boiled eggs by the end. Father said, this will help you stay strong and have energy for dancing! And we passed right through all the cities—Ufa, Samara, of course Moscow. I just watched everything through the window. It didn't matter though, when I got in. The happiest day of my father's life, he told me.

"You know, it's funny. My son and I took the same train. And I packed the same foods for Farkhad and me, even though I was sure he'd hate it as much as I did back then. He doesn't yet know what's good for him." The man smiled, his eyes shining with memories.

"Children take so long to realize anything, and then it's too late," Mama said.

"It's all right though, isn't it?" The man raked his hand through his son's dark hair. He continued, non sequitur, "You know, Nureyev was a Tatar Muslim."

"Was he? Well. So did you dance for a company?"

"I did, for a time in Nur-Sultan. Then I got injured . . . Back then, there wasn't much you could do if your hip was finished, not like these days. Now I do contracting work."

When people were starting to tire of waiting, and even Farkhad's father fell silent, a teacher came out to tell the parents to leave. She stood aside so the children could walk into the foyer on their own. The moment I was inside, I knew that this was the world for which I was born. It was home—the walls painted in the light gray of

February, the smell of aged wood, the blue-carpeted staircase, and the framed pictures of all the legendary graduates since 1742. I recognized the ethereal Anna Pavlova from her poster that had hung at my school, and instantly committed the others to memory. Nijinsky, Balanchine, Baryshnikov. And as I looked around in amazement, a clear sign assured me that I would pass the audition: there was music in my head that I'd heard only once before. It was from the ballet on television that day when Sveta told me I was a jumper. I could now recall the music note by note; I'd kept the score in my subconscious all this time. The very strangeness and improbability of the premonition made me feel absolutely certain that it was real.

But as I went through the physical exam and choreography, I realized I was far from the best. It was evident that most of the auditioners already had years of dance and gymnastics—whereas the extent of my training was doing splits in the living room when Mama wasn't watching. The other girls seemed extraordinary in my eyes, but the teachers grumbled "stiff back," "weak turnout," "too short," "too short *legs*," "too muscular," and in one horrific instance, "too fat," loudly enough so that everyone could hear. Mine was "bad feet." Not one, not two, but three board members muttered this while watching and prodding me as I stood or moved to their commands only in my underwear. On the second day, a doctor—one of those rather numerous people who look as though they were born middle-aged, wearing bad shoes—explained in more detail, as if comparing potato varieties in his garden: "You have a classic Greek foot. This will create problems later, on pointe."

After the second-round medical exams, Svetlana came out and posted the results on the bulletin board. I didn't have the strength to face it and let others push past me. There was a girl called Berezina who also hung back near me, looking frightened. She was vivid but delicate, like the wings of a butterfly. With her white leotard and white chiffon skirt, long-lashed dark eyes, and perfectly centered black bun, the only part of her that felt human was her bright pink earlobes. She was the one auditioner who hadn't gotten any disparaging remarks—she had no discernible flaws. A girl near the board turned around and called out to her, "Nina, we both made the final round!" Only then did Berezina work up the courage to move to the front. I heard the friend say, "What would make you nervous, Nina? You're one of the best girls here."

My heart was beating right underneath my skin, which had become as thin as a balloon. Even other children had been taking stock of the competition, just as I inevitably noticed Berezina, and no one had singled me out or stared at me with envy. Then my mortification turned to fury, which pushed me to the front of the board. My heart nearly stopped when I saw my name with those who passed.

By the final round, the remaining fifteen auditioners resembled one another like apples at the grocery store. Small head, willowy neck, slender shoulders, supple spine, long thin legs, narrow feet—the Vaganova look, one they say is more delicate and graceful than any other school in the world. Differences in physique had been weeded out; girls simply standing in their underwear already had a pleasantly unified effect of a corps de ballet. For a second I couldn't even locate myself in the mirror. Then I saw my reflection—same litheness, my skin stretched taut over my ribs, high and sculpted hips, sticklike legs, dark brown hair pulled back into a bun. Identical to all the others, no deviation worth mentioning except my bad feet.

"Girls, in one long row. Sixteen sautés in first, sixteen in second, sixteen changements," one of the board members said, using her hands to show us the jumps. She cued the pianist.

In the mirror, the girls jumped together in unison. Then one of them—my reflection—rose higher than the rest. It was the force of all I'd been suppressing; I felt like I could reach my hands and tap the ceiling if I wished. The board members were now pointing in my direction. Murmurs and gasps. *That's a jumper.* I sprang even higher. I could fly to space and touch the stars if I wished.

When the piano stopped, I finally came back down to earth, my cheeks warm with the other girls' stares. I stood with my back straight, feet folded into a perfect fifth position, while the board members muttered and scribbled at their long table. Then they seemed to reach an agreement; the ones at the corners who had walked around the back to talk to other colleagues returned to their seats, and Svetlana cleared her throat.

"We are taking two," Sveta said. Two out of five hundred girls.

"Natalia Leonova. Nina Berezina. The rest of you are dismissed."

I SAY GOODBYE TO NINA and return to the hotel at three in the afternoon, the most ambivalent hour of the day. My curtains have been shut since I arrived, and the air is dense and warm. I pull aside the drapes and open the French doors, and a pale, foamy light pours into the room. Outside is a tableau of corniced buildings, cars, and people, mixing in and out of the frame, each in their own worlds. At the precise moment when I turn away from the balcony, my eyes catch the first of the cream roses drop a petal. It whispers softly as it touches the coffee table.

After I shower, I hobble out in a towel and collapse on the bed. An iron weight has been tied to every joint in my body. I feel I could fall through the many floors, to the lobby and to the center of the earth, until I put a Xanax on my tongue and float back to the surface. The cool breeze and the diffuse sound of traffic lull my eyes to close. Sleep crashes in like a wave, and I dream of a black bird—with shiny jet feathers, a curved yellow beak, and large eyes like dots of oil. I have seen this bird before. It flies ahead of me and I follow. Then more and more black birds appear, thickening the sky. Their cawing envelops me in a veil of sound, carrying me up to their height. They begin swirling upward in formation around me, creating a vortex of feathers above the clouds, just before plunging to the ground and taking me with them all the way down, down, down.

OF ALL CREATURES IN THE animal kingdom, birds are the most social. Even an albatross, which flies alone in the ocean for up to several years without ever touching land, sleeping midair and never seeing one of its kind, eventually returns to its colony—the exact place of its birth.

ii

MY ROOMMATE AT VAGANOVA WAS SOFIYA. SHE WAS A TYPE I'D SEEN BEFORE AT school: she dressed neatly and laughed easily, and always had about three other, like-mannered girls around her. With her upturned eyes, small nose, and champagne-blond hair slicked back into a bun, she looked more French than Muscovite—that is to say, she had *délicatesse*. In the early days, after turning off the light and crawling into our respective beds, she told me that her father owned a mining company and her mother used to be a ballet dancer herself—a corps member at Bolshoi. I told her that my mother was a costume maker for Mariinsky, that such and such soloists came to our apartment to do fittings specifically with her. I loved hearing the envy in her voice as she said, "I wish my mother did something like that—all she does now is go shopping and take care of my sister and me."

But then, little things began to accumulate. During center combinations, I positioned myself in the front instead of staying with her in the back of the room. After stumbling in a turning combo across the floor, she would giggle and shrug with the others, whereas I would repeat it by myself on the sidelines—until I'd executed it correctly, five times in a row. I always showed up first to class, at least fifteen minutes before Sofiya came in with her entourage. I knew that the other girls thought I was showing off in front of the teacher, but I didn't care about their approval. Sofiya also wanted us to wear matching Grishko warm-up sweaters. Each one cost Mama's weekly salary in those years of vertiginous inflation, when everyone became poorer except the wealthy. I told Sofiya no without going into the particulars.

The final straw was that I wanted to finish my homework no matter how late or early, or how tired Sofiya was from the rehearsals for *The Nutcracker*. To be fair, sometimes it was Sofiya who kept me up by inviting another girl to our room to gossip and listen to songs on her cassette player. Her impressive music collection was yet another thing that set Sofiya apart. She didn't mess around with homecooked cassettes dubbed from other counterfeits or recorded at underground concerts and passed down from older cousins, the prized possessions of upper-level students. She had a row of authentic records by Kalinov Most, Aquarium, of course Kino's entire discography, and even Madonna, Mariah Carey, and Whitney Houston with pristine J-cards in their clear plastic cases. Sofiya and the girls liked those power ballads the best, and even I listened while pretending to be bothered by the noise. "And ahhhh-i-ahh-i, will always, love youuuu—" the girls would croon at the top of their lungs, and I wouldn't be able to resist humming along. When the sound skipped, Sofiya popped out the cassette and turned the wheel with her pinky to tighten the thin brown filmstrip. The music returned, cocooning us in momentary esprit de corps, and she went back to painting the nails of her perfect, almond-shaped feet.

I WASN'T FAZED BY THE other girls, but I was terrified by our teacher Vera Igorevna. She showed me that a person could be honorable and cruel at the same time, and that bullying could create miracles.

Once, she gave us an epic rond de jambe en l'air combination until my right hip was only hanging on by being jammed into the socket. At the end of the combo, I stretched my leg fully out to the side, perpendicular to my body, in an à la seconde balance. Vera Igorevna held out a hand to the accompanist, stopping him midphrase.

"Release the hip, Leonova! Release it!" Vera Igorevna screamed. What was she even asking—weren't your legs supposed to be attached to your body? I tried to somehow detach my right hip from my socket without my leg falling lower than ninety degrees. Vera Igorevna, gnashing her teeth, stormed over to me and yanked my right leg out to the side by an inch and lifted it higher. "Like this! Yes! Now hold it here! Music, *pozhaluysta*!" When she took away her hand, my leg stayed floating out of sheer fear, while the accompanist meandered through the polonaise, clearly enjoying the sight of all of us shaking uncontrollably.

Despite her soft, dumpling-like silhouette and an unfashionable gray shag that I at first misconstrued as nurturing—or at least, easy—Vera Igorevna's character was as forceful as a general's. While we lifted our trembling legs and held it with our last remaining breath, she regarded the room with a distant and grim air, as if envisioning a field of battle. As much as she corrected each student with an unfailing sharpness, her true focus was on raising an entire class of dancers more than taking care of any one girl. She didn't play favorites like the other teachers, with the result that none of the students felt attached to her. She ended every class with her preferred form of torture—a never-ending loop of relevés on pointe. My toes felt like they were being skinned with a flaming vegetable peeler, but my fear of Vera Igorevna kept me going.

One of Vera Igorevna's other tendencies was to go past the end of the lesson. Because of this, all her students were late to the subsequent class, and she had been at war against the general-subjects teachers for decades. In the changing room, I barely had time to glance at my bleeding toes before shoving them in sneakers. They ached and throbbed through math, Russian, French, and science, during which I sat and wondered whether the blood had soaked through the socks and reached the lining of the shoes. This happened without fail, six days a week.

One day at lunch, I searched for Sofiya at the canteen. She was usually easy to spot: a champagne-colored head surrounded by two or three darker ones, shimmering in a mirage-like atmosphere of laughter. My eyes found her quickly, although for the first time ever, she was seated across from Nina and—the person I wanted her to sit with even less—Seryozha.

I froze, unsure whether to go somewhere else, but Sofiya raised a Grishko-sweater-clad arm, waved it in my direction, and piped clearly, "Natasha, come sit with us." Both Nina and Seryozha turned around to look at me with an uncertain smile, as though they hadn't quite decided what to think about me—and I was hurt, not by Nina of course, who had no reason to like me, but by Seryozha.

I walked over to the table and sat next to Sofiya, facing Nina and Seryozha, who no longer blushed like a beet in my presence. I hadn't seen him so up close in months—maybe even since before he auditioned and moved into the dorms. He hung around a lot of new friends and no longer seemed to need some old neighbor from his apartment building. Although he was sitting, it was noticeable that he had had a growth spurt of several centimeters. His body had lost its downy look and hardened into sinews, but his blue starburst eyes remained the same—the color of deep ice under the snow. I heard myself speak, "Hi, Seryozha," and his strange familiar face softened into a smile.

"Natasha, I don't know how we didn't cross paths earlier," he said, sitting up straighter in his white uniform T-shirt.

"Wait, you two already know each other?" Sofiya asked, and Seryozha obliged with the story of our shared apartment building and former school, leaving out the Reznikovs' New Year's party. Sofiya, who valued friends for specific reasons, dawned with the realization that I could offer something other than proximity as her roommate. It was not talent or sincerity that she sought in her closest companions, but connections to other interesting people—especially a boy like Seryozha—which made it easier to create a *group* of friends. If such a thought process were not so evident in her suddenly warmer expression toward me, I would have blamed myself for being cynical. But for whatever it was worth, Sofiya didn't try to mask her ideas or feelings, and her shallowness had a refreshing honesty to it.

Like Seryozha, Nina was popular, and therefore worthy of Sofiya's active interest. Nina and I had both been learning the role of Little Masha in *The Nutcracker.* There were five performances scheduled, and only one of us would be the A cast, getting the opening and the final night. Naturally, we hadn't become close.

As we ate, I found out more about Nina than I had in the past several weeks of rehearsals. With an engineer for a father and a teacher for a mother, she was from a solidly middle-class family without strong roots in the arts, as she herself put it. "But I want to make it. No, I'm *going* to make it," she said with surprising resolve, clenching her translucent hands. I also observed that, although Nina was always orbited by her friends, she didn't take so much comfort in the safety of numbers as Sofiya did. This was evident in the way she sat back from the conversation instead of seeking approval or consensus, gazing impassively with an air of someone much older listening to little children's chatter.

After the classes ended, Nina and I went to the warm-up room to get ready for the 5:30 rehearsal. Without Sofiya to create incessant noise, we fell silent, but in a way that didn't feel wholly uncomfortable. I sat down on the floor and slowly peeled off the socks crusty with dried blood. My toes had been blistering, bleeding, scabbing, and reopening every day for weeks. If I could have just two days without pointe shoes, I thought my feet could heal. But our only day off was on Sunday. At the prospect of this cycle continuing forever, a soft moan escaped my throat.

"Are your feet okay?" Nina asked, sitting wide straddle on the floor. I nodded—apparently unconvincingly, for she craned her neck toward me and winced. Immediately, she rooted around in her dance bag and pulled out a roll of white tape.

"Wrap it around your toes. It doesn't help much when you already have blisters, but it won't hurt. Just take this one—I have more in my room," she said, offering it to me. I hadn't known Nina was as angelic as she looked. One hoped that someone so pretty and well-liked by everyone would be hiding an ugly soul, but Nina was not.

"Thank you," I croaked, before winding the tape around my toes and wrapping them in lambswool. They already felt better inside my pointe shoes, and I rose with a renewed burst of energy. That was when the door opened and Vera Igorevna walked in, along with Vaganova rector Ambrosi Kobaladze.

Like many successful artistic directors, Ambrosi Simonovich was a short and unremarkable-looking man of indeterminable middle age, who would forever appear anywhere between forty and sixty. As was Balanchine before him, he was a character dancer rather than a danseur noble. His greatest role had been Bluebird in *The Sleeping Beauty*, not a prince or a warrior who must carry an entire ballet. A few decades hence, Ambrosi Simonovich gave the impression of a midlevel bureaucrat on a holiday or someone's papa with a fondness for golf shirts rather than a former magical creature. As was his habit, he strode in quickly with his lower body while keeping his upper body cool and calm, paused in front of us, cupped an elbow with one hand and with the other, pulled thoughtfully at his neatly trimmed beard. Vera Igorevna, who wasn't much shorter than Ambrosi Simonovich, followed her superior with an uncharacteristic air of deference and positioned herself just slightly off to the side and back.

"Both of you girls have been working very hard these past weeks," Ambrosi Simonovich said in his slightly nasal voice. Nina and I muttered thank you, and he nodded impatiently.

"You know how important Little Masha is—right after Big Masha. Most, if not all, Mariinsky soloists and premiers at one time played the lead in Vaganova's *Nutcracker.* I myself played the Nutcracker Prince. Vera Igorevna was Little Masha in her day—were you not, a few years before I matriculated?" He glanced at his colleague, who proudly nodded and responded, "Big Masha, too, in my final year"; it then struck me that Ambrosi Simonovich was rambling, which kind people are wont to do when they feel pressured to act harshly.

"So, we've decided on the casting. The opening night will be danced by Berezina. Three performances in total," he said, and all the blood rushed away from my head. "Leonova, you'll dance the remaining two performances."

Ambrosi Simonovich's furrowed brow softened with relief, and I realized he expected us to thank him. A dutiful *spasiba* left my mouth, and the rest of the evening was a blur. When I regained a sense of awareness, I found myself in my bed. Sofiya was either doing homework or watching ballet videos in the television room, and a comforting darkness surrounded me. I was curled under the blanket, looking at the golden sliver of light beneath the door. Every time someone passed in the hallway, their shadow moved through the thin rectangle. The muffled sound of conversations and laughter made me even more aware of my solitude. Was I alone or lonely? The boundary between the two states was a door with no threshold that I crossed many times a day.

A shadow glided across the gap of light and stopped, followed by a knock. When I didn't answer, the handle turned slowly. Then the room was flooded with the garish glow of the hallway lamp, which set in relief the figure of Nina Berezina. She had showered and changed into a clean T-shirt and warm-up pants; against her chest she was clutching a bottle of what looked like vodka and a bowl.

"Hey, Natasha. Are you asleep?" she said, although I was sure she'd already seen my open eyes. "I brought you something."

Then curiosity got the better of me. I sat up on my bed.

"What is it—vodka?"

Nina laughed. "Yes, but it's not what you think." She motioned for me to swing my feet out from under the covers and poured the vodka into the bowl.

"Again, this is best if you do it *before* developing blisters. But soaking your feet in vodka helps toughen your skin. It will sting now, but keep doing it a few times a week and it will get better." She placed the bowl next to the bed and looked at me eagerly. I took a deep breath and plunged one foot into the bowl—a moment so painful it expelled my soul from my body. When the worst passed, I pulled my toes out, opened my eyes, and saw I was gripping Nina's hand like a woman in labor; then the ridiculousness of everything hit us at once—and we started giggling.

"Should we drink some?" I asked, and Nina pretended to pour the contents of the bowl into her mouth, and we laughed until we were both tearing up and gasping for air.

Ballet is vast—but the ballet world is intimate. People with whom we took classes, dined with, and competed against would be the same people we'd fall in love with, marry, keep as lifelong friends or rivals. Between the two of us, it was Nina who first decided we were better off as friends, for reasons that have never been clear to me. Maybe it was because she thought she would always be slightly ahead of me—that's a reassuring quality in our condensed world. Maybe she really cannot dislike anyone—a problem I've never had.

For my part, I accepted Nina because she was the one person who let herself in through my door. Back then I was too young to know what causes two people to gravitate toward each other. Only time has shown me the truth: we can choose the minor friends and the minor lovers, but we don't have any choice in the matter of the people we truly love.

Who are the people we truly love? I don't think it's people we like, but the ones we keep thinking about. I have met scores of wonderful people, men and women, with whom I shared intimacies, laughter, goodwill—and then never thought about again after I moved on to the next theater and engagement. Some had even captured my imagination fully for months, but after we parted, I never felt their absence. They hadn't taken up any room inside me. Then some others occupy a huge part of your mind, and your heart, for years and maybe your whole life. Maybe they take up space inside your soul, so you can never really lose them without losing yourself, too. I think often of my childhood friends without feeling a particular wish to rekindle what we had. I even miss the way I miss them.

Between classes, meals, performances, and late-night confidences, a delicate balance had been struck between us by the time we reached our fourteenth year. Sofiya, the luminous daughter of fortune. Nina, who had an earlier birthday and had turned fifteen already, with her air of gravity and grace noticed by teachers and students alike. Seryozha, universally beloved for his sunny candor and goodness. And me, self-conflagrating in the worship of ballet, always the first to arrive at the studio and the last to leave, who would have been destroyed if not for the mollifying effects of friendship. It was an unspoken rule that we didn't compete against one another; if one of us was unhappy, the others flocked to console, and if another succeeded, we shared in that triumph. None of us overpowered the group. Like the geese that fly in formation, the leader at the tip of the V naturally replaced by another when it is tired, we took turns being the focus of attention for a while—always returning to an effortless state of inertia. Moving, but resting.

This was disturbed by a hairline fracture, itself begun by something so inconspicuous and banal, that only years of reflection led it back to my phone call with Mama one Saturday afternoon. When she heard me, her voice brightened like the old costumes she treated with lemon and baking soda in our bathtub. Not new, but newish—not happy, but happyish.

"Natashka. How is school, and when are you coming home?"

I mumbled some excuse about the packed rehearsal schedule, and she didn't resist my hesitation—in fact she sounded a little relieved, despite the fact that months had passed since I last visited. Although I was too old to be whipped by a belt, spending a lot of time together was a strain on us both. Mama was often stressed and, I suspect, sad, and she could take things out on me unexpectedly. One minute we would be having a laugh, and the next she'd shout at me over something as simple as forgetting to turn off the bathroom light. And I'd aged out of being soothed by sleeping in her bed that we'd always shared. I still longed to love and be loved by Mama, but she made me tense, anxious, and wary. Mama did wish me to feel happy; and it was all the better if she knew I was being raised by this hallowed school, learning exactly what I wanted. This was the best solution for everyone. Sometimes a family was better apart than together.

"Natasha, I have good news," she said in her rare cheerful voice, and I pictured her twirling the corkscrew cord around her forefinger, a girlish habit that kicked in when she was on the phone with Sveta.

"I just got a raise at the theater. One hundred rubles more a month." This was about the cost of five liters of vodka. "We can get you a new coat. The one you have is getting short in the arms."

"Thank you, Mama," I said, and we hung up a few minutes later. I couldn't bring myself to talk about the real reason I'd called. It was our teacher Agrippinia Alekseyevna's seventieth birthday in a few weeks, and fifth-year girls had agreed to pool our money for a gift. Sofiya, who so naturally took to the organization of social obligations, was in charge of the gift and soon asked me for my contribution.

"I couldn't get ahold of Mama. She's been working late at the opera house," I told her. "Can you take care of my portion, too? I'll pay you back after the break."

"Sure," Sofiya said, narrowing her eyes. But ten minutes later, her need to talk about Seryozha overcame her annoyance with me, and she was back to gossiping happily while plucking her eyebrows down to slender Cs.

The day before Agrippina Alekseyevna's party, Sofiya's mother came to pick her up at the dorm on their way to the department store. There was a soft knock of a long-nailed hand on our door, like the scraping of branches against our window on windy nights. Sofiya bounded out of bed and threw herself at her mother, and then they were locked in a tight embrace, rocking side to side.

"Mama, this is Natasha." Sofiya nodded in my direction, and her mother smiled at me using just her lips. She had elbow-length blond hair and thin legs clad in low-rise jeans, which was then entering the dawn of its golden age among fashionable Muscovites. Her frosted blue eye shadow struck a chord deep within me as a remarkable discovery. They left arm in arm, looking like a pair of sisters. Three hours later, they returned with a beautiful amethyst necklace for our teacher, as well as many more shopping bags filled with Sofiya's new clothes. As Sofiya prattled and put away the purchases, I wondered whether she might say "Oh here, saw this and thought of you," pulling out something very small and inexpensive. Something that she wouldn't even want for herself.

When the last bag was emptied without unveiling any gift and Sofiya trotted off to take a shower, my face burned from shame. There was only one thing worse than being poor, and that was *acting* poor—expecting generosity from people who have more. So what if Sofiya's wardrobe was filled to the brim and arranged by color, and my identical one next to it was half-stocked with worn and faded things, like a pre-perestroika grocery store? It still wasn't Sofiya's responsibility to make me happy. Instead, I imagined being on the other side one day, undressing my own handbag or high heels from its layers of silky tissue paper; putting them away in a closet lined with shelves, each level full of objects exuding the intoxicating scent of wealth.

This was just one of the countless things I wanted to do when I was older, inspired mostly by Sofiya and Nina and their families. Take Mama to the department store, buy fresh flowers for myself every week, wear cardigan sets, read *The Master and Margarita*. I never told them that their habits were the visceral images after which I was seeking to fashion my own life.

On Wednesday, Agrippina Alekseyevna celebrated her seventieth birthday in the Petipa studio, surrounded by her former and current students and esteemed colleagues. Along with the amethyst necklace and other gifts, many bouquets of flowers were heaped upon Agrippina Alekseyevna's tiny body; a magnificent tiered chocolate cake was cut and laid out on little plates, but no one touched them except for the boys. Ambrosi Simonovich delivered a wonderful speech, heartily kissed Agrippina Alekseyevna, and then made everyone roar with laughter by suddenly lifting her overhead in a beautiful arabesque. We gazed up at her in amazement: when she posed like that, she did not look a day over twenty-one. At the end of the party, Agrippina Alekseyevna turned to me and asked, "Would you help me carry the flowers back to my car?" I was thrilled; being singled out like that to help a teacher was a special honor. I packed her car full to the ceiling with flowers so that Agrippina Alekseyevna laughed about not being able to see the rear window. The headlights of her car cut paths of lead-tin yellow through the evening air, and I stood waving at her for a long time as she rounded the corner.

On Thursday, when we filed into the studio for our technique class, Agrippina Alekseyevna was nowhere to be found. Five minutes after the hour, Svetlana walked in as our substitute teacher, but she refused to answer what was wrong with Agrippina Alekseyevna.

By Friday, my concern turned to distress. I kept recalling how she poked her birdlike face out the window, saying she couldn't see anything in the rearview mirror with all the flowers in the way. No one would tell us what happened to her, and I felt certain that there had been an accident—and that I'd played a part in it.

Then over lunch on Saturday, Sofiya revealed that it was indeed the flowers that caused the trouble, but not in the way I imagined.

"It was her cat, Tybalt. He was having bloody diarrhea, and Agrippina Alekseyevna thought he was struck by stomach cancer," Sofiya said, impaling a baby tomato with her fork to underscore *bloody diarrhea*. "But after some outrageously expensive tests, the vet told her he probably just ate some plants."

"So he's fine?" Nina asked between bites of lettuce.

"Yes. She'll be back on Monday. But rehearsal tonight is still canceled!"

We hadn't had a Saturday evening off in months. As we may never be blessed with another case of feline diarrhea before graduation, Sofiya immediately set into motion the plan to best spend our freedom. Mariinsky was performing *Swan Lake* that night; furthermore, it was the twenty-one-year-old prima ballerina Katia Reznikova's debut as Odette/Odile; *furthermore*, we got free admissions with our Vaganova student IDs. Within minutes, Sofiya invited Seryozha and Andrei, a sixth-year from Novosibirsk, and we agreed to meet in the courtyard at half past five.

My mind was racing toward the evening so that I barely minded that Vera Igorevna was teaching our afternoon technique class instead of Agrippina Alekseyevna. Vera Igorevna had become more sharp-tongued than I remembered, telling Sofiya in front of everyone that she should concentrate on her general subjects, as she wouldn't get anywhere with ballet. Even Nina wasn't free from criticism. "Why are you hopping? Root your supporting leg down. Try again," our teacher snarled. When Nina still hopped out of her attitude turn, delicately and almost apologetically, Vera Igorevna groaned, "You look like a three-legged baby goat." Then when I was least expecting it, she pointed at my face and said, "Leonova, do an attitude turn."

I did a clean triple and landed in an allongé. For once, Vera Igorevna didn't seem to have anything to say. Then she added sullenly, "*Vot tak.* Yes, like that."

After class, the mood in the changing room was at an all-time low for the beginning of the weekend. I caught up to Sofiya, but she lowered her eyes and shook her head without speaking. Nina was more composed, promising to shower and meet us outside shortly. Sofiya and I climbed the winding stairs to our room. When we opened the door, the sun was throwing its last rays into the snow-covered courtyard. A bare-branched tree spun the light on the tip of its upturned finger, sending it over onto Sofiya's bed, where she collapsed facedown and lay motionless.

"Hey, we have to get ready." I tapped her shoulder gently.

"You guys go without me," Sofiya mumbled into the bed.

"You're the one who got us all excited. Come on." I grabbed her hand and pulled, but she swatted me away. I sat next to her, suddenly flooded with exhaustion.

"She's bitter and jealous of young girls who can dance, like she used to." Even as the words left my mouth, I knew that they weren't true. Vera Igorevna was mean, but not mean-spirited.

"She's right. I'm not good enough." Sofiya moaned, her head still buried in her pillow.

"Stop saying that. You've been doing really well," I said, patting her back. "And everybody has off days."

"*You* don't have off days."

I didn't know what to say to that. It had been a long time since I'd endured the terror of doing worse than the day before. At some indiscernible point, something had clicked into place within my body. My weaknesses—toes rubbing inside pointe shoes, graceless port de bras—were gone, and my strengths—speed, turns, jumps—were intensified. Ballet hadn't become easy, but it made sense to me the way chess made sense to a great player. Mostly it was an awareness of what you could do with all the pieces. Then you could get creative, even playful. Sometimes it was a negotiation with ballet—what you gave it and what you asked in return. Since reaching this point, every morning felt like the first day of summer, awash in warm blue, exhilarating and limitless.

"Hey, it's almost five." I tapped Sofiya again. "If you don't come, Seryozha will be disappointed."

Instead of shrugging my hand off, Sofiya stayed dead still, and I pressed on.

"Weren't you planning on wearing that new velvet dress? You look so good in it. Come on," I said, pulling on her arm.

Sofiya put on a halfhearted show of resisting me, but in the end I succeeded in getting her out of bed and into the shower. The boiler was broken again, for there was no hot water. We shrieked while splashing ourselves as much as we could endure, jumped out after a few minutes, and immediately pulled on thick knit hats over our wet heads. When we were finished dressing, I scanned the courtyard and saw three dark silhouettes, bracing their elbows and shifting from hip to hip. They waved at us frantically; Sofiya shouted with gusto, "We're coming!" and we ran downstairs, skipping two or three steps at a time and giggling for no reason.

As soon as we left the few blocks around Vaganova, I lost any sense of direction. It was Sofiya and Nina who knew their way around the city; Seryozha, Andrei, and I stuck close and let them lead. The night was lovely because we were young and in a mood to be moved. Everything seemed important to remember, and the world was speaking to us in secret signs. On the asphalt black and glossy from old snow, stoplights were painting their brushstrokes of red, yellow, and green. The fog was fresh and cool against our faces. We were brimming with jokes and the relaxed cheerfulness of being guided by someone you trust. It is a happiness to know nothing about where you're going, except that you'll end up somewhere wonderful.

Where we ended up was a fast-food place, a palace of fluorescent lights and french fries. Nina, Sofiya, and I had been eating primarily buckwheat and salads for months, and the rich smell of oil reached up not just to my nose but all the way to my brain. I had enough money for a small order of fries and two tiny paper cups of ketchup. I carried these on a plastic tray and took a seat next to Nina. Seryozha sat next to Sofiya, and Andrei grabbed a chair from another table and put it between Nina and Seryozha. We talked first about Agrippina Alekseyevna and Tybalt, and then the conversation drifted to the brilliant Katia Reznikova.

"I saw her dance Paquita last year—she is extraordinary," Sofiya said, taking a dainty bite of her burger. "She makes me wish I had a big nose and fiery red hair. So elegant."

"I like your blond hair. And your little nose," Seryozha said, just sheepishly enough that I could still believe he was the same boy I saw growing up in our building. Otherwise, he was unrecognizable. There was the sharp ravine between his pectoral muscles, the veins wrapping around his arms like the ridges of a tree, and the area where I wasn't supposed to look but couldn't help, the triangle above his legs. Smiling,

Sofiya laid a hand on his thigh. They locked eyes for a moment as though they were about to kiss—but he picked up his soda, and she disappeared behind a napkin. On the other side of the table, Andrei and Nina were deep in conversation about his Jean de Brienne variation at the upcoming Vaganova recital. I caught Nina telling him not to worry because he was splendid, he was great with everything.

"Oh no, not everything," said Andrei, a dreamy smile spreading across his well-defined, princely face. "I'm horrible with adagio. It's, it's . . ."

Nina leaned toward him sympathetically; at the same time, she whispered to me, "Do you want some of my sandwich? And my fries? I can't eat it all." She did this sometimes when I still looked hungry after finishing my food.

As I took a bite into her sandwich, Andrei said with relief, "It's too slow." Nina's eyes twinkled in admiration, as if he'd just revealed the most profound insight about the human condition. Andrei was quicker of body than of mind, but it was impossible to hold that against him. In fact, it added to his charms by making his exceptional beauty seem more human and reasonable. Watching Andrei and Nina incline their darkly handsome heads toward each other, I realized that they were the perfect pair for a ballet blanc—a flawed nobleman and a devoted sylph. Seryozha and Sofiya, with their golden hair, resembled Apollo and his Muse. I made a mental note to share this observation with the girls later. In the unchecked exuberance of our teens, we had been talking about ourselves increasingly in terms of what we could be, not what we were.

When you have more life ahead than behind, dreams are more real than reality.

Little by little, we were beginning to understand that life itself was the ultimate casting, and we wanted to know what our roles would be. It was the only thing that fascinated us endlessly, other than Seryozha and Andrei.

WHEN WE ARRIVED, THE THEATER was glowing in its plaza like a ship in a darkening sea. The crowd swelled around the entrance, murmuring excitedly about the new Odette. It was a full house. Every blue velvet seat was taken, packed from the orchestra pit to the Tsar's box with its monogram, then the belle étage, and all the way to the gods—the cheapest seats right underneath the ceiling, painted with the immortals. It was a rare honor for a dancer to be named a prima ballerina and the Swan Queen in the same year, only her twenty-first, and expectation coursed through the air like a live wire.

But the show set off to a poor start: no one came to *Swan Lake* to see the prince's birthday party, and that night the audience was visibly impatient for Siegfried and his pals to wrap it up. What they were waiting for finally began with the swell of tremolo on the strings. It reached up to the very last row—an unmistakable quality of Tchaikovsky—and Ekaterina Reznikova swept onto the stage as the White Swan. Thunderous applause at her mere entrance. What Sofiya said about her big nose and fiery hair was true. You could clearly see her aquiline features from a mile away—the highly arched eyebrows, piercing eyes, pronounced cheekbones. Her arms and legs were stupendously long and limber, even for a Mariinsky ballerina. She danced Odette not like a frightened and fragile bird, but like an exiled queen who must endure her fate with dignity. Even when she encountered Siegfried with his crossbow, she forewent the traditional fluttery, fearful bourrées and maintained her commanding poise, as if daring him to shoot her, at his own risk.

When the curtain fell on Act II, the theater almost quaked from the roar of the audience. But they were waiting for Reznikova to prove herself as Odile in Act III. It's said that Aurora in *Sleeping Beauty* is the most technically difficult female role; however, the ultimate test of a ballerina is *Swan Lake* with its dual roles of Odette and Odile. I knew from watching her in Act II that Reznikova would suit Odile even better, and soon she confirmed that was true. Because of the sheer length of her legs and feet, she was not a true bravura dancer made for the Black Swan's fouettés and pirouettes; there were more natural turners in the ranks of the Mariinsky, but she had fire, she had style, she had *attack*. When the coda ended, the audience reaction went past rapture and reached a level of panic.

We walked home by the Fontanka, its black surface gilded by the streetlamps. Somehow Sofiya, Nina, and Andrei were walking ahead, and I found myself side by side with Seryozha. I'd noticed that he talked easily with Sofiya or Nina, but remained silent with me—which I no longer minded as much as I once did. Seryozha flirted with Sofiya and commiserated with Nina, but his silence with me made me feel that he trusted me the most.

"Katia is going to be the reigning prima, isn't she?" I said, forcing my feet to keep moving forward. It had been a long night at the end of a long day.

"I think so. Hard to believe she was a student like us, not so long ago." Seryozha smiled. "I wasn't actually that close with her. She was nice to me—but it was her parents who really liked me. They still send me New Year's cards."

To my right, the river was flowing slowly and a little secretively, the way it always did at night. I paused and took hold of the guardrail, and Seryozha asked me if I was all right.

"You've never talked about that party or the Reznikovs, ever since." My words sounded more accusatory than I intended. "It's just that I thought you were—maybe ashamed of me."

Seryozha opened his mouth in surprise. I found myself trying to discern the starburst pattern in his eyes, but it was too hard to see in the orange light.

"Natasha, I could never be ashamed of you," he said, shaking his head.

"The truth is, when you dance, it's impossible to look at anyone else." Seryozha's breath turned to fog within fog. Mist was rising from the river, the clock struck midnight and tomorrow dissolved into today, and everywhere I sensed the hard edges blending, blurring. Our friends were calling us from up ahead; their voices were three distant lighthouses. He started walking again as though nothing had happened—but with one sentence, everything had changed between us.

iii

A FEW WEEKS BEFORE THE ANNUAL EXAMS, SOFIYA'S PARENTS TOOK HER to Yalta for a long weekend. She always worked herself up too much, it wasn't good for her to have no other life besides dance. It would balance her emotionally and physically to have a few days off on the beach. She returned with a marvelous tan and a handful of photos from her point-and-shoot camera. The sapphire-hued Black Sea lapping against a pebbly shore. Striped parasols and orange towels. Sofiya in a bikini top and white shorts, walking up to a fairy-tale castle on a promontory by the water. She seemed to have brought back the warmth of the Crimean sun underneath her translucent brown skin. Then on her first day back, Vera Igorevna berated her for a full five minutes, ending with "If you dance that badly at the exams, you'll get me fired." Before her trip, this would have made Sofiya cry miserably in our room. But this time, emboldened by some outside influence—the sea, the wider world—she took a radically different attitude.

"I could take this as yet another thing where I have to prove myself, to show that I am better than what I actually am," she said. We were sitting on our desk chairs pulled close to the window, which was open to catch the breeze. With her legs crossed Turkish style and her pink hands laced around a cup of tea, Sofiya looked like one delicate and beautiful knot.

"Or I could think of it as a process of learning. I have never done this before—finishing my seventh year at Vaganova—and so, how would I *know what to do*? All I can do is be curious and learn." She paused to take a sip from her cup, and I did the same. The weather was quite warm, but we still liked our hot drinks, which gave the sensation of being full.

"I think that's a really healthy perspective," I said, and I meant it.

"Seryozha says so, too." Sofiya smiled the way she did only when talking about Seryozha. It was unconscious and irrepressible, a natural phenomenon caused by another human being—like the rain falling or the sun rising simply because you gazed at someone. Because of her, I learned what someone looks like when they're in love.

"If you think about it, there's nothing that we've experienced already," I said, drinking from my cup of chamomile. "It's all new. And we just have to live each thing as it comes."

She groaned and shook her head.

"*You* don't have to find mental strategies to cope. All you need to do is just be exactly who you are, and you're brilliant. You don't know what it's like to always fall short of everyone's expectations, including your own."

One of life's ironies. Everyone expected Sofiya, ideally formed and born of a former dancer, to live up to all that she'd been given. Especially her mother, who was one of the best in her year at the Bolshoi school, even if she only made it to the corps at the company. On the other hand, everyone had always underestimated me, which gave me endless motivation to prove them wrong. This happened so much that when people discounted me, I was *more* confident that I would succeed. Since no one outside of our group wished me particularly well, I essentially felt invincible.

ON THE DAY OF THE exam, we filed into the Petipa studio to dance in front of our teachers, répétiteurs, and administrators of both the school and the ballet company. There was the diminutive Vaganova rector, Ambrosi Simonovich, gesticulating dramatically about something while charming Svetlana; and next to the imposing figure of Ivan Stanislavich Maksimov, the Mariinsky director, Vera Igorevna was glaring at us with such an expression as to make even the innocent blurt "I'm so sorry." The seats on the balcony were filled by students from other levels and parents. I'd tried to get Mama to stay home, saying I would be able to concentrate better without her—but in the back corner closest to the door, I found her sitting quietly like someone else's shadow. After the exams, Mama would suggest we go for *stakanchik* ice cream. She thought I still loved it; she had no idea I hadn't eaten sweets in years. So I would sit there barely touching my *stakanchik* while Mama worked through hers, trying to make conversation to bridge our lives that no longer had anything in common.

Mama met my eyes and gave me a shy wave. I kept my pose but tried to show her with my expression that I knew she was here. I'd lied to her: Mama didn't break my concentration. It just made me feel a little sad to see her, but I was calm. In the past three years, I'd received perfect marks in all categories. I'd already been told that I would represent Vaganova at the Varna International Competition in July, along with Seryozha and Nina.

The accompanist played generously that day, attuned to our wishes. His music moved us from the barre exercises to the center, then to allegro. I didn't have to think consciously about the choreography, which had been drilled into us for months leading up to this.

After the final révérence, we returned to the corridor and wrapped one another in hugs. Nina said, "I lost my balance slightly at the end of the manège, but I don't think it was that noticeable. Otherwise I'm happy." Sofiya was flushing and trembling from the rush of adrenaline. "For me, it went better than any other run-throughs we've done," she said, exhaling with a hand over her chest. Nina draped her arm around Sofiya's shoulders and squeezed. This was the last time we three would ever be together, though we didn't know it yet.

Neither Sofiya nor Nina asked me how I'd done, and I didn't have to explain. I was already the best at Vaganova, including the eighth-year students who were now graduating. I was only curious to know whether I would be the best at Varna, against everyone else in the world who also thought that they were the best. Naturally, to be once in a decade required nothing less.

THE ETYMOLOGY OF THE NAME Varna was unclear, possibly meaning "fortress," "flowing river," or "black," according to the city map I picked up at the hotel lobby. Vera Igorevna gave us our keys—Nina and I in one room, and Seryozha in another—and ordered us to rest and then get ready for class at six in the evening. Of course, as soon as Vera Igorevna's back was turned, Seryozha came over to our room and said, "Yours is a lot bigger. But mine has the better view." When we saw his room, Nina and I both screamed. Beyond the window, the city of red roofs, white walls, and lush gardens spread out like a cool stone mosaic floor in a chapel. And all the way to the eastern horizon, there was the achingly blue ribbon of what could only be the Black Sea.

I proposed that we go to the beach before class, but Nina was against it. In the end, she decided to rest and take a nap, and Seryozha and I ventured outside. The first thing I noticed: the directness of the sun, which was bleaching the stone paths and anything not shaded by the abundant gardens. As my eyes adjusted to the southern brilliance, I was struck by how much older Varna was compared to Piter—by a factor of millennia. The walls, roads, and cathedrals of this city were ancient, and people were as unharried as the red flowers that streamed down from windowsills. In Varna, heavy things felt heavier: the stones, the sound of church bells, the weight of time. And light things felt lighter: shadows of trees, the smell of roses, children's laughter, and my own feet—which barely needed to touch the earth, realizing that this was the very first time I truly proved myself. I'd fulfilled my promise to leave. Being far away from everything I knew gave me the sense of another sun rising in my world.

Seryozha asked if I wanted to get iced coffee. I was in fact thirsty, but I wanted to make it to the beach. Seryozha agreed, as he always did—that's how he partnered me as well, graciously letting me take control. I puzzled out the streets on the map as the sun bore down on us, but the sea had disappeared from our view and we lost our way before long. After an hour, Seryozha said we should head back to the hotel.

"We'll get another chance to go to the beach. The stage is right near there."

"But once we start competing we won't have time," I said, folding the map. Another thing about Seryozha was that he thought there was always later, that it would all work out in the end. For me, it had to happen in the right moment to be right. (Once, while coaching us on our *Don Quixote* pas de deux, Vera Igorevna growled, "Seryozha has time, Natasha has timing. You each have to learn from the other. Otherwise you're *both hopeless*.")

When we showed up just minutes before the class started, Vera Igorevna shocked us by not berating us for the first time in our memory. Instead, she warned all of us, including Nina:

"Stay close to each other and don't talk to or look at anyone else."

We nodded; then Vera Igorevna motioned for me to stand aside.

"At the barre, you stand between Seryozha and Nina," she said in a low voice. "Natasha, you want too much to prove yourself. That might feel helpful now, but it will poison you later, like arsenic. No true artists are driven by the desire to be the best."

The other competitors were streaming into the studio, pulling on their leotards and pushing an extra pin into their buns. It was time for me to go, but I couldn't resist asking.

"Then what are they driven by?"

She shook her head impatiently, and it suddenly struck me that this was the very first conversation Vera Igorevna was having with me one-on-one, in all these years.

"That, Natasha, is the one thing I cannot teach you. Now go, before the good spots are taken."

IT STARTED TO RAIN LATER that night. Vera Igorevna made us promise to go to bed immediately so we could be fresh for the first day of the competition. We nodded as one, but five minutes later Nina and I snuck into Seryozha's room and watched the storm cover Varna in a blind rage. A yellow lightning split the sky in half, and thunder followed like the sound of giant chariots. Nina and I draped a scratchy blanket around both of us, and Seryozha passed us an open bottle of vodka. Nina shook her head—she was not going to take any chances. But Seryozha and I convinced her that a few drops would help calm her nerves.

"Did you see the kids from the Bolshoi school?" Seryozha asked, and Nina nodded enthusiastically.

"Am I really the only one who followed Vera Igorevna's orders?" I snorted. We knew that when she told us to ignore other competitors, she really meant our rival school in Moscow.

"The girls were beautiful but a little soulless, if I may say so," Nina opined; no one but we knew that despite her angelic appearance, she had a sharp eye. "But there was a guy who was spectacular in grand allegro. The one with longer hair. Natasha, you really didn't notice?"

"That's Alexander Nikulin." Seryozha grimaced, taking a swig from the bottle. "The enfant terrible of the Bolshoi. The new Baryshnikov. The best."

"We weren't supposed to be checking out the competition," I said. As Seryozha pulled a bit of our blanket over his lap, I explained what Vera Igorevna said to me about not seeking to win.

"But I never wanted to be the best, or to prove myself." Nina hugged her knees to her chest. "To me, ballet is beauty above anything else. It's enough that I get to be a part of that beauty."

"And you, Seryozha?" I turned to him, and he chuckled.

"Honestly—I dance because I want to impress girls." By now I'd gotten used to this quality of Seryozha's. Flirty, but a little silly and self-deprecating.

"Is it working thus far?" I laughed, taking the bottle from his hand and bringing it to my lips, conscious of where his mouth had just pressed into it.

"I don't know—is it?" Seryozha said. Another lightning illuminated the whole city, and then the room fell into an even greater darkness.

THE STORM CALMED IN THE early hours of dawn, but the outdoor stage in the Sea Garden was still flooded up to the ankles. The crew spent all day pushing the water off with brooms, chasing away frogs, and blasting the stage with what looked like a giant's hair dryer. Without a run-through, it was impossible to know what type of floor we'd be dancing on, how much force and counter-balance we'd have to employ to account for the grippiness and rake. Use too much force on a slippery floor and you could fall flat on your face at the smallest imbalance; and then too much hesitation on a grippy floor could knock off a few turns from what should be six, seven, eight pirouettes. We practiced on raked floors at Vaganova, which prepped us for the tilted stage at Mariinsky—but many other theaters around the world were flat-floored. This was on top of the fact that in ballet, no matter how good you are, you can't ever know whether your movement will be executed perfectly. Each time you step into something as simple as a piqué arabesque, you risk not being on top of your leg. Every second, the conditions are changing—your muscles, energy, mentality, the floor, humidity, the atmosphere, your partner.

"It'll be all right," Seryozha said as we waited behind the ivy-covered wall wrapping around the stage. Floodlights shone through the greenery and dappled the costumes of dancers as they passed in and out of the darkness. We wished each other *toi toi toi* and made the sign of the cross. God bless and protect. A stagehand gave us our cue. We took each other's hand.

The bright staccato of clapping enveloped us as we stepped inside the blinding light. I instantly realized that the floor was slick, and Seryozha held my hand tighter. But the music began, and everything else receded into the distance. There was just us, dancing together, in the chiaroscuro between the night and the light. Why I long for the stage: it strips you bare. Even my hunger, my fight, my desire dissolve away until only the most essential part remains. That part is more than just beauty, more than just love.

I waited behind the wall during Seryozha's variation, but I didn't need to see him to know how he was doing. He was playful and flirtatious, but not rakish or destructive; his young lovestruck Spaniard had a sunny sincerity, like picking ripe tomatoes. When he finished, I ran onto the stage for my solo. Kitri's variation had never troubled me—it simply required the fleetness and coquettishness of a girl who knows who she is and what she wants. Kitri is a huge red rose, a brilliant-cut diamond. She's no great mystery, but that doesn't detract from her acknowledged attraction and popularity. Not everything has to be dark to be worthy.

After my solo, the coda hurtled to the end—and the only thing to do was give people what they expected from *Don Q*, which was fireworks. The moment we landed our last tour and pirouette in unison, all I could hear was my own ragged breathing—then the force of the applause almost knocked us over. Whistles—*bravi*. Seryozha handed me off toward the audience, I curtsied deeply and then returned to him for a final bow together.

When the first round ended, we found out that Nina, who danced the Aurora variation, did not advance to the second round. She cried over breakfast, and Seryozha and I took turns rubbing her back and offering her tea. A hundred people had been eliminated, and there were forty remaining. Out of these, only one dancer—male or female—would leave with the grand prix.

Seryozha and I had prepared separate solos for this round. The audience gave my variation a standing ovation; but I knew I'd done my best when Vera Igorevna said, with a frown, "Some little details could have been better. Overall, however, that was nearly there, Leonova."

In an unprecedented mood of laxity, Vera Igorevna decided that I'd earned my right to watch some of the other dancers. Leaving Seryozha to warm up, Nina and I made it to the seats by ourselves. I began truly paying attention to the contestants for the first time. There was a Cuban boy who nearly set the stage on fire with his Actaeon solo: he spent more time in the air than on the floor, then finished off with a nine-pirouette and a huge grin on his face like a talented colt breezily winning his first race. That's how I learned that the Russians and the Cubans both prized bravura, but the Russians made it look like art and the Cubans made it look like a party—they were dancing for joy and for each other. The English were more restrained, less interested in gymnastics or exaggerated proportions of the body; the Americans were generally athletic although too much of a hodge-podge to express a national style. Other than the Romanians and the Ukrainians, who clearly favored the Russian school, the only ones who showed distinct academicism were the French. Both Vaganova and the Paris Opéra Ballet School were often called elegant, but the former had soul, *dusha*, and the latter had what could only be described as fashion—a quality that made others want to copy them.

"Ah, Nikulin is next, Natasha," Nina whispered as the French Giselle walked off the stage. "It's the new Baryshnikov from the Bolshoi."

I didn't tell her it bothered me slightly, this tone of utter marvel at someone who wasn't one of us. Nikulin was at least half a head taller than every other male dancer in the competition. Clad only in the blue harem pants and gold chains of his Ali the Slave costume, his muscles were not nobly lithe, but heavy and dense and animalic. His hair was blond, but different from Seryozha's creamy ash; it was garishly yellow and fell straight almost to his shoulders. Even from a distance, I could make out the hard-set jaw and self-possessed stare, as if he didn't care at all about the audience or the jury.

"He looks nothing like Baryshnikov," I whispered, and Nina nudged me to be quiet.

Stillness fell in the amphitheater. When the music came on, Nikulin did something unthinkable—he sprinted across the entire length of the stage during the four-count preparation before his solo began. The Ali variation is not something for which you want to be out of breath under the best of circumstances; at a competition, under nerves and pressure, it's suicide for most people. But Nikulin was actually *smiling* while running downstage to end up in a flawless attitude balance, and he was breathtaking for the same reason Baryshnikov was—because art at its highest form is dangerous. He began slicing across the stage in a diagonal, doing a version of a pistol jump that I'd never seen before. His body threw off all expectations of heaviness and became explosive in jumps of unseen revolutions and height. Watching him was like watching a volcano erupt in the black of the night, rejoicing in the glowing red of liquid fire and fearing death at the same time. Beauty, violence, life, destruction, perfectly expressed in one body.

This, I realized, was something meaningful. They say that male ballet dancers fall under two archetypes: airy and crystalline Apollonian, and earthy, magnetic Dionysian. There was something about Nikulin's quality that was utterly Dionysian, but before I could figure out what that was—temperature or texture?—he had already moved on. He was shredding the stage with his grand pirouette that became faster and faster toward the end; then he threw his body into two consecutive double tours, ending on his knees in a devilish backbend.

Deafening ovation like a storm. Nikulin stood and then bowed reverentially, still in character as Ali the Slave. Nina tugged at my elbow, and besides, I couldn't possibly remain sitting—that would be like lying. We rose and added our clapping to the overwhelming cacophony.

In the third and final round, Seryozha and I danced the Gamzatti pas de deux from *La Bayadère*. This was what Vera Igorevna had prepared as my secret weapon, the true showcase of my qualities, with the most jumps of any female classical variation. And after Nikulin, I was no longer complacent—I was angry enough to fly above the roofless amphitheater. When I leaped, I hung on to the air before coming back down, and the audience gasped in unison—a reaction to which I'd become accustomed since age ten, yet relished at that moment more than ever. Something had possessed me and was dancing through me, more beautifully than I was humanly capable of.

And yet when they called me up for the women's gold medal, and not the grand prix that was awarded to only one dancer, I was not astonished. That went to Alexander Nikulin, who beamed as he accepted the prize onstage. I tried hard to watch his face—was he genuine, arrogant, shy, or shallow?—but it was almost impossible to figure out someone who was ecstatic. In brief moments of true happiness, people are remarkably similar. It's the rest of the time that reveals their differences.

The ceremony ended, and attendees filtered out through the Sea Garden. We followed the crowd, sighing and breaking into exhausted smiles. With a puffed-up chest like a defeated Napoleon, Vera Igorevna was grumbling about the lack of finesse in the Bolshoi style—all flash and no substance, no *integrity*. She cleared her throat and solemnly said, "Natasha, you did very, very well." Then in a moment of human weakness, she let slip something that she'd warned me against: "Better than that Nikulin." I felt a strong wish to hug her but decided against stressing her out with too much familiarity. Instead, I curtsied deeply.

We were catching a six o'clock flight the next morning. Vera Igorevna and Nina started walking ahead of us, and Seryozha and

I followed behind. Our path was like a tunnel in the darkness, but it wasn't frightening, just intimate. I wanted both to walk this way forever and to end up where I hadn't been, someplace wider, a new world even outside of ballet. Such vague yearnings were so sharply felt at seventeen; I took a deep breath to ease the pang. Seryozha was tugging at my wrist.

"There's something we need to do," he said. "Let's go to the beach."

"It's so late already. And what about Nina and Vera Igorevna?" I eyed their backs, already disappearing behind other dancers and coaches.

"They won't miss us for an hour." Seryozha smiled, extending a hand to me. I took it and he pulled me southward, where the garden soon opened out to a crescent of a beach. The night cast everything in ink blue, and the moon traced a silvery path from the horizon to where we were standing barefoot on the sand. I squeezed Seryozha's hand a little tighter. St. Petersburg was right on the Baltic, but you forgot that—the sea was hardly the point there. I breathed deeply in and out, almost panting. It hurts your heart when you see something and realize what you've been missing your entire life.

"What about Sofiya?" I asked him, without letting go of his hand.

"You know, there never was anything serious between us. We're still so young! We never said we were . . ." Seryozha muttered.

"I know, but she really likes you."

"Sofiya didn't pass the exams, Natasha. She's not coming back to Vaganova—she's going home to Moscow." He inhaled sharply. "And I really like you."

In my mind flashed everything Sofiya had that I wanted. It didn't seem so outrageous that I should have just one thing that *she* wanted. And in Moscow, she would forget Seryozha and find another source of fascination. We all had the emotional stability of an atom missing an electron. I'd kissed a few boys simply because they had shown me interest; it seemed rude not to at least check what the fuss was about. Nina and Andrei, Vaganova's most constant and even-keeled couple, had had at least five mini breakups before getting back together again. Our entire class was in the throes of fumbling in the dark, sneaking into beds, and crying in the bathroom; relationships flared and died in the span of a few days like in *Romeo and Juliet*, only both parties revived and went on falling passionately in love with others.

We stood with our hands interlaced, eyes fixed on the crashing waves. Then suddenly, I started giggling.

"Fortress—that's me," I said. "Flowing river—that's you. Black. Well, that's obvious."

"What are you talking about?" Seryozha, who didn't understand, nonetheless took this as an encouragement. He drew me in, and we kissed; the warmth and the smell of his body—like rain and fresh plaster—loosened something hard inside me. For the first time in my life, I *tasted* happiness: not earned at the end of some struggle, victorious and alone, or even basked in the communal glow of friends, but received from someone who intended it just for me. It was freely given, without any reason, like true kindness and true friendship. But this feeling was more intoxicating than those things—this heady sweetness that coated the inside of my mouth, the inside of my entire being. Yet it was not Seryozha that I was thinking of as we stood, our bodies knitted against the wind. It was Nikulin, his inhuman gifts, and what I had to do to surpass him.

YES—YOU NEVER RECOVER FROM THE first time you see beauty like that. Talent was common in my world, such that a middling amount of it could even seem vulgar. Everyone I knew, even students who were expelled, were prodigies by any normal standards. But they were the shallow seas visible from the shore, and he was the open ocean, so vast that direction lost its meaning; water as far as the eye could see, creating its own weather, its own laws and logic. Above all, dangerous. I was frightened and tempted, and now live with the consequences of that wreckage in my own body.

PAIN RADIATES EVERYWHERE AFTER JUST one company class at Mariinsky. My feet and ankles are so red and swollen, I feel afraid of walking to the bathroom. I don't return to the theater, and spend the day holed up with room-service vodka and numbingly inane TV shows. And somewhere between my second and third glass, I realize how possible it is to give up and accept defeat. How pleasant, even. I have nothing to prove to anyone—I don't have to *be* anything. I used to look down on people whose only objective in life is going to work, coming home, eating dinner, watching a show, and going to bed, and now their simple satisfaction in the mundane seems to signify maturity and wisdom. Tomorrow, I will book the next flight out of Piter. I'd have to hire someone else to make arrangements for Mama. Pack up the furniture in my apartment in Paris, buy a cheap place in the country, find some regular routine. Live quietly until money runs out—which should not be in at least several years. I can't picture what happens next, but again that's asking too much of myself for no reason. I've lived my entire life as though swimming upriver, and now I'm ready for the lovely, whole surrender of letting the current carry me down. My mind thus made up, I fall into a dreamless, unmedicated sleep for the first time in months.

Before I order breakfast in the morning, Igor Petrenko calls me from the lobby.

"There's a visitor who is asking to see you," he whispers into the receiver. "It's Madame Nina Berezina."

I tell him to send her up. Within minutes, Nina walks into my room, looking and smelling as fresh as blue wildflowers. She hugs me, closes the door behind her, and puts down her handbag in one multitasking movement that nevertheless doesn't register as chaotic, only lively. It reminds me why she is so wonderful, among many other reasons.

"Why haven't you answered any of my texts?" she asks.

"Oh. I wasn't feeling well. I haven't been looking at my phone at all." I fumble around searching for my phone until it is discovered facedown on the vanity. Twelve unread messages, all from Nina.

"Get dressed. You can't just stay in here like this," Nina says, casting critical glances at the tangle of sheets, empty glasses, and towels on the floor.

"Let me at least take a shower first," I protest, but Nina shakes her head.

"No need. We're going to the *banya*."

We don't talk much on the way to the bathhouse. Nor do we start chatting amicably while stripping down in the dressing room. I haven't observed my naked body carefully in a long time, leaving the light off while taking showers at the hotel. I flinch when I see myself in front of the mirror. My eyes are ringed by dark circles, my triceps hang loose, and even my cheeks are saggy.

"I look like shit," I say.

"You do not look like shit," Nina says automatically, and then glances in my direction. I can see her judging and then trying so hard not to judge my body, because that's what real friends do. Nina would rather sit next to a crying baby in an airplane than tell me that I'm fat.

In the sauna, I watch the sweat bead on my skin and gather inside the folds of my body. Drop by drop, like collecting water in the desert. Once the heat becomes unbearable, we plunge into the cold pool, which makes all my nerves spring back to life. We then retreat to the *predbannik* and settle on a bench with cups of fresh cranberry purée, at which point Nina finally decides we're ready to talk.

"Have you gone to see your mother yet?"

I shake my head. Nina lets out a small sigh.

"Do you want me to come with you? Maybe after this. I don't have to be home until evening."

"You're so kind, but I'm definitely not ready," I say, stirring the red pulp with a spoon. My eyes begin to sting and I push the cup away from me. Nina makes a sorrowful face.

"I'm sorry. We don't have to talk about this right now. I just wanted you to know that I'm here for you," she says, patting me on the back. "When you have a giant mess of a knot, the thing to do is find the easiest single knot to untie, and then the next one, and then the next one. For now, we should focus on getting you back on your feet." She rises, signaling that we're ready for another round of steam and cold plunge.

After the *banya*, Nina asks if I would like to come over for dinner.

"I wouldn't dream of it. I'm sorry I took so much of your time. It's your only day off, you should have spent it with your family," I say.

"You are my family, too." She wraps me in a hug. "Drink less and eat more, Natasha. And come to physiotherapy tomorrow. Dmitri arranged for Svetlana to work with you privately. If you don't show up, it will be terribly disrespectful."

I SHOW UP AT THE theater the next day at quarter to eleven, and Sveta is waiting for me by the elevator. She has started wearing glasses and looks slightly shorter than I remember, but her hair tied back in a low bun is still as black as it was twenty years ago. She rushes over, kisses me on both cheeks, and says, "Don't worry. I'll take good care of you."

"Sveta." I pause, my voice caught in my throat. "Everything has gone so wrong. So, so wrong."

She gazes into my eyes, her hands cupping my face. "I know. But nothing this painful lasts forever."

With her Russian tolerance for pain, Sveta believes that my retirement was a mistake and that my French physio team was simply incompetent. She and I start working on rebuilding the strength in my feet, going over the same basic movements that I hadn't done even in my first year at Vaganova. There is no dancing to speak of. No music.

Sveta says, let go of expectations of when your body will heal. Think about this one tendu, this one relevé. Her idea of a "treat" is sixteen grand battements each to the front, side, back, and side, which is both exhausting and boring. When I complain, she says that the great Marina Semyonova taught and demonstrated this combination into her eighties. "Maybe if you practiced this before, you wouldn't have gotten injured," scolds Sveta.

Despite Sveta's restraint, every morning I wake up wondering if that would be the day I jump. Every afternoon I go back to the hotel with swollen ankles and feet. Every night I soothe myself with Xanax and vodka, without which I can't fall asleep. But if I fall asleep, black birds surround me, smother me, their feathers in my eyes, throat, all over my back. Plumage bursts through my skin like crocuses pushing their way out of the earth, my arms become wings, and my lips harden into a beak. I try to fly but I fall, spiraling and scattering tufts of black down for what feels like eternity—and then I wake up, the sheets drenched and tangled around my legs. As I adjust to the solidness of the bed beneath me and the powdery smell of the linen, my mind forms these words on the ceiling—Will I finally jump today?

A month passes like this, and I still haven't attempted a single pirouette let alone danced on pointe. Our conditioning sessions are increasingly gloomy, despite Sveta's superhuman efforts to maintain crisp optimism. The sun is already setting earlier and earlier, and people's smiles as they lounge outside have a bittersweet resignation that yet another summer is waning. My performance is scheduled for October.

"I can't dance Giselle by then, Sveta. We might as well tell Dmitri now," I say one day, my legs sprawled out in a wide V in front of me.

"You're doing great, Natasha. *Ktoh ni riskuyet, tot ni pyot shampanskava.*" He who doesn't take risks, doesn't drink champagne. Sveta plants her hands on the barre and bends her graceful torso in a half-moon shape, stretching out her own body in the middle of my dispirited break.

"What if I don't want to drink champagne?" I lay my back on the floor, cushioning my head with interlaced hands. "Why don't I stop now? What difference does it make ultimately? We're all slowly dying anyway."

"Do you remember when you were a kid, a little seamstress's daughter, and no one told you to dance—in fact, discouraged you from trying in every possible way?" Sveta crouches down to my level. "No one believed in you then, except yourself. Now it's the opposite—everyone believes in you, but you coldly refuse all that faith."

I push myself up onto my elbows. "That's not exactly true. You believed in me back then, you told me I was a jumper. It's my earliest memory, Sveta. You made me become a dancer."

She smiles. "Honestly, Natasha, it was a passing comment on my part. I didn't know you took it so much to heart. Even if I hadn't told you anything, you would have found ballet one way or another. Become one of the greats, one way or another."

Sveta extends a hand and pulls me up to standing. After we finish the rest of the exercises, I text Nina that I'm ready to go see Mama now. An hour later, Nina meets me outside the entrance, a white practice tutu slung over her shoulder like a cupcake liner.

"Are you sure you're ready?" she asks as we pile into a cab, and I nod.

"It sounds awful, but today is the first time I'm really missing her."

We head southeast to the suburbs. Just past a rye field and an abandoned monastery, we stop the car in front of a little Church of St. George. It's surrounded by birch trees, which part to reveal a gravel path leading to the back. Each crunch of our footstep releases a fresh smell of moss and lichen into the air. It doesn't take me long to find her in this place. Soon I am standing in front of a very simple stone, which holds her life reduced to a few simple words: ANNA IVANOVNA LEONOVA, 1961–2019. We stand in silence, heads bowed and hands interlaced, as the sky darkens and the wind blows with the first husky chill of autumn.

"I didn't even remember to bring flowers," I finally say without turning to face Nina. She puts her hand on my shoulder and squeezes gently. I can't speak, I can't even cry. Nothing feels right when you visit your mother's grave for the first time.

iv

BEFORE MY FIRST SEASON AT MARIINSKY BEGAN, I MOVED BACK HOME. Mama was still living in the same cheerless apartment facing the courtyard. Rather than sharing her bedroom as I did before Vaganova, I decided to sleep on the couch in the living room. Mama apologized every time she accidentally kicked my open suitcase or saw me folding the comforter and putting it away behind the sofa. She would say, "Wouldn't it be better if you slept in my room? The couch is bad for your back."

"It's only until the season starts and I get paid," I said to her, more to signal that I'd be leaving soon rather than to assuage her fears about my back. She obviously saw right through me. Her eyes widened and just the right part of her upper lip lifted from the lower lip, as if the two sides of her face were in an argument about how to feel.

"I'm going to save everything I can. I'll spend only on rent and a little bit of food, and give you the rest," I continued, as I often did instead of telling her I loved her.

"On a corps de ballet salary? Will you have a lot left over to splash around?" Mama asked, but her lips were twitching in a near smile.

"I'll also get performance bonuses. And I assure you, Mama, I won't be in the corps long." I put my fists on my hips, as if daring her to disagree, but she didn't. By now, if I'd told her I would be the first woman to dance on the moon, she would have believed me.

"I don't need your money, Natasha. What would I do with it?" She threw her hands in the air, as if exasperated by the suggestion.

"You can do whatever you want. Buy yourself a pair of nice shoes. Go out to dinner. Get a pet poodle," I said, drawing a husky chuckle out of her. I liked making her laugh, although she wasn't far off: on my monthly salary of 10,000 rubles, I couldn't get an apartment of my own or give her any money for a while. I realized I would have to move up quickly to be able to afford anything, even food and practice clothes. Many corps members were only able to keep dancing thanks to family money. Nina was moving into her older sister's apartment, which her parents paid for, and Seryozha was going back to his parents' home, too.

July dawned hot and restive. In Petersburg summers there was always something implacable in the air, pale arms bared in sleeveless tops, people drinking on the quays watching the bridges crack slowly upward to let a ship pass through. A light-purple sky at midnight. Music rolling in waves across the Neva. No one going home. Fullness of the sun returning before anyone has had much rest. Elliptical days long on the light and short on the dark, like the keys of a piano.

In the middle of July, the middle month of summer, my friends and I had a picnic in the Field of Mars to celebrate my eighteenth birthday. Nina made piroshki and cucumber dill salad. Andrei procured a bottle of vodka. Seryozha brought a bottle of champagne and a birthday cake. We laid two small blankets side by side and clung together like sailors adrift on a raft. The grass shone and rippled in green waves. A playful wind rifled through our hair and knocked down empty paper cups.

After a while, Andryusha and Seryozha got up with a Frisbee. Nina and I propped ourselves up on our elbows and watched the boys play fetch with each other. Taken out of their usual setting and practice clothes, they looked both more ordinary and more handsome in their jeans and T-shirts. Anyone passing by wouldn't have seen us as ballet dancers but four university students on a break. I let myself be pulled into a fantasy of a less difficult life. Less pain, less discipline, less disappointment, less pressure and competition—but less of other things, too.

Nina's mind was running in a completely different direction, however. "I'm so happy we're all going to be in the company," she said, fidgeting with a lock of her midnight hair. "And Andryusha and I will get to spend a lot more time together." Andryusha had graduated a year earlier and was already a coryphée, and Nina had been secretly worried that he would leave her for someone at the company. I never thought princely Andryusha capable of betrayal—he always looked like he would make the most terrifically bad liar.

"You don't feel like you'd be hanging out too much?" I asked, just as Andryusha threw the Frisbee high above Seryozha, who jumped like a trout to catch it with one hand.

"No, of course not. I feel I could spend every day with him and not get tired," Nina said, wrapping a satiny ribbon of grass around her finger. She unwound it when she saw Andryusha and Seryozha walking toward us, laughing at something and shaking their heads.

"Girls! Is it time for the cake yet?" Andryusha said, settling down next to Nina and pouring more champagne into all the cups.

Seryozha planted eighteen candles in the cake like saplings and lit them one by one with a match. Then they sang me happy birthday, everyone's faces glowing, everyone's voices out of tune. After I blew out the candles, Seryozha grabbed my hand and twirled me into a kiss. When we came apart, I was left with a metal object in my palm. It was a key.

"What's this?" I held it up, and Seryozha smiled.

"It's the key to our new apartment," he said bashfully as Nina and Andryusha clapped. "I found a one-bedroom apartment, not very big but close to the theater."

"With what money? I don't understand."

"Ambrosi Simonovich helped me rent it on the cheap, it's his cousin's apartment."

So that was why Seryozha had been busy these past several weeks, conferring with Ambrosi Simonovich and disappearing for hours at a time. The rector had a special place in his heart for Seryozha; I knew he wouldn't have done it for me. It irked me that Ambrosi Simonovich had more of a say in where I would live than I did. Didn't Seryozha wonder whether I might want to decide for myself? But I made an effort to smile at him, who didn't see any reason I would be less than thrilled.

Everyone wanted to immediately see this apartment. We packed the barely eaten cake, rolled our blankets, and took the Metro to Vitebskaya Ulitsa. It was on the fifth floor of a brick building near the end of the street. We huffed and puffed up the stairs in our inebriated state. When we got to the door, Seryozha insisted that I use my key to open it.

Long, low western light everywhere. Humble at a first glance, the apartment revealed its idiosyncrasies one by one—although, as it was tiny, uncovering its secrets didn't take long. There was a little kitchenette as you walked in, some space where you could put an entry table or a shoe closet, and a bathroom with a book-size sink, a standing shower, and a questionably low toilet. The living room was as big as a large mattress, and the floor was tilted very badly. I felt I could fall over just walking across that steep slope.

"Here's our very own raked stage," joked Seryozha, doing a pirouette and making me laugh. He reached over to grab my hand and led me around the rooms, opening various cupboards and drawers. He pointed out where I could put my foam roller and yoga mat, where we could sit and eat breakfast together. I began to notice certain charming details, like the built-in bookcase in the only bedroom. This pride of the apartment had a surprisingly high ceiling and two large windows that gave way to the west. If you leaned out at one of them, you could see over the tops of buildings the tiniest trace of the Neva like a mirage.

"Isn't that the river?" I pointed at the horizon.

"I don't know—is it?" Nina craned her neck.

"Very hard to tell." Andryusha cocked his head.

"Of course it is. We have a river view, friends!" Seryozha boomed, pouring the last remaining vodka evenly into our four cups.

"To Natasha's birthday!" Nina said.

"To you three making the company!" Andryusha said.

"To friendship!" I said.

"To our first home!" Seryozha said, and I embraced my friends in the simple, animal rush of contentment. Such things that people took for granted felt so new to me, I could weep.

IN THE FIRST WEEK OF the season, Seryozha and I had just arrived at the studio and started warming up when Andryusha sidled next to us. "Congratulations, Natasha," he whispered. "You've seen the casting for *La Bayadère*?"

We hadn't. He warned us in a low voice, "I would try not to say much about it in front of the others," as we both rushed to the bulletin board. I'd gotten the Second Shade, a short but coveted variation usually danced by soloists. While Seryozha had gotten only corps parts, I was thrilled for Nina that she was tapped for the Third Shade. But the cascading ranks of the company that swarmed around the announcement kept their faces carefully impassive. It was the only way one could survive the constant competition with any dignity—and more importantly, to not incur the wrath of anyone who thought they deserved your role. I was already inured to such dynamics from Vaganova and knew how to act. Stay indifferent, impenetrable, and focused on the job. Don't gloat at the compliments and don't break down at the slights. What I didn't count on was the fact that company members had far more ego than students cowering under their pedagogues. They had all been the best in their class; many had earned a medal or two. The pay difference per role, not to mention by rank, was tremendous. Naturally, the ones at the top didn't want to help the junior dancers take over their roles. But before long, Ivan Stanslavich pulled me aside with an inclination of his majestic, silver head, and told me to seek Katia Reznikova's help with my variation. The director spoke as if it were an afterthought, but everyone knew he didn't intend anything he said to be taken lightly.

"Katia has a reputation for being more generous," Andryusha advised over lunch. "She's Ivan Stanislavich's favorite, and she's still only twenty-five. She doesn't have anything to be afraid of."

I waited until a break in Katia's Gamzatti rehearsal to approach her. The music tempted me to peek inside the studio, but I knew not to distract her to satisfy my curiosity. Only when the pianist went to the restroom did I step inside and face the whole reality of Katia in her element. She took company class with the soloists, and I with the rest of the corps. So most days, it was easy to ignore her solar luminosity and magnetism, around which even other premiers orbited dim and powerless. But now, as she stood on one hip, swigging from her water bottle, her mere presence was more vital than most dancers in the act of performing. She was one of the gods, who could not help but shine and reveal their divinity when disguised among mortals.

"Katia, I'm sorry to disturb you," I approached her with a smile. But as soon as I said her diminutive name, her face froze—and somehow her eyes turned a more vivid shade of green. She'd expected to be called Ekaterina. She was not much older than I was, but it was not for me, a new corps member, to determine the formality between us.

"Natasha, isn't it?" Katia slowly screwed the cap of her water bottle back on, and I nodded.

"I've admired your dancing for such a long time, ever since I saw your debut in *Swan Lake*. I don't know if you remember, but we first met years ago at your parents' New Year's party. I was there with Seryozha Kostiuk."

"Ah. I remember Seryozha," Katia said, fixing her gleaming eyes on mine. "I saw he just started in the corps."

"Yes, we both did," I said, encouraged by her acknowledgment. "Ivan Stanislavich said I should ask you to help me with the Second Shade variation. I'd be so grateful if you could spend a few hours with me."

"Oh, no. I couldn't possibly," Katia said. "I'll talk to Ivan Stanislavich so he understands." She didn't offer any false apologies. It seemed that she considered excuses, regret, and social lubrication as beneath her. She unscrewed the cap and took another slow sip, just as the pianist returned and sat down on his bench. I didn't have any choice but to walk out of the studio, my face burning and my heart pounding.

Later that night in bed, Seryozha said, "Maybe she simply doesn't have the time or the energy, Natasha." His T-shirt was shapeless over his torso; his eyes were crusty with fatigue, unrecognizable from back in the day when they were bright and faceted like cut ice.

"It wasn't just that. And of course you don't understand. No one ever dislikes you." I roughly peeled off the hand that he laid on my shoulder. He looked back, mouth open, confused by the notion that someone could be hostile to him when he hadn't done anything wrong. His whole life, he'd had the benefit of people who got along with him, who treated him with fairness and, very often, generosity. I was the opposite: until we formed our group of friends, no one gave me any extra warmth, and often less than what civility demanded. A part of it had to be that Seryozha was a boy—both men and women were almost always more gracious to boys than to girls. But that didn't explain everything. Case in point: Nina, who attracted goodwill as universally as Seryozha did. Once, I'd asked her why people liked her more than me, and she'd said with seriousness, "Oh but I actually care *a lot* whether they do." That was the extent to which I figured out why I didn't win people over.

Seryozha scooched closer to me; when I didn't roll away, he kissed me. His tongue ran over my lips until they parted. We only kissed with tongue when we had sex—or more precisely, when he wanted to have sex. I had a vague sense that this wasn't the way it was supposed to be when we were young and in love. But Seryozha didn't seem to mind. He slipped his hand underneath my T-shirt and touched me in the exact same sequence he always used while I lay beneath him, exhausted and naked only from the waist down.

The next morning, I waited for Ivan Stanislavich to talk to me about Katia's refusal to coach me; but he marched away as if he'd forgotten me completely. Ivan Stanislavich was as different as possible from our Vaganova rector. He was a legendary premier in his day, coached by Galina Ulanova herself, with the height and bearing of an exemplary danseur noble. Under the full gray hair and prominent eyebrows, he had the perpetual look of analyzing your dancing, even your character, with the impersonal attitude of an X-ray machine. He employed nothing of Ambrosi Simonovich's good-natured circumlocution before delivering a difficult decision, a habit I now saw was rooted in parental feelings. On the contrary: the Mariinsky director did not serve children or insecure dancers—all he served was ballet, the art and the institution both. Since he didn't bring up Katia first, I would have only made myself appear needy by asking for his advice.

I began rehearsing Second Shade on my own, watching videos for reference. Once or twice, Ivan Stanislavich stopped by the door as I danced to a CD, watched me for a minute with his subzero glare, and walked away without saying anything, his footsteps ringing like those of a chatelain in his cold stone halls. At first, this made me nervous; then as I came to understand Ivan Stanislavich's nature, I ceased to worry. Although Vera Igorevna was harsh and sometimes cruel, there was still something in her that made you want to dance better for her.

I suppose it's because she believed in you, even though she did her utmost to hide it. On the other hand, Ivan Stanislavich didn't "believe in" a dancer. Either a dancer had what he wanted or he moved on to the next one. Since our relationship was going to be a transactional one, I wasn't anxious about disappointing him. I didn't owe him anything; I really felt I didn't owe *anyone* anything. I even felt a kind of relief at this, as a kite that is cut off might soar gladly for a while before realizing the hopelessness of its situation.

Before, much of the reward of dancing had lain with satisfying and honoring my teachers, especially Vera Igorevna. Stripped of the others, however, I now had to go deeper for fulfillment, to a mysterious place where music and movement met and blended, like an underwater lake at the bottom of the ocean. It was peaceful, beautiful, and terrifying all at once. And this was especially true of *La Bayadère* with its divine score. Every time I rehearsed, I fell into this secret space until the boundaries containing me dissolved. I wanted to disappear between music and dance. Dancing *well* was, in a lot of ways, besides the point.

On opening night, I got ready in the women's corps dressing room with Nina, pinning each other's hairpieces as we had done since we were ten. Then we scurried backstage and hid ourselves among the set props to watch Acts I and II. Daria, a feline blond prima with a reputation for precision, was dancing Nikiya, the beautiful temple dancer who is betrayed by her sworn lover, Solor. Daria was the only dancer in the company who had the power to reject her partners, if rumors were to be believed. It wasn't Ivan Stanislavich's pleasure to tolerate such usurpation of his authority—yet Daria always delivered exactly what she wanted, and that was a priceless quality in our world. Although she was magnificent as usual, my attention was trained on Katia's Gamzatti, the single-minded princess who marries Solor. Based on my recent encounter with her, I now knew why Katia was so well cast as Gamzatti: she could be genuinely adversarial. The two biggest divas of the company dueling onstage made all of the corps watching in the wings want to grab popcorn.

"Ivan Stanislavich knows what he's doing, pitting them against each other," Nina whispered, adding more rosin to the heel lining of her shoes. "They are evenly matched."

"I hate to say this, but Katia won this round," I replied, smoothing the white chiffon sleeves of my costume. The curtain fell on Act II and the stagehands set the multiple backdrops spinning all around us. Dancers stripped their wet costumes down to their waists and limped back to the dressing rooms. The air was dense with sweat, adrenaline. I reached my hand to the floor to feel its grip before the curtains rose again on Act III, the moonlit Kingdom of Shades.

The next morning, *Kommersant* published the following review:

> Daria Lubova is unquestionably the most technically flawless ballerina in Mariinsky's current roster, making her ideal for pure academicism of Aurora or Balanchine's Diamonds. In Nikiya, a role that demands emotional subsumption more than perfectionism, Ms. Lubova is less convincing. Opposite her, always enthralling Ekaterina Reznikova commanded the stage regally as Gamzatti, evoking another legendary redhead in the role: prima ballerina assoluta Maya Plisetskaya. There were two noteworthy debuts, both from new members of the corps de ballet. Almost as soon as Natalia Leonova appeared onstage as the Second Shade, her lofty cabrioles caused the audience to collectively gasp and break into an early applause. In just over one minute, Ms. Leonova demonstrated that rare effect when choreography dissolves and all movements seem a spontaneous and natural extension of the dancer's soul. She was followed by Nina Berezina, an exceptionally elegant and nuanced Third Shade. With their inspired and fresh performance, both recent Vaganova grads gave the impression that they are destined to leave the corps de ballet before long.

V

IN MY FIRST SEASON: GULNARE IN *LE CORSAIRE*, MASHA IN *THE NUT-cracker*, a Flower Girl in *Don Q*, and the Diamond Fairy in *Sleeping Beauty*. On top of the soloist roles were the corps de ballet parts, meaning double the number of rehearsals. Days passed by with relentless and numbing intensity, like a book where a character gets killed off on every single page. In the morning I woke up in our apartment, which was so cold that we could see our foggy breath. Seryozha would jump out of the bed, make tea, and bring back bowls of steaming kasha for both of us. I shimmied on my clothes under the covers, and when we could no longer tarry, we took the Metro for the 11:00 a.m. company class. Dancers would be stretching and doing calisthenics quietly in the dark, too tired for words, until someone flipped on the light switch with a click. That moment—profound and silent misery for everyone in the room, each and every day. Slowly warming up until more or less balanced and in tune. Fifteen minutes for lunch, usually a banana or a salad. Then hours of rehearsals, a little break where we'd try to nap or eat something, performance, stumbling out of the artist entrance at 11:00 p.m., going home, taking a shower with the water turned all the way up to scalding—the saving grace of the apartment—and collapsing on the bed next to Seryozha. The following day, the cycle would continue. Wash and repeat. Wash and repeat.

Though Vaganova had been demanding, the company was what taught me the different levels of fatigue: there was the fatigue where my eyeballs felt like falling out of their sockets, and one where, after a particularly grueling *Swan Lake*, I had to crawl up the stairs to our apartment (thankfully, with gloves) because I didn't have enough strength in my legs. I hadn't anticipated this much physical pain when I was still only eighteen going on nineteen. But no one besides

Seryozha, Nina, and Andryusha knew how weak I felt every single day. No one commiserated with me for having the nerve to get soloist roles in my first season, and then even more in my second season. The stars like Katia openly shunned me, the middle were similarly wary, and the rank and file didn't treat me as "one of them," either. I still made corps salary and counted every ruble at the grocery store, so the only reward for my social banishment was the performance bonus, which I saved and presented to Mama whenever I went to the costume department for fittings. I couldn't always score a comp ticket, but she seemed to get almost as much thrill from this postshow ritual. "This thousand rubles is for which role?" She'd say out of the corner of her mouth, a pearl-ended pin in her mouth. "Ramzé in *La Fille du Pharaon*," I'd answer, and her face would light up with recognition—not of the choreography or the music, but the turquoise-embroidered bodice and tutu. I would tell her about the breathtaking Sphinx and painted Egyptian columns, the clip-clop of a real white horse pulling a golden chariot across the stage, and she would laugh huskily, showing the gums of her teeth.

On the nights when Mama came to see me dance, I glanced up at the Duke's box at the end of my variations and saw her clapping longer and harder than anyone else in the auditorium. And at curtain call, I offered my bows to only her. I came to cherish my solos for these moments with Mama more than just for my own sake. For the first time in my life, I felt close to her without the fear of getting hurt.

LIKE OTHER ASPECTS OF COMPANY life, the curtain call was replete with both tradition and hierarchy. The corps dancers always bowed first, followed by soloists of ascending importance, and finally the principal roles. This was actually quite simple: the stage manager called out who was going next, so that no one could offend anyone by mistake. Other rules were more subtle and unspoken, although you were still expected to know exactly how to behave. One night during the curtain call for *Raymonda*, I (Henrietta) was lining up to curtsy next to other "friends of Raymonda" when the coryphée who played Clémence suddenly dropped her knee to the floor. The rest of us stiffly did our half-curtsy, horrified at what had taken place. This was obviously more than just an issue of uneven height; honor was at stake. Then we watched Katia, who danced the title role, step into the spotlight for her bows and touch her knee to the ground—the unspoken prerogative of the prima ballerina.

Katia rose to standing, smiling regally as if she hadn't noticed Clémence's indiscretion. She walked to the wings and led the conductor by hand to the center stage, where he bowed deeply from the waist. He was shockingly young for his position—no more than thirty-five—with a sophisticated, tanned complexion and black hair. He took Katia's hand again and kissed it gallantly, the same way conductors always do to the prima ballerina after every performance. But something about it was nonetheless different—maybe just a split second after that kiss, when he still held her hand and their eyes met—and I realized that they liked each other and were doing their best to keep it hidden in front of the 1,600 people in the audience.

After the curtains dropped for the last time, I returned to the corps dressing room and pulled off my pointe shoes next to Nina. She'd played a noblewoman in the castle, and was covered in setting spray from her headdress to her chest. Each time her makeup-remover wipe went across her face, a new swath of her clean skin revealed itself in the mirror. I stepped out of my tutu and unhooked the bodice until I was naked except for my tights. I loved how close I felt to Nina when we were going through the postshow rituals side by side, all pretenses gone, and purely comfortable and accepting in each other's company, like a couple of battle-worn soldiers in the trenches sharing a smoke after a day of bombardment. Tired but buzzed from the adrenaline, we gossiped about Clémence's presumptuousness and how Katia would mete out just punishment. Then, once we were both covered up, I finally told her what I had noticed about Katia and the conductor.

"He's handsome, and terribly talented. They'd make a brilliant couple," Nina said. Then worried that she might have betrayed me by sounding too complimentary, she added, "Of course, he would soon find out her true colors."

"I don't think she'll be nasty to *him* at all," I said, shrugging on a fleece zip-up jacket. "What struck me was how she was looking at him. I— Can you keep a secret?"

Nina's eyes brightened. She loved secrets and nodded enthusiastically.

"I can't remember the last time I looked at Seryozha that way," I said, hugging my elbows close to my body. "Is that normal?"

Nina sighed and pulled on her gloves. "You've been together for three years. It's okay not to be so infatuated anymore. In fact, that's how you can build something stable." She smiled at me in the mirror; she and Andryusha had just gotten engaged in the New Year. The news wasn't surprising to anyone who knew Nina. She was only a year older than the rest of our class, but she had always been much more mature. She'd skipped ahead of our adolescent and early-twenties dating roulette and put her money into the one lifetime savings account that was Andryusha.

"So you stay together until the relationship loses its fizz and then you get married?" I said, only half-jokingly. Nina took a sharp inhale through her nose, losing patience with me despite her determination to be a good friend. It was getting late.

"I think I'm just tired. That's when I get these thoughts," I said. We both zipped up our coats and walked out to the elevator.

"Listen, Natasha. It's not that I'm not excited about Andryusha anymore. It's that I'm excited about *different things* now. Living together. Taking care of each other in all ways. Building our family," Nina said as the numbers above the elevator lit up one at a time. It arrived with a ding and we got on.

"Can I ask you something, Nina? What if you could only dance with Andryusha for the rest of your life—how would that make you feel?"

"I'd be absolutely thrilled. Wouldn't you, with Seryozha?" Nina pushed the door open, and we found ourselves outside the artist entrance. Before I could answer her, a dark shadow approached us and called out, "Are you Natalia Leonova?"

"I am," I said nervously, glancing at Nina for support. "How can I help you?"

"I'm so, so delighted to meet you." The stranger stepped forward into the light, revealing a pair of ruddy cheeks under the hood of her parka. "Come on, kids!" She hailed behind her, and two little girls hopped next to her like bunnies and stared up at me with huge eyes.

"My girls just started taking ballet and we're your biggest admirers. You were unforgettable tonight, as always. We were wondering if we could get a photo with you—would you mind?" She produced a camera from her purse and looked hopefully at Nina.

"Of course, I would love to," I said, and Nina took the camera while the girls and their mother grouped themselves around me. Then two more people—an older gentleman and a young woman in her twenties—shyly lined up and asked for my autograph on their programs. Afterward, they ran off into the darkness.

I stood still for a while, ignoring the cold. Then Nina called my name, her voice getting edgier with fatigue. We started walking, the snow clinging thickly to our knit hats, erasing our footprints almost as soon as they appeared; and I remembered what I was despairing of just before the fans descended on us. A secret too bizarre and shameful to tell even Nina. It wasn't Seryozha I imagined dancing with for the rest of my life, but someone I'd only seen once before, from a distance, and wasn't even sure I would like.

IN HIS BAR OFF PLACE des Vosges, Léon said that people told him secrets all the time. Because he was a bartender, they felt that he was immune to judgment. It liberated them to see him unsurprised by anything. One man went to the library every Sunday and ripped off the last pages of books. "He was like a serial killer of books," Léon said, pouring me a Bordeaux.

"*Absolument fou*," I said.

"Yes, but believe me, Natasha. Everyone is crazy in some way." He put his fingertips together next to his temple and burst them open with a *peww* sound.

"Tell me more."

The most common secret people had, according to Léon, was that they weren't in love with people they were supposed to be in love with. The couples who came into the bar were often not in love with each other. Sometimes they told him this while their partner was in the bathroom, but he could figure it out just by looking.

Once, a man came in alone and ordered a martini at the bar. A well-bred American of the sort you see around the First Arrondissement. He said he'd always wanted to visit the Victor Hugo museum around the corner, and finally did it that afternoon after living twenty years in Paris. He left home after he broke up his sister's engagement to a perfectly dashing young man he knew from university. Made up some lies about the fiancé, convinced his sister that he wasn't right for her. People eventually assumed that he was in love with his sister's fiancé, and he let them believe it. But it was really because he was in love with *her*. Did this surprise Léon? The man wanted to know. No—but Léon asked why he was telling him this now. Because I'll never see you again, of course, the man said. Léon figured he would run into him the following week with his wife, coming out of Chanel. That was normally how things happened after people told him their secrets. But the next day, Léon saw in the news. An American expat drowned in the Seine.

EVERYTHING BECOMES MORE POWERFUL WHEN it isn't told. Fears, sadness, desires, dreams.

There is a secret about Mariinsky that I haven't told anyone. One day I climbed to the gods, drawn by the massive chandelier and the dancing divines encircling it. At the end of the very top row, there was an unmarked door, which led to a dark vestibule with a narrow, steep staircase. This ended at a heavy steel door marked DO NOT ENTER that I believed would be locked. I still pushed it, and all the light and fresh air of a warm March afternoon burst inside as if from another world. The cool, clear, earthy smell of spring pressed against my face and nearly sent me reeling in a vertigo. It was so unexpected, this beauty. All of Petersburg lay at my feet.

I walked to the ledge and leaned over the balustrade to take in the city. The golden cupolas shone between the rows of trees, whose tips were sparking live with the tiniest green of new leaves. Slate-gray roofs stretched from horizon to horizon, broken up into orderly pieces by the canals. A gale was herding the swells of clouds across the soft blue sky, like sheep on a meadow. Everything was moving slowly, in the sunlight, without struggle—the opposite of my entire existence, from the day I was born. I wondered if I'd ever be able to live that way. I'd been performing almost every night for the past four seasons, still in the corps and dancing soloist roles. My body and mind had already reached a breaking point. Tears came into my eyes, and I gasped and shivered, desperately trying to keep them down. I could hardly complain to Seryozha, who had been working just as much, but only dancing small parts. Nina was even busier—she was devoting any free time she had to planning her wedding, which would take place in June.

With five minutes to go before my next rehearsal, I climbed down from the rooftop. When I returned to the studio, the office manager poked her head in and said, "Natasha, you had a last-minute change for the Friday performance. Daria caught the flu."

"I haven't been her understudy," I said.

"Actually, Katia will be stepping in for her in Nikiya. You'll do Gamzatti instead of Katia," she said, flipping through her clipboard.

"Where is Ivan Stanislavich?" I asked.

"In stage rehearsal. He'll be done in a few hours—"

She was still talking when I stormed off. I swung open the door to the auditorium, and the dancers onstage momentarily paused before returning to their work. Ivan Stanislavich was sitting in the middle of the orchestra level, directing the dancers on the microphone. He looked at me behind his shoulder, frowned, and turned his focus back in front of him, all without a break in his instructions. I strode to his row and said, "I need to talk to you."

Ivan Stanislavich grumbled into the microphone, "Kolya, less thrashing about in pure fear. It's *Le Jeune homme et la mort*. La *mort*! Be seduced." As I still stood glaring at him, Ivan Stanislavich held the mic off to the side and said, "What do you want?"

"I need to talk to you about *Bayadère*."

Ivan Stanislavich cleared his throat, knitting his impressive gray eyebrows together. "If you want to talk about casting, wait until I'm done."

"No. It has to be now. You can stand to give me ten minutes of your time."

The dancers on stage fell silent. Kolya paused his danse macabre with the woman in yellow, who stood openly staring at me. Ivan Stanislavich said to them, "Take five," and turned to me with an alive expression I'd never before seen in him. He was always inscrutable, dispassionate, like a crocodile that lies motionless on the riverbank; I'd managed to surprise him, and would now see the consequences of unnerving someone powerful and dangerous. My heart pounded so loudly that I was afraid that he would hear it. But my anger was greater than my fear, and I kept my hands balled up at my sides as we stepped inside one of the boxes.

I thought that as soon as the partition hid us from the dancers, Ivan Stanislavich would pour diatribes against my conduct. But he indicated a chair to me—like many in his position, he retained the mannerisms of gallantry, in gesture if not in intention—and sat down himself. He crossed his legs briskly, folded his arms over his chest, raised his chin, and said, "Speak."

"You just dumped me into Gamzatti without any warning, two days before the performance. How do you possibly expect me to prepare this properly?"

"I know you don't need much time to polish up the grand pas de deux. You did well with it at Varna."

"But not the other scenes. This isn't fair. I've been dancing in the corps, at your beck and call for the solos, working twice as many hours and making less than half as much."

"What are you saying, Natasha?" He narrowed his eyes and breathed sharply in through his nose.

"I want to be promoted. Not to coryphée. Nor second soloist. First soloist." I tried to keep my voice level—and was proud of myself for succeeding. Ivan Stanislavich raised his eyebrows and shook his head in disbelief; this time, I really did strike his nerve.

"You've put in a few years' hard work. I'm not denying that, but—"

"This is my fourth season, actually. I'm turning twenty-two this summer. You made Katia a principal when she was twenty-one." I knew that wouldn't go in my favor, but I couldn't help myself.

"Don't compare yourself to others, Natasha," he said with a smirk, raising his hand as if he'd heard enough. "It makes you sound like a little girl." He rose, signaling the end of our tête-à-tête.

"I'm dancing many of the roles Katia, and all the other principals, have done." I stood up and blocked his way out of the box. At this display of impertinence, Ivan Stanislavich's face turned an unsophisticated shade of purplish red. I'd genuinely appalled him. But I saw something else, too—a kind of spark in his eyes that wasn't there when he was analyzing his troops with his X-ray vision. I realized then that it wasn't a coincidence that Daria and Katia were his favorites. Obedience bored him.

"Fine," he spat out, slowly returning to his normal color and grasping the back of a chair for support. "But under one condition."

"Speak," I said coolly—two could play at this game.

"It's not just me who gets to decide these things. The general director, the administration. Yes—the administration. Truthfully, we have no plans to move up any of the women in the next few years—" He hurried to finish his thoughts, seeing my expression of horror. "And they'll think a promotion isn't really called for. Unless you show that you're at that level."

"And how?"

"This year is Moscow International. Bring back a medal and we'll sort out your promotion. It's a big purse—$30,000 for Women's First Prize. That's—I think, 900,000 rubles."

I nearly stumbled in shock, and tried to hide it by shifting my weight. That was more than five times my annual income. Ivan Stanislavich knew this, of course, and smiled in a condescending way that I found truly revolting.

"And the Grand Prix?" I asked, looking straight into his eyes.

"Let's be realistic, no one's asking you to win the Grand Prix, but—if I recall correctly, $100,000."

My heartbeat was vibrating throughout my entire body. Alexander Nikulin, singularly explosive, a nuclear reactor made for dance. Beauty so true it felt violent. Moscow International was hosted by the Bolshoi. It took place every four years, so there was just one chance for young soloists in their prime to enter. Of course he would be there.

"Don't worry about the Grand Prix. Any of the three women's solo prizes would work," Ivan Stanislavich said, indicating with his head that he was ready to be set free. I stepped aside for him, and he returned to his orchestra seat with a visible sense of relief. He seemed to regain his sangfroid with every step, so that by the time he grabbed his mic, everything about him was as controlled and contained as before.

"Take it from the cigarette part. Blow the smoke in his face and tempt him to die," he ordered, sending the dancers flying back to their positions. On the stage, Death in her yellow dress put out her cigarette, slid down the length of the young man's body, and clung to his waist with her legs in a center split, her head to his crotch, swinging just above the floor like the pendulum of a clock.

ON FRIDAY EVENING, I WAS getting ready for my debut as Gamzatti when there was a knock on our dressing room door. I opened it and discovered one of the many theater employees whom I recognized only by their faces. She was in her forties, with very pale skin and dyed orange hair that she wore slicked back into a bun. Her sharply cropped bangs always seemed like a warning sign against bothering her without good reason.

"Natasha? I'm Tanya," she said in a haughty voice as she marched in. "I'll do your hair and makeup today."

"I've always done them on my own—" I started to say, but stopped at the look that Tanya gave me.

"It's your debut as Gamzatti, yes? Your first principal part, yes?" She took a step forward a bit menacingly, pointing a hairbrush at me like a pistol. "I do the hair for the primas.

"If you want, you can learn to do it yourself, after I show you." She paused and put the brush to her lips. "You're Anna Leonova's daughter, right?"

I nodded, and the vertical lines between her brows softened a little.

"I got your mother her job at the theater. Anna is a good soul. Now sit."

I'd done other major roles before, but none as important as Gamzatti; and I had the feeling Ivan Stanislavich had personally ordered this, as he pulled on the strings of every major and minor event at the theater with astonishing exactitude. Perhaps he thought it would appease me after the confrontation in the box, or he just innocently wanted my debut to be a success. Or he was inciting Katia's wrath by steering her own makeup artist in my direction, so that our animosity plays out onstage with real venom. Ivan Stanislavich was capable of manipulating anyone to get the precise effect he wanted.

I sat down and tried to catch Nina's eyes in the mirror, but she busied herself with fixing her hair jewel. It was the first time since we were ten years old that we weren't pinning in the pieces for each other. Earlier in the week, when I'd told her of my argument with Ivan Stanislavich and his counterproposal, Nina had clasped her hands to her mouth and whispered, "Natasha—you know what this means?"

"It means I'm going to win even if it takes the last breath I have. And he's going to make me first soloist," I'd said, staring in confusion at Nina's fear.

"But if you don't get a medal, he'll have the perfect excuse not to promote you for years—perhaps ever," she'd said, with the air of an adult teaching a child how the world works. That shade of condescension and lack of faith had bothered me; she'd sensed it, and we'd barely spoken ever since.

Nina left early for Act I, so by the time Tanya was finished ("There—that's much better than when you do it yourself, yes?") I didn't have to awkwardly wish her *toi toi toi*. The signal for intermission summoned me behind the curtains, where the stagehands were wheeling in the palm trees and the sun-warmed palace of the Rajah for Act II. The corps dancers in their marigold costumes were gossiping and warming up by the colossal statue of the Buddha. They stopped whispering when I passed by them. Behind the giant tiger prop I spotted Seryozha, who was dressed as one of the background warriors again—he had understudied for the Bronze Idol, but never gotten a chance to perform it. He strode over, wrapped me in his arms, and gave me a tight squeeze.

"Are you feeling okay?" he asked, pulling away a bit to study my face. I nodded. It took too much energy for me to make small talk before a show, and he knew it.

"*Merde*," he said with a smile.

"Thank you. You, too." I untangled my arms from his, but he held on to me just a second longer and brought his lips close to my ear.

"You know you've always been my prima ballerina. I'm so proud of you."

A sudden impulse caught hold of me and I gripped his upper arms. *Kiss me*, I wanted to say. I pictured the soft pink of our lips open and hungry for each other, my arms tightly wound around his back and his hand running up and down my spine. But then I imagined how embarrassed Seryozha would be if I even asked. *Here, in front of everyone?* he'd say. Kind, loving, patient Seryozha. I did love him, but I wanted to want him more than I wanted him. Instead of a kiss, I gave him one last squeeze and walked away.

I meandered to the center center—the middle of the stage, the center of gravity in our universe, to which everyone—dancers from the corps to the principals, the conductor, the orchestra, the light designer, stagehands, and even the director—was inexorably pulled. I lay down on it and spread my arms and legs wide. The spotlights transected my field of vision in wide, white shafts; the shining nautical star remained on the underside of my lids when I closed my eyes. It was almost peaceful now with the warmth of open strings vibrating across the auditorium, the twittering of the flutes and the oboes, and the floor holding up my body with unasked-for generosity—a force equal to gravity.

Of course, this takeover of the center center would become yet another reason for Katia, her friends, and followers to think I'm arrogant and insupportable. For Ivan Stanislavich to think I was amusingly headstrong. Seryozha to think I was wonderful. Nina to think I was changed. And not one of them knew the real me—sometimes *I* didn't even understand who I was anymore. But when I was here in the center of the universe, then and only then did I know exactly what I was. Beneath my skin, every part of me was pulsing with the molten force I'd always kept in check, ever since I could remember. I wanted to unlock the dam and let them see it.

On the other side of the curtain, the orchestra quieted to an attentive hush. The maestro raised his baton, and the violins and the celli filled the theater with their lush interlude. My skin prickled from the sound of fluttering costumes as dancers took their places. One minute until curtain up. I opened my eyes with a start, like someone swimming up from the deep and breaking the surface of the water. I pressed myself to standing and saw, across the beams of tangerine light, Seryozha staring at me with an expression of awe—and something even a little like terror.

With her long limbs and innate grandeur, Ekaterina Reznikova's Gamzatti has long been the calling card of Mariinsky's *La Bayadère*. On Saturday night, St. Petersburg witnessed an artist at the peak of her maturity subverting expectations in another role that had hitherto been denied her: Nikiya. Her Act I pas de deux in particular was tender and sweet as this critic has never seen before in Ms. Reznikova's dancing. She spoke through her exquisitely pliant back, through her beautiful feet, and even to the ends of her long plait of auburn hair. Does the transformation owe itself to her romance with a certain associate conductor, if one is to believe the rumors swirling around balletomanes like pigeons in Palace Square? The famously private prima ballerina only seems willing to speak through dance.

But the biggest surprise of the night had yet to come. In Act II, another revelation arrived in the form of Natalia Leonova as Gamzatti. In her first season at Mariinsky, she had made a splash as a darkly mystic Second Shade, a moonbeam dancing on an icy stream. This time, Ms. Leonova

> danced Gamzatti like the radiant sun bound for the zenith, touching the ceiling with the arc of her glorious saut de chat. But her allure is greater than the sum of her wickedly fast turns and breathtaking jumps; it's how she transmits the very fullness of life through every gesture, glance, and connective tissue of the dance. With each new triumph, the ballet world asks, will Ms. Leonova be promoted? Or will she languish in the corps forever, destined to become one of those who debut a few principal roles early on and settle downward to dancing bit parts? This is a familiar pattern at Mariinsky, a troupe not known for advancing its women. Besides Ms. Leonova, there are a dozen female first soloists who have been stagnating for a decade or more, much to the consternation of their loyal supporters. If next spring also passes without a promotion, it would not be the first time Ivan Maksimov resists public pressure and chooses to keep his top ranks small. And who could complain? Mariinsky has failed talented young dancers before, but Mariinsky does not fail.

A BELLHOP TIPPED HIS RED felt hat to me as I rushed into the Grand Korsakov Hotel. Another set of stained-glass doors swung open, and then my heels sank into the soft, hand-stitched Persian rug snaking across the porphyry floor. In the lobby, art nouveau splendor: dark bronze statues and towering urns of miniature orange trees; the gold-leaf cupola with its frozen waterfall of a chandelier, drawing people's eyes upward so that they instantly walked taller and more smartly. I caught sight of a manager and said, "I'm looking for the Berezina wedding."

"Up the stairs and on your left, in the ballroom," the manager replied. I thanked him and hurried up the steps, only slowing down when I heard the laughter, murmurs, and cheerful chimes of silverware and glasses. A server wearing a tailcoat opened the door for me, and I entered.

It was a setting reminiscent of Nijinsky's *Le Spectre de la rose.* A vast skylight of pale blue stained glass ran along the soaring, barrel-vaulted ceiling, anointing the room with the glaucous glow of the White Night. Another stained-glass wall—a depiction of the god Apollo—illuminated the rounded niche at the far end of the room, like the apse of a church. Guests were seated with the pristine tablecloths spooling at their laps and falling to their ankles, and craning to talk over the long-stemmed candles, the snowy bunches of hydrangeas. They were white, but looked a little violet in the twilight atmosphere of the room.

At the head table, Andryusha's father was finishing up a toast. He was as handsome as his son, and his wife was elegant and charming. Near them sat the newlywed couple, laughing, blushing, and drinking far more than eating. Nina was wearing a simple silk dress cut very close to her body—she didn't want anything frilled and beaded that would remind her of a costume. A tulle veil flowed from her low bun to her hips. I had always been transfixed by Nina's beauty but never more than at this moment. She saw me and beckoned with a wave.

"You're entrancing," I said, hugging her and then Andryusha, then Nina again. "I feel I'm going to cry, seeing you like this. Congratulations, Nina. I'm sorry I missed the ceremony."

For a long time, we both sniffled and laughed in each other's arms. We hadn't cleared the air since arguing about Moscow International, using our respective packed schedules as an excuse to avoid a frank conversation. Now the months of awkward politeness fell away as naturally as ice melts on the first hot day in spring. After giving me one final squeeze, she pointed at a table and said, "I seated you next to Seryozha. Go eat now and then we'll catch up later. I'll come find you."

Seryozha was talking and laughing with other guests, emanating ease and comfort. When I reached him, he stood up to kiss me and pull out my chair. He looked dashing, too, in a sharp new suit that he'd bought with an unexpected bonus: he'd danced the Blue Bird in *Sleeping Beauty* the other night, and Ivan Stanislavich had even complimented him after the show. This had been the biggest coup of Seryozha's career thus far. He touched my shoulder and said, "I need to take a picture of you in that dress."

It was a red silk chiffon dress I'd grabbed from a sale rack in the slim window between rehearsals and shows. I had never spent so much on a single item of clothing before, but I thought I'd earned it. All spring and summer, what little free time remaining had been devoted to preparing for Moscow. Earlier that afternoon, I'd danced a matinee show and gone back to the studio to work with Vera Igorevna. My hair was still crinkly from being pulled out of a sweaty bun.

"I came straight from rehearsal. Didn't even get to take a shower." I sighed, taking a sip of champagne. "How was the ceremony?"

"It was beautiful. To see them like that—" Seryozha paused, no doubt thinking of our Vaganova days when we were all legs and gap-toothed smiles. And then Seryozha and I went back even further than that, to that courtyard building strewn with rotting apples and wet leaves and cawing crows. It was dizzying to think of how we had ended up in this place, with handsome, sophisticated, and well-dressed people, looking and sounding exactly like them.

A server laid a dish of canapés in front of me, and I started eating in silence—I hadn't had any food since the morning. When I'd worked through half of it, I saw Nina glide toward me, her veil trailing behind her like mist. She laid a hand on my shoulder and said, "Come with me to the ladies' room."

We were silent on the way to the restroom. Once we were inside its gilded walls, Nina bent forward from the hips, pressed both her palms on the polished zinc counter, and breathed out a huge sigh, like a frustrated professor about to give a lecture. She sniffled with the beginnings of a sob, then laughed in embarrassment, fanning her flushed face.

"It's just been so overwhelming—preparing everything on my own for months, and then worrying whether the day would go well. Andryusha didn't help much. But really, it all turned out beautifully."

"Everything has the mark of your genius in it," I said, patting her arm and resting my hip on the counter.

"You know, I asked Andryusha to write the address on our invitations and mail them out, and then they *all* came back to us. Because he mixed up where to put the sender and the addressee! It was the *one job* he had. He is so—" Nina choked up. "So amazingly dense sometimes!"

"But you love him?" I asked, and her frustration melted away in an instant.

"Oh god. I do. I love him so much." Her voice trembled now for an entirely different reason, and her eyes brimmed with unchecked devotion. "Sorry! I'm so emotional today. I can't help myself."

"You don't need to apologize for loving your husband on your wedding day. It makes me happy to see you so happy."

"Me, too. I'm glad we're finally married—and that we'll soon have a family."

"Isn't it a little early to be thinking that?" I slid off the counter and stood straight, dusting off my bottom. "I mean, you're twenty-three and still in the corps. You'd be giving up on your career if you were to have children before making first soloist."

Like those days in July when the sun disappears and the entire city looks up simultaneously at the sooty sky, waiting for the inevitable downpour, Nina's eyes turned obsidian in an instant. I tried to steer the ship in another direction. "Remember when we were in our first year at Vaganova, eating lunch together at the canteen, and you kept saying 'I'm going to make it'? We both wanted the same thing, like two horses running side by side on the racetrack, but somehow never competing. Always best friends."

"Don't tell me how to live my life, Natasha." Nina crossed her arms over her body and shivered, as if some cold draft blew into the pleasantly warm room. It was the kind of thing she would never have said to me before—and that gesture was so foreign to her, she seemed like a different person entirely. Then I knew.

"You're pregnant. I'm so sorry, I didn't realize—" And then without thinking, I made things even worse. "So you're definitely going to—"

"Yes!" Nina shrieked. "Of course I will, because I married the love of my life and we both want a family. I actually want something beyond myself."

"That's not fair," I said, weakly, so as not to deteriorate the situation further. Nina kept going, however; once she began, she seemed unable to stop.

"Oh, there were lots of times I wished I could warn you not to live that way, but I kept my mouth shut. You want to know what I think? You treat Seryozha badly. Stringing him along when you don't even love him. He deserves better than you."

"That's enough. I got your point," I managed to say, as my heart threatened to jump out of my body and my cheeks became hot, dry, bloated.

"And speaking of best friends? Remember how you started dating Seryozha right after Sofiya got kicked out of school? Nothing can come between you and what you want. That's the real you."

I tried to speak, but the words were caught in my throat. How long had she been holding this in? She'd never taken Sofiya's side or reproached me before, but she had to have nursed this grievance for years. Nina always did things by the book—of course she would have disapproved. Probably talked to Andryusha about it countless times behind my back. Were our years of friendship even real? I couldn't breathe. The shimmering walls of the restroom seemed to close in on me from all sides, turning into a gold coffin. "I'm sorry you feel that way," I muttered—or I think I did before running out of there. The lobby blurred past, and then cars and the beautiful buildings lit up by flood lamps, and I kept limping away as quickly as my tired feet would allow.

When I gathered my senses, I was standing next to the Metro station where a group of teenagers were skateboarding and evading parental authority. Their cigarette smoke glinted ghostlike in the fading light of a summer night.

From somewhere over my shoulder came the clear keening of seagulls and crows. I turned around and found a grizzled man in a wheelchair feeding a loaf of bread to a large flock of birds. They surrounded and kept inching closer to the man like gang members threatening to mug him. He didn't seem fazed and just kept throwing bread crumbs, muttering to himself. A deranged old man, feeding savage criminal birds late at night. Someone with no place to go, no one better to care for. His actions—maybe even his existence—made so little mark in the world, even to the gulls at the end of the day. And yet. Didn't everyone live this particular insanity, more or less? Everyone was unworthy, the loved and the loving. And you knew this, but you still went through it, to be a part of the chain of beings rather than float through life unmoored. That futile attempt at love was the cord that tied you to the spaceship as you drifted in cosmic blackness, hearing your own breathing and watching everyone else on earth. Without it, there was only death.

I took the Metro back to the apartment, showered, and lay in bed, staring at the ceiling. When it lightened to pink, Seryozha unlocked the door and stumbled in. I kept my eyes closed while he took off his clothes and crawled into bed. His skin was steeped in the briny smell of vodka. Although drunk, he kissed me very quietly on my lips, thinking that I was asleep—and I ached for him, as I always did.

"Hi," I said. The honeyed sun slid into the room. A shadow of a bird flew across the wall behind Seryozha.

"I'm sorry I woke you up." He smiled, putting his hand on my waist. "Where did you run off to? Why didn't you let me know you were leaving?"

"I just came straight home." I took his hand in mine and squeezed. I'd never had to do this before—break the cord that bound me to safety and kept me alive. I took one last, deep breath before saying goodbye and spinning into nothingness at a thousand miles per hour. "I need to talk to you."

ACT II

Everything on stage should be just as complex and, at the same time, as simple as in life.

—Anton Chekhov

i

IN THE CAB BACK TO THE CITY, NINA ASKS IF I WOULD LIKE TO COME OVER for dinner. It's not good to be alone, she says. When I don't answer, she lays her scarf across both our laps. This dissipates the chill of the cemetery, which seemed to have followed us into the car. Nina has always been surrounded by people, being nourished by them and taking care of them in turn. An aspen tree is like that, growing in a forest that is actually a massive single organism with shared roots. The above-ground trees are continuously cloned from a single seedling that started the colony, tens of thousands of years before. I can't fathom how safe it must feel to be an aspen, to have roots that are—as far as humans can tell—possibly immortal. Love that runs in Nina's veins is as old as the first aspen. Her parents gave it to her and she gives it now to her children. She extends a bit to me, too, but I'm not *of* her. I thank her for the dinner invite and get out of the car in front of the hotel.

Housekeeping has left the room tidy and free of empty glasses. My eyes flit to the nightstand and see that my pill bottle is gone. Panic. How stupid could I be, leaving it lying around. I throw the pillows on the ground and pull apart the neatly made bed. Then I see it on one side of the bathroom counter, hiding behind a tube of lipstick and a moisturizer. I grab it and shake. I can't know for sure if any pills have been taken, but it seems as full as it was last night. I clutch it like a tsar snatching a firebird and make my way to the balcony.

I open the French doors and step onto the narrow, tiled space, more like a pocket hanging on the outside of the building than a proper terrace. A street vendor is selling some colorful, glowing, spinning gadgets that appear to be flying around. Tourists walk by, looking in all directions except straight ahead. Two teenage couples stroll past in a tangle of legs and arms. "Good luck with that, Mashka!" shouts one girl, and Mashka yells back the correct response to ensure fortune. "*K chyortu!*" To hell with it! It's an appropriate thing to say, not only when someone wishes you good luck but in most situations in life. It can mean equally you'll do something or you won't. A homeless man lies stretched out for the night under an awning, a bottle each of vodka and mouthwash lined up by his head.

A pink sparkling gadget floats up to my level and hovers like a hummingbird before falling into the darkness. It's noisy, ugly, ersatz, and meaningless, like most things humans make. The teenagers whoop in delight and buy those toys from the vendor. I open the bottle and shake out one, two, three, four, five pills. That seems like a sufficiently harmful number. Then just to be safe, six. Seven. Eight. Nine. Ten. There was a fashion designer who lived in our quartier, a younger girlfriend of a very old and famous rock star, who quite unexpectedly killed herself one evening. No one understood why she did it, even though the papers weakly suggested her business was under some debt. Her boyfriend was worth half a billion euros, it just didn't make sense. I get it now. Perhaps she was also watching the street below her balcony and realized that there was no difference either way. For people like Nina, the aspens of the world, their absence would matter. But I'm utterly alone and can disappear without really hurting anyone. The two teen couples appear to be competing against each other to see whose toy flies higher. A pink one and a purple one threaten to flutter all the way into my balcony. I step back and close the doors, yelling, "To hell with it!"

I take the fistful of pills to the bathroom and throw them into the toilet. Before I fully realize what I've done, I pour out the rest of the bottle and flush. They don't all go down so I flush again, and the last one circles dramatically around the bowl for a while before joining its friends in the netherworld. I imagine it squeaking *Goodbyeeee* . . . in a tiny voice that pills must have. And then I laugh. It sounds so unhinged that I'm simultaneously startled, but I can't stop. Tears leak from my eyes, yet mirth still gushes out of me like a torrent. My body is shaking with its last remains as I realize I hadn't laughed in over two years. I must have smiled sometimes, but I can't recall ever finding anything funny. It's as though all the laughing I hadn't done during that time has exploded and burned out of me in one go. My body feels empty, in a not-unpleasant way. I lie down in bed—regretting how frantically I unmade the nicely tucked corners—and will myself to sleep.

I can't sleep.

Every time I open my eyes, the clock has moved by an hour. My heart is a ticking bomb and I hold it down with a shaking hand. Am I having withdrawal effects already? Or is this just in my head? I go back to the bathroom and force myself to drink a few cups of water. In the darkness, I get a strong feeling that if I look in the mirror, I might see something frightening I keep my head lowered and watch my tears drip down into the sink I'm afraid I'm afraid I'm afraid

THE SUN, AGAIN, INTRUDING IN everyone's affairs. I thought that I closed the balcony doors last night, but they are wide-open now, curtains flapping their wings to the morning wind. I'm curled up on top of the sheets and can't remember how the rest of the night passed. Must shower, must get back to session with Sveta. I limp to the bathroom and, against all odds, the hot water inspires hope again. If I can stay alive today without breaking, I think I'll be okay. To encourage myself, I even take my time moisturizing and dabbing on some lipstick, although it costs me a great effort to face the mirror. In my right eye, there is a burst blood vessel the size of a pomegranate seed.

Downstairs, I have toast and jam with a glass of fresh orange juice. My heart is ticking again, so I practice counting my breath. Inhale to ten. Hold to ten. Exhale to ten. All those years of performing, my heart felt like it would explode every single time I went onstage. But I knew how to use that adrenaline rush, even welcomed it. It made me fly. As though to punish me for regularly putting it through such extremes, my heart now races uncontrollably. Allegro. Presto. Prestissimo.

I walk out of the hotel and stand on a corner to hail a cab. A murder of crows has gathered across the street, their feathers gleaming like black opals in the sun. They're being fed by the homeless man I saw last night—the one with the vodka and mouthwash—and then I freeze in recognition. I've seen him before, a long time ago. A shiver runs through my spine; someone is playing a joke on me. Someone much more powerful than I am, and with not such good intentions at heart. Did the man just look up at me and wink? I run back into the hotel lobby and cling to the back of a chair, gasping for breath. A hand grabs my arm. I shriek.

"Natalia Nikolaevna! Forgive me, I didn't mean to startle you." Hotel manager Petrenko is so shocked and contrite, his eyebrows knit together in an upside down V. "Are you all right? I just wanted to make sure you're okay."

"Igor Vladimirovich," I can barely manage words, I am so happy to see him. "Can you please order me a cab to the theater? And wait with me until it arrives?"

"Of course, Natalia Nikolaevna. Do not worry." He pats my elbow and goes out to the curb. He returns in a few minutes, carrying a to-go cup. "It's tea with raspberry jam. It will calm your nerves."

When the cab arrives, we walk out together. The homeless man is gone. Crows, gone.

"Igor Vladimirovich, did you see a homeless man across the street? He was there just minutes ago."

"I didn't notice anyone like that. Was this man bothering you?" Igor Petrenko says, opening the cab door for me. I shake my head no, and he smiles. The manager believes I am telling the truth, and also that the man was not and is not there. These two contrary facts can coexist without disturbing him, and I cling to his version of reality.

"Natalia Nikolaevna, I know I always say this, to everyone it seems—but if there's anything I can do for you, please let me know. I really do mean it," he says reassuringly.

"Thank you, Igor Vladimirovich," I say, climbing into the seat. "I really do mean it, too."

When I arrive at the theater ten minutes late, Sveta is waiting for me, lips thinly pressed and arms crossed. But her frustration turns to concern when she sees how I look.

"What happened to your eye, Natasha?"

"Nothing. I just didn't sleep very well," I say. "Yesterday, I went with Nina to see Mama. Afterward I had a bit of a—tough time."

Sveta frowns and shakes her head, and I can't tell if she's still angry with me.

"Oh Natasha. I've been wanting you to do this for a long time," she finally says, wrapping me in a hug. When she detaches herself, my shoulder is a little damp where she was resting her head.

"Sveta, since I did something you approve of, can you also do me a favor?" I ask. She raises her eyebrows.

"Music. I need music, Sveta. It's the only way I'll be able to get better."

She agrees without much struggle. I select *La Bayadère* on my phone, and then immediately my heart starts beating more normally. Moderato. Andantino. Sveta leads me through our exercises on the floor, and then at the barre. With music, everything feels twice as easy as before. Even Sveta notices and says, "I think you'll be ready to do some center in a few days."

"No, Sveta," I say. "Let's start tomorrow." She narrows her eyes in mock disapproval, but her lips are twitching in pleasure.

At the end of the session, Sveta invites me to come eat with her. I shake my head. "I just want to check something." As I make my way to the elevator, my heart starts beating faster again. I realize my feet and ankles are swollen and red, as the anesthetic effect of music wears off. For the first time today, I wish I hadn't so nobly thrown away my pills.

The elevator dings and opens to a quiet corridor. It's dark and deserted all the way to backstage. Strange, as it is always bustling with people setting up for the night's show. The painted backdrops of chandeliers and sateen stand as weary and faded as a beauty after two in the morning. The curtains have been left raised, so that when I stand on the stage, I can see the half-lit auditorium filled with blue velvet chairs. I lie down on my back and close my eyes. Against the bare skin of my arms and back, the black linoleum feels powdery and caressing.

The sound of footsteps stops about a meter from my hips. "Is it comfortable, lying like that on the floor?" asks a voice that is teasing, but not brazen. Almost sweet. When I open my eyes, I realize with inner tremor that it's Alexander Nikulin. He smiles in the relaxed manner of one who knows his own power and is withholding it as a matter of courtesy. Lights pour over his body and create a sharp outline, dividing the world into him and all else.

The Bolshoi stage is huge. Vast. I prop myself up to sitting, frowning to hide my excitement at being alone together with him. He moves downstage and starts doing grand pirouettes with such nonchalance that I almost doubt that he was talking to me. Perhaps I misheard, and he wasn't saying anything at all. But he speaks again.

"'There is no stage so comfortable, the most comfortable in the entire solar system, in the entire universe, as the Bolshoi!'" Nikulin says in a singsongy voice, facing the empty seats covered in red velvet.

"Maya Plisetskaya," I say, and he snaps his head toward me. No—let me explain better. His body still turned toward the auditorium, his neck twists slightly back so his face in profile is engraved by the golden lining of the spotlight. Next to his casual perfection, my voice is gravelly and my body, ordinary. Maybe that is why he walks off the stage without responding to me.

As soon as he leaves, other competitors file in, whispering among themselves. Many of them know each other from Bolshoi, the academy or the company. There are also dancers from Ukraine, Germany, the United States, and Japan. Cameras follow us like bats backstage. The footage will air live on the state TV channel, overlaid with dramatic music and a double-headed eagle. The correspondents speak in hushed voices: "Moscow International is unique not just for its legendary stage but for the extreme rigor of its jury. At the last competition, the Women's Solo First Prize, the Women's Pas de Deux Third Prize, and the Men's Pas de Deux First and Second Prizes were unrewarded by the discretion of the jury. In the entire history of the competition, the Grand Prix has been awarded only four times . . ."

But these noises and distractions fail to shake me. During the whole competition, my mind is focused only on Nikulin. I'm conscious of dancing for the one person against whom I desire to win. I want him to fall to his knees and feel a little violated, as he's done to me. I want him to shake from a mixture of fear and envy and ecstasy. And despite my ignoble intentions, I know that something divine is occurring. Abandon everything the world has said about the impossibility of perfection: I know it exists, because I am it. Everyone is watching me from the audience, the wings, and the TV cameras. Their fear and envy and ecstasy feed my dance like dead leaves in a fire. That is, everyone's except Nikulin's, who disappears after his solos and doesn't stay to watch the other dancers. He returns only for the award ceremony. When they announce the Grand Prix and call out "Natalia Leonova," all the applause and flowers in the world, even the prize money, feel like nothing compared to the carefully composed expression on Nikulin's face. The very fact that he's so inscrutable shows that I've taken him by surprise. He cannot ignore me anymore because I've wounded him.

I'd brought my suitcase to the theater so that I could take the overnight train back to Petersburg immediately after the award ceremony. I took off my makeup and changed into jeans before heading out to catch a cab on Petrovka Ulitsa. I positioned myself on the curb by the swell of cars. Once the euphoria had the chance to circulate around my body, it was settling into a strange, melancholic numbness. I'd just experienced the happiest moment of my life, and I had no one to call. It made me proud to imagine Mama watching the competition on TV, but I wasn't in the mood to talk to her. I couldn't call the people I'd learned to love since starting ballet, Seryozha and Nina. Even some of my obsession for dance and yearning for Nikulin was fading. In its place bloomed a sense of emptiness so pure that I almost forgot what my name was, why I was standing there amid the red glow of traffic.

The true cost of accomplishing something you want with your whole being is that the moment you get it, you realize that it's not enough.

I gazed inside myself and saw a barren and empty landscape, like the Sahara stretching endlessly under cold blue stars. Or someone who is shipwrecked in a storm and after days of drifting on a piece of wood, finds herself washed up on a deserted island. She utters only two words left in her dry, salt-crusted mouth: *What now?* Dazed and trying to stay rooted, I peered at the glossy black surface of the car windows. Beneath the coral streetlamps and a neon billboard of the TSUM department store, I looked tired but—it was the first time I consciously thought this—beautiful.

"Congratulations, Natalia."

I jumped, expecting Nikulin—but in the next moment, I realized I was looking at the paunchy figure of Mikhail Alypov, the general director of Bolshoi Theatre. We'd been introduced briefly during the competition, but his reputation preceded our meeting. He had graduated with a degree in theater in the 1970s, immediately gone into administration over regional companies, until finally assuming the top post at Bolshoi. As such, no one under his reign—opera singers, dancers, instrumentalists, and artistic staff of respective troupes alike—truly respected him. Some called him "monkey" behind his back not only because his ears stuck out but also because he was great at swinging from vine to vine to the next opportunity. Of course, publicly they kowtowed to the most powerful man in Russian performing arts.

"Good evening, Mikhail Mikhailovich," I said to him, wheeling my suitcase around. He smiled by moving his heavy cheeks toward his prominent ears, like someone doing an unpleasant but necessary exercise.

"Are you leaving? Why not stay the night and head back tomorrow morning, refreshed."

"I already booked my overnight train," I said. This time, Mikhail Mikhailovich let go of his mannered expression and guffawed in earnest.

"Natalia, you just made three million rubles in one night. You won't need to worry about missing a train, from now on. Besides, I can reimburse you for the wasted ticket. Let's go to the Metropol. You can't leave Moscow without even visiting it."

I had no choice but to accept his offer. We crossed Petrovka and reached the Metropol, a pre-Revolution hotel that took up a whole block. It was reminiscent of the Grand Korsakov, but on a magnified scale—like everything else in Moscow. The bar's manager recognized Mikhail Mikhailovich and immediately ushered us to a corner table.

"I always sit here. It was Prokofiev's table, when he lived at the hotel," said Mikhail Mikhailovich, before asking the manager for a bottle of Dom Pérignon. The champagne was opened with a perfunctory pop like the stamping of a bureaucrat's seal; neither Mikhail Mikhailovich nor I cheered. The manager poured the Dom into our coupes while a waiter laid out dishes of blinis, smoked beets, and cream. Mikhail Mikhailovich and I raised our glasses and mumbled our toasts.

"I didn't know Prokofiev stayed here," I said. Then I hurried to add, "But I love him."

"Oh? What about his music do you like, Natalia Nikolaevna?" the director said luxuriantly, wiping his mouth with a napkin.

"He has irony." I watched Mikhail Mikhailovich's heavy-lidded eyes grow a bit wider. "What he means is different from what he's saying. There's a great deal of ambivalence in his music, like a mind divided. Isn't it just like life?"

Mikhail Mikhailovich pondered this. "Perhaps, perhaps. It's hard for me to say, I'm not really in the business of making art. I'm in the business of making artists." The director added with a self-satisfied grin, "And *unmaking* them, too. Sometimes that is inevitable."

I sat in silence, wondering which way he'd decided about me. It suddenly occurred to me that I was having drinks with the general director of Bolshoi at the Metropol, when I'd never so much as shared tea with Ivan Stanislavich, the ballet director of Mariinsky. Heat rose to my cheeks.

As if he didn't notice, Mikhail Mikhailovich said, "The thing about Prokofiev that I like is that he was a genius. He wasn't a diplomat. Stravinsky, Shostakovich, they all hated him, but in the end, they respected him. I often find that this is what happens to people at the top."

I couldn't bring myself to say what I was thinking. But the director didn't need my encouragement, now that he was warming up to the effects of the Dom.

"Yes, I know what they say about me behind my back. I mean, Prokofiev and his enemies were composers, pianists—the most rational kind of artists, and still they almost came to blows. You think ballet dancers are emotional? Imagine being the object of scorn to a hundred and fifty opera singers. They are astonishingly dramatic."

We both laughed, shaking our heads. "Don't upset them, Mikhail Mikhailovich—they will start singing!" I said, and the director guffawed, slapping the table.

"I knew we'd get along, Natalia. You and I are not as different as you think," Mikhail Mikhailovich said as the last weak strains of laughter left his body with a sigh.

"I wasn't some old Muscovite. Just a son of farmers from Lithuania. No one took me under their wing. But I was more intelligent, more focused, and more willing to sacrifice than anyone else around me." He paused to take a swig of his champagne, and I nodded.

"And so, eventually, you could say that I won." The director smiled. "That's how success works, Natalia, as you found out yourself tonight. Tremendous moments like these never happen by chance, they happen by your own will and work—but they also don't occur many times in life. So listen carefully.

"I want you to come to Bolshoi as a prima ballerina. It's what you need to dance the way you deserve. You're not a Vaganova dancer at heart. You jump too high, turn too many times, and you're altogether too unique—all of which makes you ill-suited to Mariinsky, and perfect for Bolshoi. I might also add that this wasn't my idea."

"Whose idea was it, then?" I asked, and Mikhail Mikhailovich pointed at the ceiling.

"Your performance caught the attention of the highest levels. It goes up, and up, and up."

I didn't know what to think. I took my champagne and gulped down the nearly full glass. The drink watered my hollow inside like rain in the desert.

"Are you saying you're going to make me an artist?" I said, mostly because he seemed to need an answer of some kind. The director reached out his hand across the table, and I took it.

"An artist is made, but a genius is born. You've yet to be the former. You've always been the latter," Mikhail Mikhailovich said, shaking my hand.

I SPENT THE NIGHT AT the Metropol, with compliments from the Bolshoi director. In all my years of touring henceforth, I have never slept in a more wonderful bed than that first time. After soaking in piping hot water in the marble bathtub, I buried myself in the softest sheets and pillows like layers of a mille-feuille. I was so happy that I was still smiling when I fell asleep. I didn't know that was a real thing and not just some cliché from movies.

Next morning, I took a flight back home—again, courtesy of Mikhail Mikhailovich—and showed up at Mariinsky. Ivan Stanislavich was in his office, looking over several rehearsals simultaneously through his live camera feed. When I walked in, he swiveled his chair away from the screens and said mildly, "Brava, Natasha. Well done."

"Ivan Stanislavich, I am moving to Bolshoi. Mikhail Alypov offered me a contract as a principal dancer," I said, wasting no time with small talk. Ivan Stanislavich's ironclad face crumpled, but he soon regained his composure.

"Is this your way of bargaining? Fine. I could give you a principal contract here."

"No, you can't change my mind," I said. "And it's already been decided at a high level, you understand."

This drove Ivan Stanislavich over the edge. He enjoyed a bit of pushback now and again, but all within reason; he didn't take well to dancers who left him, rather than being abandoned by him. Then the real blow was that the Bolshoi general director Alypov conspired against him and bested him in a game of influence. There was nothing more he could do, other than warn me: "Once you go out today, you're never coming back to Mariinsky. I will personally ensure that you are banned from this building."

Although I had no love for him, hearing this made my heart seize up inside my chest, and with great effort I kept my tears from welling up. After four years of my life and hundreds of performances, I was nothing to him or to Mariinsky. When I gathered myself enough to speak, my voice sounded convincingly cold.

"If I have any choice in the matter, I will not step foot here again."

"WHAT ARE YOU DOING HERE, Natasha?" I hear Nina's voice and open my eyes. She's standing over me, the spotlight making a halo around her head. Behind her, I see stagehands rolling backdrops and lighting crew doing tests for the evening performance.

"I just got done with rehearsals and went looking for you—Sveta told me to check the stage." Nina pulls me up by the hand. "I need to go home, but why don't you come over for dinner? It will do you good."

I nod because I can't think of a single excuse. Nina ushers me out through the artist entrance to the street, where Andryusha is already waiting for us in their silver Lada. He gets out of the driver's seat, shouting, "Natasha, how many summers, how many winters!" He then wraps me in an enthusiastic hug that takes me by surprise—I hadn't known that he liked me so well.

"Haven't seen you in ages," I say, and he squeezes me one last time before letting go. "Andryusha, you are even more handsome than before."

People in their teens and twenties have the beauty that they have been given. After the age of thirty, their looks are determined by what they give—to themselves and to the world. Andryusha had been almost unfairly handsome in our school days and the early years at the company. Now his deep-set eyes, easy smile, and taut body—everything somehow broader and more open than before—tell me he has been giving generously to both himself and others, by being kind and loyal and working hard without losing the pleasure of it. Andryusha smiles at my compliment but doesn't betray even a trace of vanity that I would often elicit in men by offering my attention.

"Thank you. You look beautiful, of course, Natasha." Andryusha gives his wife a quick kiss and opens the car door. "Petya, go to the backseat. Lara, scoot to the middle so your brother can sit next to you. Luda, you can sit on Mama's lap. Natasha, you sit in the passenger seat."

Andryusha gives me a regretful glance to apologize for speaking to me as if I were one of his children. First thing I notice about them is their spotless and soft skin, like *porosha*—snow that has freshly fallen overnight, lying undisturbed and shimmering in the morning sun. As a child, Nina had the same otherworldly quality, which has over the years dimmed down to a whisper. The family grumble and shuffle themselves around the car like bees in a hive, and then we're off, the car threading its way through the mauve fabric of the night. I've always loved driving in a city after dark—the ugliness obscured, the beauty intensified, everything rushing by with a sense of promise. The peaceful feeling doesn't last, however. Andryusha keeps asking Petya and Lara if they said hello to Aunt Natasha, they keep insisting that they did (they didn't), Luda is so hungry after her gymnastics practice that she's about to melt down, and no one is happy until Nina allows them to play with her and Andryusha's phones. There is blissful silence until we arrive at their apartment and the kids run off to their respective rooms.

"I made pizza dough earlier. It'll take me a few minutes to put those in the oven. You girls want anything in the meantime?" Andryusha says, picking up Luda's jacket from the floor and putting it in the closet.

"Just some tea. I'll get it." Nina goes into the kitchen, and Luda follows her, whining about her hurt knee. The two older kids have come out of their rooms and are now fighting over the remote; Petya wants to watch Zenit St. Petersburg play their archenemies, the CSKA Moscow, and Lara complains that it's her night to choose and *Frozen* is playing.

"But, Papa, it's an important game and Lara's seen *Frozen* before!" Petya, who is eleven, shouts in the direction of the kitchen. He is the replica of the young Andryusha I first saw at Vaganova. Eight-year-old Lara is close to tears. "It's—my—night!" she yells, punctuating each word with a smack to Petya's shoulder.

"Okay, watch ten minutes of the game, then ten minutes of *Frozen*, back and forth, until dinner." Andryusha gives his verdict from the kitchen as Nina emerges bearing a tray of tea. She and I sip without talking as the kids sullenly watch soccer and then the magical Nordic princess for ten minutes at a time. The apartment fills with the cheerful smell of olive oil and tomatoes. When the pizza is done, the kids all beg to eat in the living room. Andryusha spends some time negotiating so that the TV remains on—*Frozen*—while everyone eats at the dining table. Peace returns for a while, and then Petya runs mid-dinner to the living room to change the channel and discovers that Zenit has scored in the past ten minutes. He screams in frustration over missing it, and then when CSKA scores two goals in the last ten minutes of the game, thus securing their victory over Petersburg, he breaks down and runs to his room, trailing fat teardrops in his wake. Andryusha sighs and goes after his son, while Nina clears the table. She motions for me to sit down, but I help carry the dishes to the sink.

"I should wash them because Andryusha cooked but I just can't," Nina says, leading me away from the dirty pots and pans. "Let's go talk in my room."

Once Nina closes the door behind her, she collapses on the bed without turning on the lights. "I'm sorry, my life is very chaotic."

"It's lively." I sit on the floor, and Nina pats the space next to her on the bed. "No, it's fine, it's comfortable on the rug," I assure her.

"Come up. It's not like we ever do it in this bed anymore."

This takes me by surprise because Nina never talked about sex except with the greatest delicacy, even when we were teenagers. I hop on and lie down next to her.

"I can't even remember the last time we had sex. It's not that I don't want to at all. I can *imagine* a situation in which I'd be in the mood. That's never the reality, though. Does that make sense?"

"It makes total sense," I tell her. "What kind of situations?"

Nina peers at the door and moves a bit closer to me.

"There's this bakery I go to. The pastry chef is a young guy, always in a clean white uniform, and he gives me samples. Unnecessarily so. I don't know if it's the smell of fresh bread, or the free rolls he puts in my bag, or the fact that it's the one place where I'm not a dancer or a mother or a wife, just Nina—but I find him quite fascinating." We giggle, and then she hurries to add, "Of course I'm not saying I'll ever do anything."

"Andryusha made pizza tonight. I bet he would be open to role-playing a hot baker."

"He's a great papa." Nina's smile fades from her lips. "He also uses that against me. Ever since he got injured and had to sit out this season, he's been acting like he's some selfless hero, sacrificing everything for his family. What about the fact that I sat out three seasons while being pregnant?" She stares at the ceiling. "And please don't say 'I told you so.'"

"I wasn't going to."

"I never thought I'd become a principal in my early twenties, like you. But it does upset me that I'm going to retire as a first soloist. I had talent, too. It could've gone differently." She covers her face with her hands. "My kids don't even take after me very much. It's all Papa this Papa that. Petya wants to be a footballer, Lara is obsessed with pop stars. Luda is interested in dance, but only time will tell."

"Nina, I'm sorry to break this news to you, but they look exactly like you." I smile, but Nina is unrelenting.

"What I mean is that family isn't everything," she says.

The door bursts open and we pick ourselves up with a start. It's Luda, a tiny ballerina with her braided bun and tights. She crawls into bed between us and Nina cradles her; they fit together perfectly like one of those hugging salt and pepper shakers at museum gift shops around the world.

"I should go home. It's getting late."

"Andryusha will drop you off."

"No, there's no need. I can take a cab." I lean over and embrace both Nina and Luda, who squirms like a cat. I mouth *role-play* to Nina, and she giggles and covers Luda's ears with her hands.

I leave their apartment and stand on the curb. There is no one out this late on a residential block. An unseasonably cold draft envelops me and rips still-green leaves from branches. From one moment to the next, the security of Nina's home is replaced by a sense of being lost. I have never been in this part of the city before. My heart palpitates again under the cotton top that had seemed thick enough in the morning. My mind is a jumble, my whole body is shaking, and the only thing I can think of is pulling on the warm-up sweater in my bag. Once that is accomplished, I squat down and curl into a ball. It's not simply fear of injury or failure or addiction anymore, it's fatigue in absolute proportions. An ice wall as high as the sky that I have to scale with my bare hands. I feel as tired as a runner who has just finished a marathon and is told, "Now do that again." Over and over.

My phone vibrates. When I pull it out of my pocket, the bright screen feels like it's an actual live being, a true friend. I read a text from Dmitri.

Do you want to meet me for a drink?

This reminds me that I haven't had a drop of alcohol in about forty-eight hours. The anticipation of it is a glowing ember in my stomach.

I text him back: *Yes, where are you now?*

In my first week at Bolshoi, Mikhail Mikhailovich invited me out to dinner to celebrate. We sat in front of a towering display of petit fours and talked about art. Like most men of his type, Mikhail Mikhailovich liked to show off his knowledge rather than reveal what he liked or found moving.

"Isn't Balanchine exceptional because he was the first choreographer to eliminate the narrative from the ballet? It's *pure* movement," the director said, nibbling on a coulibiac with Italian truffles.

"I don't think any dance is just movement. No art is pure abstraction. There is always meaning behind it," I countered, yet the director didn't seem to mind.

"But what about music? Say, Mozart."

"*Especially* Mozart! He is full of symbolism. Whenever he wrote in A major, he was describing love," I said, taking a bite of a cake swathed in edible gold; to my slight disappointment, it tasted no different from a regular chocolate cake. "Every movement and position in ballet also inspires an inherent feeling, like A major did for Mozart."

"So what symbolizes love in ballet?" asked Mikhail Mikhailovich, hardly bothering to veil his skepticism.

"There are too many, but the easiest one would be . . ." I rose from my seat to demonstrate. Right foot pointing forward, left arm overhead, right arm to the side, head tilted back. "Effacé devant. It's tender. Do you see?"

I sat down. Mikhail Mikhailovich leaned back in his seat and smiled, making *hmm* sounds of agreement.

"I don't understand people who try to separate form from meaning—this obsession with 'purity.' As if art ever has anything to do with the external! Things that can be taken at face value are precisely the opposite of art. Art is what can't be seen from the surface," I said.

Mikhail Mikhailovich rested his elbows on the table, leaned forward, and said, "Do you know who you remind me of?"

"Who?"

"Dmitri Ostrovsky. Have you met him yet? He's our leading male principal."

I'd already stood close to him in company class, but merely shrugged.

"Dmitri also has a consuming interest in all the arts, not just dance. It's how I know which ones will be truly great. I've never met anyone who knows more about music, paintings, or history, than Dmitri. Like you, he has fans in the highest places. It's made him rather unruly in recent years. Even to me. I would advise you to become friends with Dmitri, if you can," the director said, and I nodded.

"If you can't, at least don't make an enemy of him. He's vindictive to the point of murderousness," Mikhail Mikhailovich said, plucking a strawberry from the tower and swallowing it whole. "Must be the Bashkir in his blood."

I smiled, holding back from telling Mikhail Mikhailovich what happened earlier that week, at my very first company class. Every ballet company has its own set of rules: at Mariinsky, the company class was divided into soloists and corps, male and female. When I realized that Bolshoi held a mixed company class, I did what any reasonable dancer would do: I waited until everyone had taken their usual places at the barre, and just as the ballet master finished giving the plié combination, I rushed over to an empty spot at the wall, far from the mirror. The pianist had already begun playing when the ballet master strode into the middle of the room with a hand held up, like a cop stopping the flow of traffic. "Natasha," he said, pointing at me. Everyone's eyes followed his finger to my face. "What are you doing there? The premiers use the center barre."

I knew which one he meant: it was the barre that was claimed by the stars, including Alexander Nikulin, who stepped forward a few feet to make room. The dancer standing behind Nikulin, with black hair, beautiful feet, and exceptionally long arms and legs, was Dmitri. He frowned when I took my place, and the other principals avoided making eye contact with me; so I knew that I'd be eating alone for a very long time. In fact, the meal with Mikhail Mikhailovich was the first one I was sharing with someone else since coming to Moscow.

It wasn't a huge loss. So many days, I would realize I'd only had tea until the end of rehearsals, and a little fruit if I had more time. I didn't care about food, just as I didn't care about sleep, friends, or anything other than dance. I rarely even talked to Mama, who had frustrated me with her ambivalence about the Bolshoi offer. She congratulated me on my advancement but couldn't see why I wouldn't stay at Mariinsky, to which (she thought) we both owed so much. During our first few calls after moving to Moscow, I tried to convince her to be happy for me.

"You can come visit me anytime you want. I will buy you tickets and take you to the Metropol. It's a very famous hotel," I said to her, pleased to be able to treat her to something special. "A box seat at the Bolshoi and dinner at the Metropol—you'll experience what only the most sophisticated Muscovites enjoy!"

But in the long pause that followed, I could picture her tensing up, her shoulders rolling up to her ears.

"Okay," she said with difficulty. "I'm not much of a traveler . . . We'll see. I'll try to come see you."

After that, we talked vaguely about flights and train tickets a few more times. But she sounded so forced that eventually I no longer suggested she should visit Moscow. Having spent nearly my whole life observing the parents of my peers, I'd realized that Mama was different from all of them. It was not that she didn't love me or that she wasn't a good mother. She was a good mother the only way she knew how to be, with her awkwardness, timidity, fatigue, and moodiness. She was whatever unkind word might be the opposite of worldly, intellectual, easygoing, naturally affectionate, and protective—as my friends' parents had been to varying degrees. It was as though the difficult start she had to motherhood soured it for both of us ever after. I imagined that some part of her was glad at the hours of train ride now separating us.

While I regretted the coolness with Mama, I let my friends go with less guilt. The memory of Seryozha was the first to recede into the deep. He'd begged for us to try to make our relationship work, and my relief in solitude let me know it would never have worked out. Already, he felt more like a brother than ever before, even when we were children. I had to keep this a secret; even someone as humble and kind as Seryozha would never forgive me if he knew.

I still thought of Nina when something funny or insufferable or beautiful happened. A few times on a day off, I lay in bed with the phone in my hand, wondering if I should call her. But in the brief interval between her wedding and the Moscow competition, Nina had resolutely avoided me. On the rare occasions when I saw her between class and rehearsals, she could be found speaking in low tones with Andryusha, their heads inclined toward each other. I would have interjected into their conversation without hesitation when they were merely dating, but now they seemed to have entered a sacred level of intimacy closed off to all others. It wasn't merely our fight—since marriage, she'd undergone a profound and instant inner shift of her values and priorities. On one side stood her family, which meant Andryusha, and on the other side stood everyone else, including me. She didn't seem apologetic about this; rather, her face glowed with the aggressive pride of someone who got what they wanted out of life. Right before I left, she stepped out of matrimonial privacy long enough to wish me *toi toi toi*, a peace accord I strongly suspected had been brokered by Andryusha. But the whole goodbye was so stiff and unnatural that it only served to remind us what we'd lost. Eventually, I stopped debating whether to reach out to her and accepted that it was time we—Seryozha, Nina, and I—learned to grow independently from one another.

With little sadness, I let dance take over the space where my friends used to be. The ritual of getting up, washing my face, boiling water, stretching, sewing and breaking in pointe shoes, taking class, rehearsing, soaking in Epsom salt bath, rubbing ointments and taping my feet before bed—all of it was a trance, much like the one that a lover goes through in the heat of passion, a kind of courtship for the ecstatic hours onstage.

MY DEVOTION WAS WORTHWHILE: I had never danced better. Even Nikulin noticed, as we began rehearsing together for my Kitri debut in *Don Q*. If he still wasn't exactly warm or friendly, he was starting to show me a begrudging respect. Every morning, he left empty space behind him at the barre, saving me a spot without saying so. He nodded in my direction as I passed him in the corridor, each time accompanied by a different girl from the corps de ballet. Although my obsession with Nikulin, or Sasha as I now had to call him, had cooled considerably since the competition, I still couldn't help but register these girls' names and faces. They also noticed me noticing them, and silently communicated to me a sense of remorse, boasting, or a mixture of both. They seemed to think that I envied them. But I didn't, because Sasha was never with anyone who struck me as better than I was. Indeed, none of them was even close to reaching *his* beauty. Sasha next to one of those girls was like a wolf taking a walk with a lapdog.

One day in September, just a few weeks before the opening night of *Don Q*, I arrived at rehearsal to find Sasha talking—not to one of his corps girls—but to Dmitri. They were laughing, and when they saw me walk in, Dmitri raised his eyebrows and left without another word. I sat down on the floor and started putting on my pointe shoes. Sasha sidled up to me with an apologetic smile.

"How are you?" he said in that relaxed voice of his, which had a disarming effect juxtaposed against his domineering body. It reminded me of the day of the Moscow competition, when I was lying down on the stage and he spoke aloud that Maya Plisetskaya quote. I still wondered if it really happened, or if I imagined it. I turned my focus back to securing the ribbons around my ankles.

"It's going. There are some little things to iron out, but we'll be ready in a few weeks," I said.

Sasha bent his knees and squatted down, resting his elbows on his thighs. "No, I mean how have you been since coming to Moscow? Getting settled in okay?"

I thought about the nearly empty apartment that Mikhail Mikhailovich procured for me near the theater. I didn't have anything in the kitchen besides a kettle—no pots or pans. The mattress was still sitting on the floor because I hadn't had time to go buy a bed.

"I don't think about that stuff," I told Sasha. He sighed and sat down next to me, stretching his legs out in front and leaning back on his palms. Then he met my eyes and smiled. It was a rare show of openness and intimacy after weeks of rehearsing together with only professional courtesy. Although I'd become used to his looks, I again became conscious of his physicality—the way he seemed to have not been born a baby like everyone else but created whole from the thighbone of a god.

"You have no furniture in your apartment, no food in the fridge, and no friends," he said. "It was like that for me, too, when I first came to Moscow."

"I thought you went to Bolshoi Academy."

"Transferred. I'm originally from Donbas. Grew up on a farm with my grandparents. We raised everything we ate. There was a dance teacher at our school, and she forced me to take ballet class so the girls would have a partner. After five years, I somehow made it here, and the others didn't take to me. The teachers just called me 'that kid from Ukraine.'" He paused and cleared his throat, as if he'd revealed more than he'd intended.

"Well, that didn't stop you from becoming a star," I said, pretending to fiddle with my shoes. "Now everyone wants to be your friend."

Sasha grinned, showing a set of incisors that were a little too sharp to be perfect. So he was human, after all. "I was lonely when I first entered the company. But Dmitri took me under his wing. And since he has the whole company under his sway, it made things considerably easier."

"Is Dmitri a kind person?" I asked, recalling the barely concealed scorn on his face as he left the studio. Sasha looked momentarily stunned, as if I'd said the most naive thing. He shook his head.

"Dima is many, many things, but *kind* is not a word that I would use to describe him. He can be generous, but not out of friendship or loyalty, only his whim—like a tsar who bestows riches on a peasant one day and then beheads him the next day. So he doesn't have true friends, but everyone bends to him like sunflowers to the sun."

I recalled Dmitri's dancing in class—his extraordinary length, supple back, hypnotic fluidity even in a simple combination. Everyone watched him, but he didn't watch anyone. He never cast a glance in my direction.

"You sound as though you dislike him."

"Oh, I do like him. He's very theatrical, and when he's in a good mood, he can be wonderful. And he likes me—he favors boys."

This took me by surprise. If there had been any gay dancers around me, they kept it secret. I only remembered one boy at Vaganova who was feminine and didn't try to hide it. He was bullied so much by the other boys that he eventually transferred to a less prestigious school. After growing older and graduating into the company, we accepted that it was polite to not ask uncomfortable questions. That Dmitri alone could defy this unspoken rule and still dance—as a star even—was almost awe-inspiring. I repeated incredulously, "He likes *boys*."

Sasha hurried to add, "I like girls."

Just then, Sasha's coach walked through the door, and we scrambled up and smoothed down our clothes. Without speaking to us, Yusupov strode across the room in his straight-legged gait and popped the CD into the stereo, and then we were on to the pas de deux.

Since I didn't have a coach yet, Yusupov was the closest thing I had to a mentor in a company where the coach-dancer relationship was particularly intimate, almost sacred. Only in his midforties, Yusupov was not one of Bolshoi's star répétiteurs, most of whom were honored artists of Russia. His wheat-colored hair in the shape of a bowl and a large, crooked nose had a look of medieval forbearance. Belying his relative youth and irregular features, Yusupov conducted himself with utmost gravitas; his eyes were serious to the point of appearing sad.

At first, I didn't understand why Sasha hadn't tried to work with someone more influential. Coaches taught not just the choreography but also shaped the entire career of their dancers. Some of them told their charges when to sleep, when and what to eat, how to dress, and even whom to date. Many took it upon themselves to lobby the management on behalf of their protégés. But I soon realized that Sasha liked people simply for who they were, not what they could do for him. In that way he had what could be called class, as did Yusupov, and so they felt at ease in each other's company. When Sasha played around creating new trick jumps and turns—this is what they loved doing at Bolshoi, in contrast to Mariinsky—Yusupov even smiled sadly at times, like a widower seeing his son at graduation. But he remained closed off to me, as did everyone else at the company except Mikhail Mikhailovich. And, little by little, Sasha.

It was two days before my debut. We'd just finished our afternoon rehearsal, the last one before the run-through onstage. Yusupov ejected the CD, nodded in our direction, and made his way to the door. Just before exiting, he abruptly turned back and called out to me.

"Natasha, be sure to rest up. And remember to eat."

I nodded, and the coach walked out. Once I was sure he'd left, I shrugged off my practice tutu and sank down to the floor. My feet were red and swollen when I pulled them out of my shoes, and I threw away the damp paper towels that cushioned my toes against the floor. I felt numb, empty, and stretched like a two-ended arrow shooting infinitely in both directions. Then another pair of feet approached mine in my field of vision, and I heard Sasha's voice.

"He's right. When's the last time you ate anything?"

I thought about it. "I had a banana and peanut butter."

"This morning?"

I'd had it the previous night after rehearsal. But to appease Sasha, I nodded.

"You know that's not good for you," Sasha said. "Let's go get dinner."

I was about to protest, but he cut me off. "We both know you have nothing else to do, no plans, and no friends."

"I have friends—they're just in Petersburg," I said. It occurred to me that I hadn't thought of any of them in weeks, and I suddenly felt very cold even in the warmth of September.

"And you have me in Moscow." Sasha reached out his hand, and I pulled it to stand up. The moment we walked out the artist entrance, a gust of humid air enveloped us. White and red petunias were fluttering in the square like tiny little flags. Cars flooded the roads. We turned right onto Okhotny Ryad and continued through Manezhnaya Square, which like a giant bowl held the golden dust of afternoon smog. To our left, the Red Square stretched south, its colorful onion domes as fanciful and vivid as a Kandinsky painting. Somewhere in the distance, a man was singing a Viktor Tsoi song and accompanying himself on an acoustic guitar. *Sunlight of mine, look at me now. See my palm has turned to a fist. And if you have powder, give me a spark. That's that.*

Sasha hummed along to the melody very softly. He noticed me looking at him and smiled. His eyes were the color of warm honey, and I felt a sudden desire to go to a cool, shaded room and take a long nap with him. We would lie in bed in the semidarkness, the windows open to let in the breeze. We would not be dancing—for once content in our stillness. We would just *be*. I glanced away so he wouldn't read my mind. But the yearning was stuck there in my head as he led us all the way to a Georgian restaurant in Old Arbat.

ii

"SO, WHAT ARE PEOPLE SAYING BEHIND MY BACK?" I ASKED, ONCE WE'D ordered dumplings, red pepper walnut dip, beet *pkhali*, and stuffed eggplant rolls. Sasha's eyes twinkled as he swigged his water.

"They're saying, 'that kid from Petersburg.'"

I smiled. "Of course that. What else?"

"Do you really want to know?" Sasha's face grew somber, and I nodded.

"I survived Mariinsky. I know how theater people are—you can't unnerve me."

"But you don't know how Bolshoi people are," Sasha said. "Back when I was still a student, some dancers in the company paid people to clap—"

"Oh, this isn't news, everyone knows about the claqueurs in Moscow," I said. Claqueurs were, like the center barre for principals, a unique feature of Bolshoi not found in Petersburg. "I heard the management pays them to cheer for certain soloists."

"Not only that. Sometimes dancers paid them to clap for their *rivals*, in the middle of a tricky variation, to throw them off." Sasha paused when the waitress came back. She laid the dishes one by one on the table, smiling at him the whole time. "I haven't seen it happen in recent years. But now you know Bolshoi is on a different level. It's best if you act like you see nothing and hear nothing. Who cares what they think, right?"

"Okay, now I *have* to know," I said, once the waitress left with a sigh in Sasha's direction. He twisted his lips, starting to speak and stopping a few times.

"People say you have a big ego. Proud. Ambitious," he finally said.

"So that means I'll fit right in." I smiled, helping myself to some *pkhali*. "They say that about anyone with a backbone. Especially if it's a woman."

"Well, there's also a rumor that you advanced not on your merit." Sasha kept his eyes on an eggplant roll, which he kept cutting into tiny pieces. "Some people think you're sleeping with Mikhail Alypov. Or someone higher up in the administration." I felt all the blood in my body rush to my head. Sasha looked up at me in alarm.

"I won Moscow International—that's how I got here," I stammered, and his face fell. "Oh, they think that was rigged, too?" I asked as nausea overtook me.

"*I* know you won because you were the best dancer there," Sasha said.

"How would you know? You weren't watching."

"Exactly. I knew you'd throw me off if I did. And it still didn't make a difference in the end." He glimpsed up from his dish and met my gaze for a second. I cleared my throat.

"And who's saying this behind my back?"

"Does it matter? I regret saying anything, Natasha. This is noise. You focus on dance and just be the best artist you can be—that's all there is. Now you know that Bolshoi doesn't care about you, it doesn't care about any of us. It hurts less when you stop caring, too."

I tried to sound cold and metallic, but instead I felt my eyes water and rushed to shield them with my hand. "You might as well tell me to stop being me."

Sasha got up from his seat, and I thought he was heading to the restroom. But he sat down next to me and laid a hand on my shoulder. His was the only touch I'd received in the past several weeks. This time, he wasn't Basilio touching Kitri—he was Sasha touching me. It made me long to touch him back, but I just stayed still with all the nerves of my body concentrated where his right hand connected to my right shoulder.

"You keep being you, Natasha Leonova," Sasha said, moving his thumb ever so lightly back and forth like a windshield wiper. I wanted to read into it, as I've wanted to read into every little bit of our interactions—but I wasn't so foolish as to think he'd be good for me. We would tear each other apart like wild animals in a cage, anyone with eyes could see this.

"Don't ever change."

ON THE MORNING OF OUR performance, I headed to the theater a few hours before company class. As I was turning the corner toward the artist entrance, I saw a line of people wrapping around the building. Near the box office, some people were even lying in sleeping bags. Their quilted nylon jackets were bright red and blue, lit up with nearly horizontal pylons of morning sun. On golden but cool days like this, between summer and fall, it is moving just to see ordinary things—people, trees, buildings—standing in the light and casting long shadows. Everything feels more similar and connected, like someone drew us all in one continuous, everlasting stroke.

I made my way up to the studio and warmed up alone for the next hour. Dancers started filtering in, one by one. Sasha showed up five minutes before class began, drinking from a thermos. He put it down next to me and rolled his neck, first one way and then the other.

"Did you see the crowd outside?" he asked, pulling away from the barre so that his spine lengthened parallel to the floor. The ballet master finished talking to the pianist, to which cue the dancers rose to their feet, pinching their tights up.

"Yes, is something going on?" I asked.

He laughed, unfolding his body. "They're waiting to buy tickets to our performance tonight. Well, they know me already. They spent the night in line for *you*, the new star from Petersburg. All Moscow is going to be watching."

I didn't say anything, drawing a curtain of indifference over my face. Sasha leaned on the barre with one hand and shifted from hip to hip, looking disappointed at my impassiveness. What did he want—for me to be thrilled? Or intimidated and nervous?

"You know, there are two kinds of dancers," I said in a low voice. "The first kind rehearses well but loses nerves onstage and performs worse than during the previous weeks. The second type of dancer always performs better under pressure than in rehearsals. Guess which one I am?" Without waiting for an answer, I grabbed his thermos and drank from it—I was expecting black tea or coffee, but it was hot chocolate.

"I like sweets, so I try to at least have them in the morning," Sasha protested in a whisper, and I smothered a laugh. The other dancers stole glances in our direction. Even the ballet master stopped explaining the plié combination to shoot us a stern look.

I knew then that each of us had finally taken off the outermost layer of ourselves, with equal senses of caution and inevitability. Between Sasha and me, there was now something alive and enticing and dangerous, like spilled mercury. Not only did we feel it, but everyone else perceived it and adjusted themselves accordingly, the way one leaves home with an umbrella because of the lightning smell in the humid summer air. Sasha lost his enfant terrible mannerisms with me, that inscrutable mask he wore at competitions. He wasn't a perfectionist asshole like I was. He was that preternaturally handsome boy in class that, instead of being snobbish and exclusive, made friends with everyone. He joked through our final rehearsal, doing spot-on impressions of other dancers until even Yusupov smiled a bittersweet smile.

When it was time for us to decamp to our separate dressing rooms, he kissed me on my cheek, lingering just a breath longer than a dry professional peck. A little part of me knew he was only getting into character as Basilio, a lovestruck young Spaniard. Another part of me thought that this was who he really was. In ballet, the boundary between you and the character blurs until you're not even sure what's real and what's pretend. Indeed, art of any kind isn't possible without its creator believing that it's truer than reality. That's the difference between art and something merely beautiful.

So when, hiding in the wings for our cue, he pulled me into an embrace and whispered *merde* in my ear, I did what I would never do, but Kitri would do: kiss him before running away onto the stage. Last thing I remember before turning into her is the sea-salt taste of his mouth.

Since Natalia Leonova's recent appointment as prima ballerina, all Moscow has been waiting to see how the import from Mariinsky measures up on the Bolshoi stage. Can the Petersburg native rise to the challenge of this, most Moscow of ballets? The verdict is in: The 22-year-old more than justified her rise on the opening night of *Don Quixote*, dancing Kitri opposite the superstar Alexander Nikulin. From her first entrance with a gravity-defying grand jeté, it was clear that Ms. Leonova was there to conquer—not with a horde of soldiers, but with her astonishing pyrotechniques and irrepressible brio.

Ms. Leonova is known as a reserved, even mysterious figure among her colleagues at the theater. Off stage, she possesses a cool modernity more than fairy-tale beauty—high cheekbones, dark and arched eyebrows, shoulder-length hair, shell-colored lips. Onstage, she was almost unrecognizable as an especially passionate, exuberant, and lovable Kitri. Offer the Cupid's bow to this Kitri, and she would say, "The bow is for cowards; give me a sword," and take what is hers as if it were her oyster. The test of her mettle came in the Act III coda, when her dizzyingly fast 32 fouettés drove the audience into a frenzy. Many shouts of "brava" and magnificent whistles sliced through the air. Hearing this ovation, Ms. Leonova answered to the hallowed Bolshoi tradition: she nodded to her conductor for an encore round of the coda and again executed perfect 32 fouettés. At this point, the nearly two-centuries-old roof of the theater seemed to lift slightly off its pillars by the ear-splitting roar of the audience. Of course, Muscovites love nothing more than a dancer who risks death onstage and comes out alive. It's heroic. And it's why we love ballet: because at its best, it is miraculous.

Ms. Leonova's partnership with Mr. Nikulin, whom the foreign presses have taken to calling "Alexander the Great," appears to be a serendipitous one. Not a typical woodland prince or Germanic cavalier, he has the raw golden look of a

> Scandinavian lord. She is dark, sensuous, and queenly. Both are bravura dancers in the mold of old Bolshoi, and each pushes the other to the limit, emotionally and physically. Mr. Nikulin supports his partner warmly—even reverentially—the way many virtuosic male soloists do not. It belies the rumors of a troupe divided by a too-swift advancement of Ms. Leonova. In a recent interview with Le Figaro, Dmitri Ostrovsky, the company's leading male premier for the past many years, decried the appointment as a travesty. "Lately, some dancers have been getting ahead simply by sleeping with certain people in the administration," Mr. Ostrovsky said, without naming anyone directly. When the interviewer asked if he meant Ms. Leonova, Mr. Ostrovsky replied with his trademark colorful non sequitur: "People will pay money to go see a flying pig, but what happens when it comes down to rest? People eat it."

THE BAR THAT DMITRI CHOSE is accessed by an unmarked door at the end of a long staircase leading down from street level. I push open the door and a very tall woman with red hair walks out in velvet platform sandals. "Excuse me," she says as she brushes me with her swimmer's shoulders, muscular but wrapped in a layer of soft, clammy flesh.

My eyes take a second to adjust to the interior, which is bathed in the copper phosphorescence of lava flow at night. Jazz pours darkly into the room. I scan the few young, trendy patrons and spot Dmitri at the onyx-colored bar, nursing a drink. When he sees me, he gestures to the bartender.

"What would you like?" Dmitri looks at me. I scan the backlit bottles lining the wall, each gleaming with seductive luster. Everything entices. After a beat, I manage to shake my head.

"I stopped drinking," I tell him.

"Natasha," he says slowly. "You're in Russia. Here, you stop drinking when you die."

I don't say anything, and he raises two fingers to the bartender. Two glasses of neat vodka appear in front of us.

"*Budem*," he says, raising his glass. When I merely glare at him, he chuckles and takes a swig.

"I love drinking under a hateful stare. It adds so much flavor." He smacks his lips. "Why are you so angry, Natasha?"

"After everything you did to me? How could I possibly be angry?" I snort. "Tell me why, Dmitri. What did I ever do to you?"

Dmitri sighs. "This is why I could never be with women. They hold grudges forever, and they always ask why." He looks off into the distance; his normally green eyes glint like rubies in this light. "Have you ever wondered what love might be like, without those two tendencies? That's love between men. It's like jumping naked off a cliff into the sea." He silently orders another drink with his finger. "In two words: no regrets."

"Or thoughtless and fatal," I say, and he grins.

"To be proper, love *should* be thoughtless and fatal!" He takes a sip of his vodka. "I once did jump off a cliff, by the way, with a certain gorgeous Michel I met in Nice. The next morning I woke up next to a note on my bed—'*j'ai passé une nuit délicieuse*.' Five words, no other explanation, and still the greatest love story of my life."

"Good for you," I say, and this draws another chuckle from Dmitri.

"You do have some steel in you. Fine. I'll tell you why." He pauses and stares into my eyes. "Back in my early days at Bolshoi, I once asked Mikhail Alypov about the claqueurs." I recall the clappers in the cheap seats, some of whom attained an aura of semiofficial employees after decades of attendance.

"I asked Alypov, why do you pay these slugs to applaud? Isn't our dancing good enough? And do you know what he said?" He pauses and raises his black eyebrows.

"He said very seriously, 'Because, Dmitri, it is *tradition*. If a ballerina does fouettés, there has to be at least three throaty bravas!'" He grins, remembering back to the theater, to the claqueurs faithfully shouting the compliments from the gods.

"How does this have anything to do with you and me?" I ask, starting to lose the thread of where we were. Being with Dmitri is always disorienting, but especially when I have been off my meds and alcohol as long as I have. My throat is parched and my eyes have a heartbeat of their own.

"Natasha, I'm trying to tell you that that's the answer," Dmitri says. "Tradition. Whatever I did to you is just tradition. You know as well as I do that when you get to the top, everyone wants you to fail, and the only way to stake your territory is to attack. Being insulted by another artist of such a caliber as I am is really the highest form of flattery."

"My head hurts," I say.

"Because you're living in the past."

His voice echoes and blurs into the copper light. I shake my head and turn around to ask for water—but the bartender has disappeared. There is no one else at the bar. The music, too, is gone, and we are alone. My heart begins pounding again. Dmitri grins at me.

"Natasha," he says, and his voice turns into something black and soft in the space between us. More soft, black things fall down like snow from the ceiling. Feathers.

"This is a dream," I say. "You're not real."

"If I'm not real, then this wouldn't matter." Dmitri reaches out and touches my cheek with his hand. I pull him into my arms. When our lips meet, thousands of black feathers rain down to cover us in darkness.

I'VE ALWAYS LOVED THE GRAY space between sleep and waking. I like it because it's soft and has no edges. No matter what they say, I am not a hard woman. I am *not* Attila. People think I spring up out of bed every morning and promptly start putting myself through another day of self-discipline, but my favorite thing is to float on a raft on this foggy lake as long as I can. I lift up pieces of dreams and thoughts with my oar and sort them as memories or fantasies, significant or insignificant. Sewing a mountain of pointe shoes. (Insignificant, memory.) Mama driving somewhere with me in the passenger seat. (Significant, fantasy. Mama never learned to drive and we never went anywhere together.) It is breathtaking how much of your identity and life consists of utter imagination, things that never happened and never will happen. Yet everything in your mind is real, and has its own mass and gravity.

Like the universe, which they say is filled with more dark matter than matter.

Sometimes in my dreams, I do complicated math sets or write an entire libretto in French—that's when I know my mind is in the mood to solve problems, but of course, the results are not usable. There is a sweet spot though where, with its speed and freedom, my unconscious creates new possibilities for my waking life. Interviewers have often asked me: What is the secret to your jumps and turns? I always answered that it's just what nature has given me, and that's mostly true. But it is in my dreams that I've figured out the torque of my back and shoulders that gives me an extra turn, or the exact arm position that produces the most *ballon*, adding another foot to the top of my jump. Then I float on the lake, holding this new idea in my hand like a stone, before the fog dissipates and I bump into the hard edges of reality.

With my eyes still closed, I think back to last night. I remember clearly the dinner at Nina's house, although what happened afterward is a mystery. A nauseating mystery, to be sure. I take a deep breath and open my eyes—to my relief, I see that I'm alone in my hotel bed. I'm naked, which is a little unusual, but not worthy of panic. I look around for my phone, and it's not anywhere in the room. My clothes from yesterday have disappeared, too. I finally find my phone on the balcony, facedown and sprawled on the floor, as if it, too, had a regrettable night. I crouch low and snatch it without being seen by the commuters below. Back in bed, I check my messages from Dmitri and my heart drops when I see his last text, the address of that copper-colored bar sent at 9:40 p.m. I'd been half expecting that whole place to be a dream.

I chuck my phone into the comforter, which my nighttime thrashing has rolled into a cloudy snail shell. I drink from the faucet before hopping in the shower, and the rush of hot water calms me instantly. I'm surprised to note that even as my mind feels like a ball of yarn that has been too unwound to ever find its shape again, my body is a degree stronger, leaner, and healthier than it was yesterday. My feet and ankles are stable and less inflamed. It fills me with a dim light of hope that cutting out everything was the right decision, even if it's also demolishing the decrepit walls of my mind.

Downstairs at the lobby, Igor Petrenko gives me a wave and rushes toward me with a shopping bag in hand.

"Hello, Igor Vladimirovich," I salute him with a touch of imperiousness. All of my delusions are renewing my instinct to armor up and not let my last remaining bit of sanity escape.

"Hello, Natalia Nikolaevna." The manager returns a friendly smile, passing me the shopping bag. "I have something for you."

I open it and pull out what I expect to be more new practice clothes from Dmitri. Instead, what I have in my hand is the outfit I wore yesterday: the cotton knit top, leotard, and warm-up pants.

"We found these this morning on the sidewalk below your room, and I recognized them as yours." The manager sounds almost apologetic. I thank him with as much dignity as I can muster while coming to terms with the fact that I must have stripped down on the balcony, at some point of the night that I can't remember. It's not that important, I tell myself. The important thing is that against all odds, I feel stronger today than I have in a very long time. The pain in my feet is barely noticeable, and energy is returning to my arms and back. Maybe thanks to the dinner at Nina's, or the ebbing of my dependence.

Even Sveta notices the changes. She appraises me approvingly throughout the barre. We trade looks of hope without saying anything. Before we move on to the center, I put on pointe shoes for the first time in two years. I'm surprised by how quickly the sensation of being in the shoes comes back to me, even if it's not quite the sensation of *dancing* in them. Sveta gives me a tendu combination and adds, "Just a single pirouette. Remember, a perfect single pirouette is harder than a triple."

For most of my life, I thought that pirouettes were the most natural things in the world. It was only when I got injured that I learned what they must feel like for most people. But today I am not afraid of them, and I sail through the combination effortlessly. Sveta and I smile silently at each other, too afraid to jinx it by speaking. We end the day while we are still ahead at petit allegro, an easy combination that I would have found boring at Vaganova. I don't care. I'm airborne for the first time in more than two years.

"I think you'll be ready to start rehearsing your variations in a couple of weeks. Today you're doing single pirouettes, but you'll be ready to go onstage in a month," Sveta says, turning off the stereo and the lights, one by one.

"You think it's possible?" I ask, folded over at the hips with one hand on each thigh.

"Of course. I went onstage one month after giving birth—and that's not even exceptional," she says sternly. "If you think this is hard, imagine what it's like after a baby." Sveta sweeps one hand down her waist and hip, as if reenacting the general concept of childbirth; but she is one of those small and wiry women whose bodies don't change much from the age of sixteen to sixty, whose firm consistency and trim shape resemble a crisp carrot, and I struggle to envision her in any other way.

As we file out of the studio, Sveta clasps her hand against her forehead and mutters, "Shoot, I almost forgot." She digs into her duffle and pulls out something wrapped in a brown paper bag. "Here, take it."

Inside, there are two glass jars of homemade soup, a roll, an avocado, and packets of tea.

"You shouldn't have," I start to say, but she waves me off impatiently.

"This is the only way I can be sure you're eating. Remember, your body won't get stronger if you don't eat."

I nod and hug her goodbye. My stomach grumbles at the sight of the soup, and I realize I haven't eaten anything since last night's dinner with Nina. I get in a cab and join the full lanes of cars on their evening commute, coiling around the city like overlapping snakes. The neon lights are turning on one by one, as if some conductor is cueing their entrance into the symphony of night. How lovely that I get to be apart from it and a part of it. My brain is turning into jelly. My back melts into the seat and my eyelids droop.

"You're a ballerina?" asks the cabdriver, and I open my eyes again.

"Yes," I say, with barely enough warmth to be polite.

"I wanted to dance, when I was little." Undeterred, the cabdriver shoots me a glance in the rearview mirror. Her eyes glitter with the reflected glow of the streetlamps. I stay silent, hoping she will take it as a hint to drop the conversation.

"But I didn't have the right body for it," she continues nonetheless. "I always felt like I was a petite girl inside a big, ungainly shell. I bet you've never experienced that. Like your body isn't your own." She catches my eyes again in the mirror, and I wonder why she looks so familiar.

"I feel like that all the time," I say, and she breaks into a husky chuckle before continuing.

"Sometimes, I get so detached from my body that I see myself from outside of it—do you know what I mean?" she says, mindlessly stroking the steering wheel with her long thumb. I shake my head.

"I once saw myself wake up, have breakfast, go to work, come home, and fall asleep—the entire day I had to watch myself like a ghost." She laughs again, and her straight, long hair glistens red behind the headrest. A shiver runs through my spine as I realize where I've seen her. Coming out of that basement bar last night, teetering on her velvet sandals. But is she following me or am I hallucinating?

We're on Admiralteyskiy Prospekt. A busy, well-lit avenue. "I changed my mind. Can you just pull over here on the corner?" I stammer.

She keeps driving without saying anything, and another chill runs through my spine.

"Stop the car," I say louder—avoiding her eyes in the rearview mirror. "Stop the car!"

Before I break down and scream, the traffic slows to a crawl—and I get out of the still-moving cab and run. I keep sprinting until I'm safe behind the door of my room in the Grand Korsakov. Except the bed and the sofa and the balcony are gone—and instead, I'm inside one of the studios at Bolshoi.

Sasha is standing in his black T-shirt and warm-up pants on a bright white shard of sunlight. He turns to me and says, "Oh, there you are. Where were you?"

iii

SASHA GRIPS THE BARRE WITH ONE HAND, HIS OTHER THUMB HOOKED over his waistband. Instead of waiting for my answer, he says, "It's a complete nightmare. Have you heard?"

I remember this day. Every moment of one's life is the beginning of the end in some way; every decision you make is a death of other possibilities. But this is the point that divides my life into before and after, a cleave line that easily breaks a diamond in half. When all the dominos of my life were lined up, ready to fall.

Sasha continues in a low voice, "Olga has disappeared without a trace."

Olga Zelenko is the queen of ballet, a People's Artist of Russia, Bolshoi's reigning prima ballerina, and the most frequent partner of Dmitri. She's been missing since the casting for *Swan Lake* was announced, naming Sasha and me for opening night, which had been hers and Dmitri's for the past seven seasons. Everyone expected a tantrum from Dmitri, but no one suspected Olga, a prim and generally polite presence, to pull this type of trick.

"I know," I tell Sasha.

He raises his eyebrows. "Who told you? I only just found out myself."

It's difficult to explain to him that I've lived this before and that he's a phantom of my own memory, so I shrug.

"I guess I'm not your only friend?" He grins.

"Oh, who said we were friends?" I say with only the faintest trace of a smile. We strip off our warm-up clothes and start rehearsing.

To dance with Sasha is to reveal our true selves to each other: it's impossible to hide or lie about who you are when you dance. And in this way we've communicated far more than with words. Since *Don*

Q, we have been paired in *Tchaikovsky Pas de Deux*, *The Nutcracker*, *Coppélia*, *Esmeralda*, *Le Corsaire*. But we haven't had another dinner together, and Sasha continues to do whatever he does with his corps girls. I don't ask, and mostly I don't care.

Yet before every performance, in the darkness (but not privacy) of the wings, we kiss. Hands cupping each other's faces like calyxes. Lips hot and hungry, overlapping carefully so as not to smudge the stage makeup. And after the performance, we go back to addressing each other with professional distance, as if we both have complete amnesia over what happened.

There are other people backstage; naturally, tongues wag over our strange behavior. I don't know what Sasha says to those who ask, but no one is brave enough to broach the subject with me. Truthfully, I am none the wiser about what's going on. At first, this brief mad interlude is enough for me. Sasha can be sweet in small doses, but he isn't someone I can rely on. It's not that he is just a shallow cad, as sometimes even great dancers simply are. Sasha could care for someone, although it's impossible to say for whom or when. Behind his ease and charm he has depth of the darkest sea, which he keeps closed off to everyone. I find his quality to be more alarming than Dmitri's—it's less mean and more dangerous. Take a peach, ripe enough to press your thumb into it; the outer layer is ambrosia, but eating the pit will kill you.

Yet as time passes, the more I imagine more. I want to take his hand and suck on his thumb. I want him to touch my bare skin all over. Backstage. In the studio. On my mattress, which is still resting on the floor.

With his arms around my waist in a supported balance, Sasha locks eyes with me in the mirror. The music plays on while we stay suspended—are we embracing because of the choreography or because of desire? His arm is damp and heavy; his warm breath tickles my earlobes.

"Natasha," he says. Not relaxed as he normally is—but careful and deliberate.

"Sasha," says a voice that isn't mine.

Sasha's arms slacken and fall as we both see the tall figure of Dmitri at the open door, accompanied by a few younger men. Sasha told me early on that Dmitri likes to handpick his protégés when they are just out of school. He coaches them on the side, helps them prepare their variations, uses his influence to get them better pay or roles. Of these, Sasha is the most successful case, although their relationship has become strained since *Don Q*—since Sasha and I have begun dancing together. After Dmitri's thinly veiled attack against me was published in *Le Figaro*, Sasha has even made a point of distancing himself from Dmitri. I haven't seen them talking or joking or practicing double tours next to each other in months. Leaning against the doorframe, Dmitri crosses his arms over his chest and calls out stiffly to Sasha while keeping his eyes resolutely away from me.

"Sasha, I need you," he says, and his entourage falls quiet behind him. "I know where Olga disappeared to."

"Where?" Sasha walks toward Dmitri, leaving me in the middle of the room.

"Her dacha. I've been there a few times." Even while affecting coldness, Dmitri's lips curl ever so slightly upward from the pleasure of showing off his privilege as Olga's favorite partner and confidant.

"Did you talk to her?" Sasha crosses his arms, sounding more cautious than relieved. He has danced with Olga several times but not regularly, and he finds her insistent and haughty—as ballerinas of his own caliber generally are.

"She's turned off her phone. But I know her ways. I need you to come get her with me."

"Me? You sure you need me for this?" Sasha asks, shifting his weight uneasily.

"Yes, I need you to come, otherwise I wouldn't have asked. If you refuse, I'll show you where the lobsters spend winter," Dmitri threatens. Then his green eyes fix on mine, and he speaks to me directly for the first time. "I need you, too, Natasha."

I look at Sasha, who frowns and shakes his head. As we deliberate in silence, one of the entourage clears his throat.

"Can I come, Dima?" He smiles at Dmitri, brushing his center-parted locks away from his forehead. I vaguely remember seeing him in rehearsals. His wide-set gray eyes turn down at the corners, and his skin is as pale, poreless, and dry as a turnip. His large nose points toward his picaresque lips, giving an overall elfish impression.

"You, Fedya? Don't you have rehearsal?" Dmitri turns to him, a black eyebrow raised to his hairline. "Stop trying to push into things way above your pay grade. First, you must dance better. At your current state, I can't possibly bring you to Olga and force her to acknowledge you by name, like you matter."

Fedya falls silent and steps back into his group. Dmitri turns to face me and continues in an accusing tone. "This company is bigger than me or you. Show that you care about more than just yourself—show that you care about Bolshoi. I'll be waiting outside." Then he turns on his heels and walks away, followed by his entourage and the disgraced Fedya.

"I don't see how this is my problem, Sasha," I say, crossing my arms, as if daring him to contradict me.

"It really isn't. It's the management's problem." He nods. "It's the theater's problem."

"I know what you're trying to do, and this 'holy Bolshoi is bigger than us' thing won't work." I sit wide-straddle on the floor and lean forward into a stretch.

"Hear me out. It might be the only chance you'll ever get to make good with Dmitri." Sasha sits down next to me. "Isn't it worth taking this chance at peace with Dmitri and Olga? Besides"—he smirks—"aren't you even a little curious what her dacha is like?"

"What's it like?"

"Oh, I have never been. She's . . . private. But I assume it would be a palace. Her Moscow apartment is paid for by a very influential admirer. Like Dmitri's apartment, which I have seen." Sasha smiles. "Dmitri's admirer is a billionaire widow, who sits in the Tsar's box wearing Bulgari emeralds. She also gave him a car with a driver so he doesn't have to use his legs for anything other than dance. The thing is, Natasha—Dima and Olga are both on another level."

Sasha gets up and offers me his hand; I take it, and he pulls me up without any effort.

"Come on, this could be good for all of us."

When we arrive at the meeting point a few blocks from the theater, I expect to see Dmitri's driver. Instead there is only Dmitri, leaning against a black sports car emblazoned with a logo: a rearing black horse against a yellow shield that somehow perfectly embodies the iconography of Dmitri. He is wearing a black polo shirt over slim white cotton pants and driving loafers, which with his olive skin and wavy black mane make him look like a rich young Roman about to head out to his vineyard. Without a smile, he tosses the Ferrari's keys at Sasha, who catches it with one hand. "You're driving," Dmitri says.

"I haven't done it in a long time," Sasha protests. "Where's your driver?"

"I sent him away. There's not enough room for three people in the back, on the return trip," Dmitri says, already getting in the backseat. Sasha sighs, puts his bag in the trunk, and signals I should do the same. He gets behind the wheel, and I sit in the passenger seat. As we make our way out of the concentric rings that enclose Moscow like a nesting doll, the car is silent save for the directions Dmitri barks out from time to time. Even though he doesn't drive, and barely seems to be paying attention to the road, Dmitri apparently knows exactly how to leave the city. The only other thing he says besides "left, straight, right" is "It's like a horrible disease—such ugliness," as we pass by a large group of flip-flop-wearing tourists. Once we make it out of the ring road, he mutters, "Until we meet again, you city of night birds and dreamers." Then he slides on his sunglasses, puts on the earphones of his iPod, and promptly falls asleep.

"Are you warm? I could turn on the AC," Sasha says, stealing a glance in my direction.

"No, that's okay. I'll get some fresh air though."

I roll down my window and breathe in the smell of the sun, damp grass, and wild berries. Green spreads earnestly in all directions. Purple and white violets wave at us from either side of the road. Dense, bright loaves of clouds roll across the sky, making the blue look even bluer.

"This reminds me of when I was little," Sasha says quietly. "We had a small orchard, kept bees. It was a simple life. I didn't have any toys or even books. During summers I went swimming in the river and caught fireflies."

"That sounds much better than how I grew up." I pause, waiting for him to ask what it was like for me. Mostly what I remember is our faded furniture, stiff curtains, and north-facing window overlooking the dank courtyard. But Sasha continues his story.

"I was very discontented—and yet, now I look back and I had so much."

"But if you had to go back to living that way, you couldn't," Dmitri says from the back, and Sasha and I raise our eyebrows—we'd thought he was sound asleep. "Don't fall under the spell of false nostalgia, Sasha. The past was never as great as you now think."

"I wasn't asking for advice, Dima."

"Just stating my opinion. You grew up in a little hovel in the middle of nowhere—so what? No one in this car wants to go back where they came from, because people like that don't get anywhere." Dmitri shrugs behind his sunglasses.

"You know, Dima, you can be such a *suka*," Sasha says. His voice is low but with an edge I've never heard before. Up until now, I've only seen Sasha act kindly, partly because it's easy for someone who has everything to be generous, partly because he has an inherent sweetness. Most people fawn on him, but even on rare instances when someone doesn't—when they lash out or ignore him—Sasha shrugs and lets things slide. One very admirable thing about Sasha is that he never talks maliciously about others behind their back. It is therefore all the clearer to both me and Dmitri that he is angry—and none of us have seen the limits of his anger yet.

"What did you just call me?" Dmitri takes off his sunglasses, his face no longer sneering as it always is—but enraged.

"I said, you're a *suka*," Sasha spits out without hesitation, pressing the gas harder with the emphatic first syllable of that word. The Ferrari roars and thrills to the animosity, shooting forward with the fury of a wild black horse. In a single breath, the white needle of the speedometer flutters up to 120 kilometers per hour.

"Get the fuck out of my car," Dmitri says. When Sasha keeps driving, he punches Sasha's headrest with shocking force. Sasha swerves, I shriek, and the car skids—stopping on the side of the road just inches shy of a ditch. At the same time, Dmitri's head bangs against the back of my seat. Sasha is bracing the wheel with his left hand and reaching across my body with his right arm. The inside of the car thuds with our adrenaline, like we're inside a metal heart. After looking around on all sides, Sasha turns off the engine with a sigh.

"Nobody gets out of the car," I say. "You are both completely fucked in the head. Do you know that? You, Dmitri, you already know what's wrong with yourself. You hate everything that isn't you—you make poison look like honey. But you, Sasha? You don't even know how screwed up you are. Always acting like you're such a charming guy, friendly to all, saying 'oh, I was raised on a farm by my grandparents'—but you're fucking every corps girl who is silly enough to fall for your tricks!"

Neither of them responds. They have never seen me speak so many words at once. Sasha shifts his eyes nervously from side to side, and even Dmitri is momentarily stunned by my outburst. And despite nearly being killed a minute ago, the afterglow of subjugating two powerful, arrogant men lights up my body all the way to the tips of my hair. It's how I learn that a brush with death amplifies such sensual pleasures.

Sasha restarts the engine and we drive on in silence the rest of the way.

It is the final brilliance of afternoon when we turn onto the long driveway lined with handsome poplars, which appear to be holding up the sky on their pointed tips. Between these stately sentinels the two-story house reveals itself, its siding painted in cobalt and the trimmings in white. Its facade is closely edged with lilac bushes, giving a primly festive impression like an empress wearing a tight lace collar. Farther out on the lawn, there are roses of yellow, orange, red, pink, white, and violet, among which an older man of about sixty is strolling with his garden shears. When he sees our car, he blinks several times until a look of recognition crosses his face, followed by a gentle smile.

"Dmitri, we didn't discuss what we'll say to Olga," I whisper as Sasha pulls over, but Dmitri ignores me, gets out of the car, and launches into extravagant kissing of the old man's cheeks.

"Alexey Arkadyevich, you look more wonderful every time I see you," Dmitri says. "How is our queen among queens?"

"She's in a dark mood. If anyone can lift her spirits, it is you," Alexey replies, then turns to Sasha and me. "And you've brought friends."

"*Colleagues*, Alexey. You've seen Sasha Nikulin dance, I presume. And here is Natalia Leonova."

"It's a pleasure to meet you, Natalia." Alexey smiles and extends a hand, which takes me aback with its firm grip. He is on the short side of average, slimly built, with the stooped shoulders of someone who spent his life reading rather than exercising, let alone dancing. But under the rolled-up sleeves of his linen shirt, his forearms are well muscled and tan. Next he grips Sasha's hand and pumps it up and down a few times, expressing wonderment at seeing him again and so unexpectedly.

"And where is Olga?" Dmitri asks, furrowing his brow against the late-afternoon light. Alexey indicates with his eyes that she is in the house, upstairs.

"Why don't we wait on the terrace? Olga is like a cat," Dmitri says. "Hates surprises. You have to let her come to you."

Alexey chuckles. "You're not wrong, Dima. Go to the terrace—it's nice and shady over there. I'll bring you something cold to drink." He walks briskly toward the house, his white linen pants reflecting the sun like sails of a boat.

The three of us amble over to the terrace on the other side of the house. Dmitri installs himself with great ease and familiarity, taking a seat at the large wooden table shaded by an awning and a rowan tree. Sasha and I arrange ourselves around him a bit timidly, like children.

"Is Alexey—" I whisper.

"Yes, her husband." Dmitri cuts me off, idly opening and closing the legs of his sunglasses. "Alexey Belosselsky-Belozersky. The most prominent Tolstoy scholar in the world. Scion of the earliest Rus princes of the ninth century. Maker of terrific homemade kvass. I hate many people—he's not one of them."

I hadn't expected Olga to be married to someone so much older. I'm still trying to rearrange my expression when Alexey comes out of a side door carrying a tray of drinks, followed by the willowy figure of his wife. Olga is wearing black sunglasses and a wide-brimmed hat that hide the top half of her heart-shaped face. Her incredibly long and thin body is obscured by a voluminous cotton shift dress with wide shoulder straps buttoned onto the neckline. In class or onstage, Olga's physicality is overwhelming—not magnetic and sensual the way Katia's is, just more elongated, flexible, extended, and arched than seems humanly possible. Together with her sphinx eyes, sharp nose, and lips that were made for pursing, Olga seems to hail from another planet. But dressed as she is now, barefoot on her terrace, she looks fragile and pale, like a grandmother who sits under an umbrella at the beach and refuses to go in the water. She walks over to greet Dmitri, who has risen in a rare show of respect. Watching them whisper and kiss each other's cheeks, I'm reminded that I haven't truly talked to her before. I haven't clashed with her the way I have with Katia, but Olga has never shown me any friendliness.

"Natasha and Sasha, you haven't tasted my famous cherry kvass yet," Alexey says, setting down chilled glasses in front of everyone. For a fleeting moment, Olga appears torn between two dueling desires—to keep ignoring us and to avoid acting utterly uncouth. Being a rude hostess is as impossible for Olga as having an imperfect rose garden. In the end, she compromises by giving Sasha and me a tiny nod, her lips drawn tight in a straight line. Sasha gives her a wave, and I silently mouth hello.

"Alexey, this is absolutely delicious. What's your secret?" Sasha asks after taking a swig. I copy his movement, and the cold, tangy sweetness of the kvass fills my mouth.

"Just cherries we pick from our garden, Sasha. I can show you later, if you like," Alexey says in his peaceful, medium-timbered voice—a deciduous tree, not evergreen. "I don't suppose you care much about things like that, though." He adds, interlacing his hands on top of the table, like a teacher resigned to disinterested pupils.

"Actually, I'd love to see them," Sasha says. The green shadow of the rowan leaves careens across his face, keeping rhythm to the breeze.

"Well, let's go on a walk. Sasha and Natasha—you haven't seen the estate," Alexey says. I have never heard anyone refer to his own home by that word, as if he were an actual medieval prince, but Alexey seems to think that it is perfectly appropriate and unpretentious.

"I've met all your trees, Alexey. I'll stay here with Olga." Dmitri props an elbow on the table, rests his chin on his fist, and squints his eyes in the approximation of a smile. So with incredible delicacy, with which he was clearly born, Alexey divides the party in two and leaves Olga in the company of her confidant. With his long-legged gait, surprisingly vigorous for an academic type, he descends from the terrace and circles around the rose garden. Sasha and I follow behind him, and soon we're walking in a half-wild field. Each of Alexey's footsteps sends panicked little grasshoppers fleeing for life, creating bouncy green arcs in the overgrown grass. There is a stream that courses over this field, narrow and just a few fingers deep but clean and cold against my sandaled feet. On its other side, a dozen fruit trees stand rather unimpressively with dusty leaves and knotty trunks. Like airplanes, we slow our pace as we approach them. In the increased stillness, the sweet scent of ripe cherries suddenly blooms in the air. Alexey turns around and says with a smile, "Yes, they're talking to you!"

We gather under the shadow of the trees. Leaning against a trunk with one hand, Alexey gives a brief lecture on the principles of orchard keeping. Throughout, Sasha nods and makes impatient, affirmative noises to show that he already knew most, if not all, of these facts. Alexey doesn't seem to mind, although he does pointedly ask if Sasha had cherry trees growing up. ("We had apricot trees—you know, Donbas is famous for them," Sasha admits. "For cherries you'd go farther south to Melitopol.") Alexey's favorite way of explaining tree life is "talking." Like most other fruit trees, a cherry tree needs to "talk" to another cherry tree of a different variety—a red cherry with black cherry, for example—in order to bear fruit. At the same time, certain varieties will absolutely refuse to "talk" to each other, and these shouldn't be planted together.

"So talking makes you a great groundskeeper?" I ask a little slyly. Alexey shakes his dignified head.

"No, it's listening," he says soberly, and Sasha again nods and murmurs, "Of course."

On the way back to the house, Alexey walks between Sasha and me.

"I find trees are similar to people," he says. "You hardly ever grow from being matched up with someone exactly like yourself. Best partnerships—in life, in dance—are born from two distinct forces coming together."

"Yes, but how do you know when you're too different, or just different enough?" I ask, keeping my voice neutral and carefully looking away from Sasha. Alexey's quick pace slows by a breath as his eyes gaze out over the untended grass, its plain white flowers like flecks of rice.

"One meets so many people in life—friends, family, lovers," Alexey says. "But those I've loved the most turned my weakness into strength."

The terrace comes into our view. Olga and Dmitri are no longer there. Our host leads us inside the house, passing through the kitchen. It is filled with objects but everything in its own place so that the whole effect is not of disarray, but of harmony and abundance. The countertop, made of velvety solid wood, is dotted with Polish ceramic spoon rests and jars of flour, sugar, and sea salt. Gently patinaed copper pots and pans hang overhead, and the long-haired gray cat is positioned at the window, staring judgmentally at Sasha and me with its forget-me-not blue eyes. An archway connects the kitchen to the dining room, which is anchored by a large, polished wooden table with rounded corners and wide, low-backed chairs with upholstered seats, like at a library. Alexey quickens his pace at this point, as murmured conversation drifts in from the living room. It is a spacious and comfortable salon, formal because of its size and the fineness of its furniture, informal because of its variegated colors and insouciant wear and tear. Olga and Dmitri have repaired to the sofa with a bottle of chilled white wine and are now in a state of joy that naturally overtakes even the most indifferent souls at summer twilight.

"I see these two have started without us." Alexey smiles. "Have a seat and I'll bring you glasses." He disappears into the kitchen and returns a moment later with glasses, another bottle of wine, a dish of cured olives, pickled tomatoes, and sliced bread. Like a townsperson played by a corps member, Alexey discreetly tops off everyone's wine without taking attention away from Dmitri, who is holding court.

"You want to know the most beautiful man I've ever seen?" Dmitri asks; Olga purrs in assent, and Sasha shrugs.

"Oh relax, Sasha. It's not you!" says Dmitri, smirking above the edge of his glass. At this, everyone laughs. Alexey says with a wink, "You're still the most beautiful man *I've* seen, Sasha," before excusing himself to prepare dinner.

"It's Yves Saint Laurent," Dmitri continues. "I met him backstage when I walked his show thirteen years ago, in Paris. He must have been in his fifties then, but nothing about his beauty was lost. Hair like the Little Prince's. Eyes, blue-gray behind horn-rimmed glasses. He was tan and had a light-brown, closely trimmed beard. He looked like a sad, desert-beaten Egyptologist who'd been forced to come to Paris for a conference. He asked me if I wanted to come home with him and Pierre."

"Well, did you?" Olga clasps her hand to her mouth, completely forgetting her ill mood and the presence of unwanted guests.

"I was about to get into their limousine and realized there were a dozen other models hanging about, boys and girls with nothing in their heads except cocaine—and I just lost the taste for it. I took off without saying goodbye. When you're dealing with le beau monde like Yves, that's the only way to make an exit. If you see them at parties, don't say hello and don't say goodbye—just say the stuff in the middle, and disappear."

"You love parties, Dima," Sasha says, as if Dmitri is forgetting a crucial fact about himself.

"But I don't love large groups of idiots, remember? That's why I never danced in the corps."

"Did you keep the clothes?" Olga asks, pouring more wine into everyone's glasses.

"Yes, it's hanging in my closet next to my first suit—this terrible, itchy polyester monstrosity that my mother bought so I could attend my first Bolshoi performance. I was fifteen. Mother kept the tag on it so we could return it after the show. It was *Romeo and Juliet*, and I'd never seen anyone so magnificent as that Romeo. I didn't know what was happening to me, it was like he had taken me in his own hands. Before I knew it—"

"Oh god!" Olga gasps, clutching a hand to her mouth.

"My trousers were ruined. I ran to the bathroom as soon as the show was over. Took off the trousers and washed it in the sink, while these horrible old men leered at me. The worst part was when Mother found out we couldn't return the suit—she beat me quite savagely."

"Why didn't you throw it away?" I ask; this is the first time I've ever questioned him about himself. "Why do you still keep something with such painful memories?"

Dmitri shrugs and pours himself more wine. "Nothing else shows more clearly how high I've risen," he says, bringing his glass to his lips. "Now, we must stop talking about my inglorious past. Alexey wants us to come to the table."

I'd thought that Alexey was making dinner by himself. It turns out that he was merely directing the cook, who sets the table with hemstitched linen napkins and gleaming silverware before taking her leave. We talk, drink, and eat until our plates are smeared with purple and green pools of beet juice and olive oil, and crescent-shaped crusts of bread litter the tablecloth. The evening air is soft and round, like the burnished moon that is rising beyond the open window. Alexey proposes we stay the night, and no one objects. Dmitri tucks into the downstairs room where he has stayed before. Our host puts Sasha and me in the upstairs guest rooms.

When I walk out of my room with a toothbrush and a towel, Sasha is standing at his door holding the same things. He pretends to make a run for the bathroom, making me laugh. Then he steps closer to me until we're standing just a hand's width apart. My instinct is to close my eyes, but I force them to stare into his. He leans his face down close to mine until I can feel his breath on my cheek. Says with his husky voice, "You definitely need to shower first."

"Liar." I push him away, laughing. It has long been a strange pride of mine that my sweat doesn't have a strong odor—it has always smelled neutral. Nonetheless, when he grabs my wrist and raises it, nosing into my underarm, I twist away hissing, "Stop!"

"You're right," he says, loosening the grip but not letting go, making his hand a warm bangle on my wrist. "Your sweat is sweet. It's like . . . cedar and green grapes."

"Okay, you don't have to go so far." I smile at him, straining to resist folding my body into his. "You should shower first."

"We could do it together." Sasha's hand travels up my arm and then wraps behind my shoulder to pull me into him. I know his body well, the shape it makes in the air when he's leaping and turning, the stark definition of his torso, the curve of his seat, and the almond consistency of his firm flesh, free of any excess. All of these things are available to anyone who watches him dance, just like any dancer's body is a very public thing. But his body in private is new to me and a soft groan rises in my throat as his chest crashes into mine. He kisses me. His hands slide under my top and ceaselessly caress my back, then my breasts. My skin dissolves and is reborn by his touch. I look up in order to see that he is also feeling this, but something about his expression—a little too self-aware—reminds me how easy this must be for him. How easy women must have always been for him. Like Dmitri said, I lose the taste for it. I pull away from him.

"You're drunk," I say, already heading back to my room. I expect him to say something—beg, cajole, or retort—but he is too proud, we are similar that way. Back in my bed, I touch myself to the sound of the water running in the bathroom. Ten minutes later, the shower is turned off and I hear his feet padding across the hall, followed by the click of the door closing. I fall asleep half hoping, half dreaming of Sasha approaching my room, opening the door, and slipping into my bed. I yearn for this so acutely that it almost feels real.

The next morning, I delay going downstairs until I hear everyone's voices congregating in the dining room. This time, Olga is standing and pouring tea for Dmitri, who is seated at the table. The voices of Sasha and Alexey waft from the kitchen.

"Some tea, Natasha?" Olga asks me, and I nod and slide into the chair next to Dmitri. Olga pours tea into my mug, just as Alexey and Sasha appear with kasha and fresh berries in white bowls painted with blue flowers.

"You are truly the most generous soul I've ever met, Alexey Arkadyevich." Dmitri sighs, cupping his hands around his bowl. "We'll get going after this."

"You don't want to stay a bit longer?" Alexey asks, expecting us not to stay.

"We have to hurry if we're to make rehearsals." Dmitri uses his spoon to sink berries into his kasha, one by one. "And Olga, too."

Olga stiffens at this, but before she can speak, Dmitri cuts in. "Olga, you've already made a big fuss, and it will be humiliating to go back and accept the management's decision—nor can you continue to stay away, unless you really want to retire. I've done a lot of thinking and there's only one way out of this impossible situation. It is for Olga and Sasha to dance the opening night. Natasha and I will dance together the next day. If the management resists this proposal, then all four of us will refuse to dance *Swan*."

This, I see, is another side to Dmitri's brilliance. Anyone who has seen him dance once would acknowledge that he is intensely intelligent, the same way a physicist is intelligent about the cosmos and a grand master is intelligent about chess—the explosive mind of someone born to question, answer, and *own* a mystery that others can't even begin to fathom. And then he knows the world outside of dance—history, culture, music, literature. But not only that, Dmitri has a singular ability to manipulate others to his own end. Even this plan, which outwardly advantages Olga, in reality benefits Dmitri, letting him push the limits of his influence within the company. Knowing this delights him—but the fact that others guess this and can't do anything about it delights him even more. He lifts his cup of tea, hiding his handsome face distorted by a lightning flash of a hyena's grin.

"I'm okay with this, but it doesn't sound like it would be up to me," Sasha says quietly to his kasha. "Olga, Natasha?"

"I think it is really up to Natasha," Olga says, casting her eyes down. Her sharply defined features project well across 1,700 people in the Bolshoi auditorium. But up close at the dining table, exposed by the morning sun, the hollows of her face look less glamorous and more fatigued. She is thirty-seven and has been a star for the past twenty years. I imagine myself as Olga, who has more dancing behind than in front of her, whose accustomed honors are going to a much younger ballerina. Inevitably, this will happen to me one day. We will all slow down, no bird dies while flying. And the best one can hope for is for your fellow dancers to save you from the worst ignominies.

"Okay," I answer. "Now, let's hit the road before I change my mind." Faces of everyone else relax visibly; Olga nods, Alexey rubs his thighs and rises from his chair, saying something about packing refreshments for the road, and Sasha meets my eyes for the first time since last night.

It is already hotter than the day before. The sun is adding a slick white gloss to the Ferrari, and everyone reaches for their sunglasses as they get in the car. We wave at Alexey—Sasha at the wheel, Olga next to him, and Dmitri and me in the back. Alexey waves back warmly, then starts tending his rosebushes before we even exit the driveway.

"He's a sensible man," Dmitri says to me while Olga and Sasha try to figure out how to roll down the top. "He's a scholar, not an artist."

The roof is rolled down and the sudden gust of air sends everyone's hair streaming backward. The whipping noise of the wind makes it possible for us to sit in agreeable silence. After we've been driving for about an hour, Olga suggests we take the scenic route and rest at her favorite spot by the river.

"There's no place to park here, Olga," Sasha complains while coasting slowly over the stretch. "I don't see a river, either. Are you sure this is it?"

"Of course I'm sure. Just park over there at the shoulder. The river is on the other side."

We park on the narrow shoulder and cross the empty road, doubt clouding over each of us who isn't Olga. There is a steep, rocky slope leading down—but beyond it, having somehow hidden itself from passing cars, a wide expanse of river is flowing brazenly blue under an open sky. Its banks are covered in colorful pebbles the size and shape of small macaroni, and trees cast shadows here and there like beach parasols until they thicken into forest. We slide and shuffle down to the water, little stones rolling off our feet. At the front of the group, Dmitri starts taking off his shirt while still walking to the water's edge. He kicks his loafers away, shrugs off his pants and underwear, balls them up, and tosses them aside. He stands for a moment with his back to us, arms spread wide toward the sun. Then he turns around and signals with his hand that we should follow him. He has unusually smooth skin with not a scar in sight, uniformly golden even over his knees and elbows—as if he were born fully formed just this morning. In silence, he faces the river again and slowly walks in until he is submerged to his hips. Olga also strips down without hesitation. Like most dancers, she's never been that precious about her body, and twice performed topless for a modern piece. The river looks icy, but Olga walks in calmly, like Nefertiti bathing in the Nile. Once she is immersed up to her chest, she turns around and smiles at Sasha and me. Before Sasha can beat me to it, I take off my clothes and dash into the water. The sun's heat on my skin is instantly replaced by the stunning cold and blue.

"Come on, Sasha," I call back to him, and Dmitri and Olga join in a gleeful chorus. "What are you, scared?"

Sasha smiles, first taking off his shirt and shoes, followed by his pants. Then he—a tiny bit self-consciously—shrugs out of his underwear. I've had the opportunity to observe that most people look better clothed rather than undressed; but Sasha is one of those rare human beings who are so beautiful that they seem more perfect when nude. As he walks in, the sun reflects on the water's surface and creates undulating patterns of light on his torso. He takes a few deep breaths and plunges headfirst—reemerging about six meters away. He repeats the process until he becomes a dot in the waves. I swim on my own, disappointed as well as relieved that Sasha has disappeared, apparently on his way to the opposite bank.

Olga and Dmitri finish their bathing and towel off with their clothes. Olga calls out that they're going to search for mushrooms in the nearby woods, leaving me alone in the river. I breaststroke around in circles a few more times and walk ashore when I get tired. I spread my clothes on the pebbles and lie down on top, knees bent, crossing my elbows over my eyes to shield them. My skin tingles from the minty sensation of a cold plunge followed by the hot sun.

"Hey." It is Sasha's voice. I hear him crouch down next to me. The fact that he is there, breathing, naked, makes my skin prickle even more. I lower my forearms and see that he's sitting on his clothes with his knees pulled up. His wet, golden hair falls in waves toward his shoulders.

"I'm sorry about last night," he continues. "You were right. I was drunk."

"Why do you do this?" I ask, flipping over onto my stomach and pressing up on my forearms.

"I'm not sure what you mean," Sasha says.

"You kiss me before we go onstage. And when you're drunk. But not when we're just ourselves—normal."

"I didn't know you wanted anything more."

"Of course I want more. You think sneaking around backstage or in someone else's hallway is what any woman would be satisfied by? Even *you* are not worth it." I take a deep breath. "So why do you do it?"

"Do you really want to know why?"

"Enlighten me, Sasha. Blow my mind with your reasoning." I glare at him, and he laughs.

"You intimidate me, Natasha. You're the most talented, intelligent, and beautiful person I've ever met. And I fear you'll find out one day that I'm not good enough for you. And then you'll hurt me, and I'll hurt you."

"We won't know unless we try." I reach out and graze his arm. He pushes my shoulder so I fall supine on my back. He puts his two fingers against my lips, like a pistol, slipping them inside as I caress them with my tongue. When he takes them out and slides them up and down my slit, I catch my breath and reach for his cock. But he grabs my wrist with his other hand and presses it on the ground next to my head.

"Don't move without my permission," he says, moving his fingers in and out of me. "You got that?"

"Yes," I say. He frowns and pins me down harder.

"Say yes, Sasha."

"Yes, Sasha."

He takes away his hand, covers my body with his and pushes himself into me. The anticipation I had for this moment is so great that I'm disappointed when it doesn't lead to a climax. Mostly what I feel is pain while he breathes out slowly through his mouth. Then he begins moving, picking up pace, and I let the waves of sensation take hold. I keep my eyes open so I can see him framed by the blue sky and the white sunburst. An idea takes hold of me—that of dissolving in this space, becoming air and light, insubstantial yet ubiquitous, eternal, powerful. In a moment of utter relaxation, a warm vibration rolls over me. He pulls out and finishes into his cupped hand with a loud groan. Once that's done, he collapses onto me, kissing my mouth.

"You want to see how hard I came for you?" he says between short breaths, and I nod. He opens his palm to show a surprisingly large amount of translucent liquid, and then rubs it off on a piece of rock. He lies down a few feet away on his back, hands on his stomach and eyes to the sky. Just when I'm about to feel crushed by his detachment, he turns his face slightly toward me.

"Your pussy has ridges," he says with a sly smile.

“It has what?”

“You have a ribbed pussy. It’s rare and feels . . . Didn’t you know this?”

“I knew,” I say. I did not—I’ve only slept with one person before Sasha.

“We should get going,” he says, as if suddenly remembering. “Dima and Olga might be looking for us.” There is no tenderness or even mischief in his voice. He springs to his feet, steps into his pants, and threads his arms through his shirt, all without meeting my eyes. I rise and put on my clothes as well, dizzy with shame. I’ve been deceived—not by Sasha, but by my own judgment. How could I have been so foolish as to think it could be anything real. He walks ahead of me toward the car, calling out, “Dima! Olga!” There’s no acknowledgment that he and I have done anything together. But when the other two shout in our direction, he glances back at me and says, “We have to hurry,” and does something I’ve never seen him do with anyone else. As we rush to join the others, he reaches out and holds my hand—and suddenly everything makes sense with the clarity of heat, water, and stone, as if my entire life up to this point has transpired to arrive at this moment.

iv

THE PHONE IS RINGING. AFTER A WHILE, IT STOPS.

THE PHONE RINGS AGAIN, AND this time it sounds long enough for me to consider reaching for it. But my eyelids, head, arms—everywhere that counts—feel made of lead. I can't move any part of my body while the phone is ringing with the gusto of a diesel-powered leaf blower. Just as I resign myself to this personal hell, my arm shakes off the invisible weight and shoots out toward the sound.

"Hello?" I answer. "Nina?"

"It's me," announces the low-pitched voice of Sveta. "We've been waiting for you for the past ten minutes. Where are you?"

I open my eyes and familiar objects come into my view—a bed covered with white sheets, a bathrobe draped over the back of a chair, and a digital clock on the nightstand indicating 11:10 a.m.

"I'm at my hotel." My voice comes out shaky. "I don't think I can go in, Sveta. I feel like I'm losing my mind."

"*We* are also losing our minds over you, dear girl. What is wrong with you?" Sveta has never said a harsh word to me before, and my eyes become heavy with tears.

"I don't know. I keep seeing things that are not real, and yet they *feel* real." I watch the tears fall and make a light-gray stain on the bed. There is silence on the other end, as if Sveta is considering what to say—perhaps conferring silently with others next to her. When she resumes, her voice is almost tender.

"Natasha, these things happen to people who are grieving. When my mother died a few years ago, I heard the tinkling of cups and water every night for months. Of course, there was no one in the kitchen. But I could have sworn she was making tea there. Was I crazy? Or was there some leak in my pipe? Or was it really my mama? It could be any of those things, but I'm not sitting here sobbing from self-doubt. No one lives a rich life or even a fairly average one without going insane at least once."

It is my turn to take a deep breath. "Sveta, who else is there with you?"

"Your partner TaeHyung Kim, of course. And Vera Igorevna. Dmitri Anatolievich thought that she'd be the best coach for you, and she agreed." Sveta's voice stiffens a bit; she's long been slighted by the prestige Vera Igorevna gained as my pedagogue, especially since Sveta herself discovered me and ensured I entered Vaganova. And while Vera Igorevna has many redeeming qualities, letting others take credit for her own genius is not one of them. Just as my thoughts drift, I hear shuffling on the other end, followed by my old teacher's gruff voice.

"Natasha, enough acting like a child. Whatever your faults, one thing you had going for you was that you were a hard worker. No, that was the *only* thing you had going." Vera Igorevna pauses; when I don't say anything, she digs harder. "If you don't want to put in the work, stop wasting my time, quit now, and never come back to dance. If you don't want to quit now, get here as quickly as you can."

In the moment, I couldn't care less whether I will lose my chance to dance forever. But it occurs to me that Vera Igorevna has already employed her strongest threats and is waiting for me to respond—and if I don't quiver and obey her, she has nothing more to wield. In her voice, there is the faintest trace of fear that her hold over me is gone and that I will quit. Crushing the pride of someone like that is unseemly, like telling your mother that you never really liked her soup.

"I'll be there in ten minutes," I say to the receiver.

Vera Igorevna is the first one to greet me when I arrive at the studio. At a glance, she hasn't changed at all since I met her at my Vaganova auditions. There are people who, after settling into a certain look of late-middle age, don't grow a day older for the rest of their lives: for some reason, teachers are highly represented in this group. Vera Igorevna's shag has remained unchanged through so many trend cycles that it has attained a kind of subversive chic or a grim sense of nobility. She is wearing all black as usual and strides up to me in her dance sneakers, barely bending her knees as if she's kept lifted high by the power of her indignation.

"I am disappointed in you," she growls as a way of greeting. We haven't seen each other in more than ten years. "I didn't teach you to be late to rehearsal."

"I'm sorry, Vera Igorevna," I say, and feeling that there should be more to our reunion, add: "I'm happy that you look well."

Vera Igorevna glares at me unhappily and whips around. At the same time, Sveta calls out to me, TaeHyung following sheepishly behind her.

"Natasha, this is TaeHyung," Sveta says as he smiles and rubs his left elbow with his right hand.

"I know. We actually met in Tokyo a few years ago." I extend my hand. He hurries to take it, half shaking it and half bowing his head.

"Well then, we're not wasting *any* more time. Natasha, we'll just do a quick barre to warm up. Tae, you keep working with Vera Igorevna in the meantime," Sveta announces sharply, as if she's loath to let Vera Igorevna do all the terrifying.

Twenty minutes later, Sveta connects her phone to the stereo and presses play. I can almost see how the music spreads from that corner and changes the atmosphere until the entire room is enveloped in that otherworldly energy. It's no longer a studio at Mariinsky—it's a village outside a specific time or place. And I'm no longer Natasha. I'm Giselle, a peasant girl who has fallen breathlessly in love with a nobleman in disguise.

Later, this man will be revealed as Count Albrecht, who is already engaged to be married to a noblewoman. I will go mad from learning of his deceit and die of a broken heart. That night, when Albrecht comes to my grave in the woods, the Wilis—maidens who have died from their lovers' betrayal—will surround him and force him to dance to his death. But my spirit will rise from the grave to protect Albrecht until the church bells sound, signaling sunrise. This is my world, my fate. I believe this so wholeheartedly that when I look at Tae, I don't analyze his physique, technique, and interpretation—I absorb only his energy and love.

As we run through our first pas de deux, Vera Igorevna barks out corrections, mostly at me, in the tone of a farmer berating a stubborn donkey: "Rounder elbow, Natasha, your port de bras has become messy in Paris," "watch the turnout of the supporting leg, Natasha." But when we finish, she says, "This wasn't as bad as I expected. Sveta said you couldn't jump yet." This is how I realize that I've gone through the partnered grand jetés without processing it.

"I couldn't, yesterday," I say—at least that's when I think I was last here. Vera Igorevna shrugs, as if it's not important.

When Tae and I are both doubled over, breathing hard with our hands on our knees, Vera Igorevna calls for the end of our rehearsal. I waddle up to her and Sveta, shoulders hunched and my weight sinking on my hips. It's a great relief not to hold my carriage high, to let gravity do what it will with my body.

"How are your feet feeling?" Vera Igorevna asks, propping her fists against her hips.

"They're not bad right now."

"From what I can tell, it's not major. How long were you out for?"

"Two years, Vera Igorevna." At this, my teacher scoffs.

"You see TaeHyung over there? He snapped his Achilles on stage eighteen months ago. And look at him now." Vera Igorevna points with her chin as she gathers her things and takes her leave.

I turn to where Tae is practicing his Albrecht solo without music—the infamous thirty-two entrechats six, as iconic for the male dancer as the thirty-two fouettés of Odile and Kitri for the female dancer. This was Sasha's signature role. And Giselle was my signature role in all classical repertoire.

As I reminisce, what I shared with Sasha takes over the room, casting it in deep indigo that only I can see. And then just as suddenly it dissipates, leaving Tae in the center, each entrechat six as crisp and clear as the last. My mind fills in the music as he jumps, clasping one hand to his heart and extending the other toward Giselle. And my god, he keeps going after the required thirty-two. Thirty-three, thirty-four, thirty-five, thirty-six, thirty-seven, thirty-eight, thirty-nine entrechats six before he crumples to the ground, pleading Myrtha, the Queen of the Wilis, for mercy. It confirms my view of Tae's primary quality: nobility, which has nothing to do with wealth, education, or even beauty. In art and in life, nobility is always doing all that one is responsible for, and then even more. Tae shows this with every movement, gesture, and glance. But at the same time, his nobility prevents his Albrecht from having true darkness, like a painting without an underpainting, a little too light and weightless. Tae hasn't yet hurt someone or something innocent. He hasn't made an irreparable mistake. He hasn't been weighted by shame. The very strength of him is his only weakness. For me, it's the opposite.

Once, Alexey Arkadyevich told me that there are people in life who turn your weakness into strength. He said that he loved these people the most—and now I see that it's true of my life as well.

"One of a kind, isn't he?" Sveta asks, regripping the shoulder strap of her tote bag. "He agreed to stay another week in town to rehearse during the break. Then he'll be away performing in Mexico City, Madrid, Bergen, and Seoul until September."

"I feel bad that he's staying in town only because of me," I say. Dancers have no freedom during the season, which at Mariinsky and at Bolshoi lasts eleven months—the most crushing of any theater troupe in the world. When August rolls around, all they want is to go somewhere else and do something that doesn't require proper shoes.

"He said he'll take a week off in Mexico before going to Europe," Sveta says. "That means we have plenty of alone time to work on your solos. You, me, and Vera Igorevna."

"I didn't even think about what you were giving up for me, Sveta." I reach out and gently hold her shoulder. "I hope I don't disappoint you. I still feel so out of sorts—just not while I'm dancing. But when I'm alone, I fall into a strange state, and afterward I can't even remember how much time has passed." The fact is, I'm even afraid to go outside the studio. Once I say goodbye to Sveta, I fear I'll again get lost in the labyrinth of my own mind.

"I know. We all agreed that it was a mistake to leave you alone like that." Sveta pauses and waves to someone at the door. "We're still in here," she calls out. Then Nina walks in wearing a T-shirt, jeans, and sneakers, her black hair loose around her shoulders.

"Come on, let's go," she says to me. "We'll pick up your stuff at the hotel, and then we'll go to my place." Then everyone begins speaking at once.

"What about Andryusha and the kids? And don't you have a vacation?" I ask.

"Nina, make sure Natasha eats and sleeps properly. You're a good girl—I'm going to go now." Sveta nods and exits the studio.

"Goodbye, Svetlana Timurevna. See you later, Tae. Grab your things, Natasha—I'll explain in the car." We both wave at Tae, who returns a smile while taking a water break from his self-guided rehearsal.

Once Nina is settled behind the wheel of her silver Lada, she tells me that Andryusha and the children have already left on a vacation to Bulgaria; she stayed behind to help me recover. I ask if she can possibly give up her chance to get away, and she laughs.

"Having the apartment all to myself, without a husband and three kids? Do you have any idea how relaxing that will be for me?"

We check out of the Grand Korsakov and stop by a grocery store to stock up on food. As we cruise around the aisles, I'm amazed by the sheer number of things Nina casually tosses into the shopping cart. There are bundles of carrots, beets, spinach, dill; shining tomatoes, lemons, a head of cabbage, mushrooms, a small sack of potatoes, sweet potatoes, peaches, frozen berries, cans of beans, crackers, pasta, a jar of chestnut jam that she deems "fun to have." When I protest that this is too much food, Nina shrugs.

"I'm used to shopping for five people. This is less than normal. Oh," She claps her hands together. "What do you usually do for breakfast?"

"Some kasha or whatever you have at home is fine," I say. She seems to think that this isn't good enough and says she'll take care of it.

After the grocery store, we make a quick stop in front of a bakery.

"Can you stay in the car? I'm not sure how long we can park here," she says, already getting out. Through the glass wall of the bakery, I watch her get in line and place her order. Behind the display, there is a young man in a white chef's uniform, and I have to strain my eyes to observe that he is attractive, but not at all as I imagined. I'd thought that this baker would be dark-haired and strong-jawed in the manner of Andryusha. Instead he is pale and lanky with rust-colored hair and a tattoo peeking out from below his rolled-up sleeves, as if he would have hobbies like skateboarding and playing the guitar. He is smiling wide as he hands off a white paper bag to Nina, whose blushing face I can see through the back of her head.

"Don't say anything," Nina says as she climbs back into the car.

"I wasn't about to," I say. "So, the bread here is very delicious. And very good-looking."

Nina's lips twist for a second, and then finally she breaks out in giggles. "Don't tease."

"I wasn't teasing. I was talking about the bread," I say, suppressing a smile. "What were *you* talking about?"

"Seriously, Natasha. You would understand if you—" Nina groans, and then rephrases her thoughts to spare my feelings. "In marriage, you need to let a little pressure out once in a while. If you go about it expecting your partner to be perfect, for *you* to be perfect, then you'll be absolutely miserable."

I haven't been married, but this makes me think of Sasha. My body suddenly goes limp.

"I do understand," I say faintly, and Nina focuses on the road until we arrive at her place.

The apartment looks bigger, airier, and more polished without the presence of children's clothes and toys. We put the groceries in the fridge and then Nina cooks while I take a shower. When I come out, she's chopping tomatoes to put in a chickpea stew. I pull up a chair in the dining room to keep her company.

"So how is *Giselle* coming along?" she asks, still working away at the cutting board.

"I'm starting to feel more like myself when I'm dancing. Then when rehearsal is over, my mind becomes a jumble. I have strange dreams—waking dreams."

Nina pauses her chopping and turns around. "What do you mean, 'waking dreams'?" She is calm, concerned, a little displeased but reassuring, as if one of her children came home with a less-than-stellar grade on a test.

So I tell her everything. How I got put on painkillers and anti-anxiety meds after the accident; how I couldn't stop taking the cocktail of pills; how alcohol kept me feeling anything at all for the past few years until I came back to Petersburg; how I flushed everything down one night; how I've been seeing people following me; that dark dream with Dmitri. By the time I'm finished, Nina has put all the ingredients in the stew, placed a lid on top, and taken her seat next to me.

"Natasha, we can go to a hospital if you want," she says, laying her hand on mine. "It's nothing to be ashamed of. Anyone who has gone through what you've gone through would be in a similar state."

"I can't go to a hospital—what about *Giselle*? And you don't even know everything that happened in Paris." A soft moan escapes my throat. "I haven't told anyone."

"You can trust me, Natasha." Nina squeezes my hand. "I'm your oldest and best friend."

But the word *hospital* has filled me with suspicion. If I tell her what happened, will she use it to put me away in some mental ward? I pull my hand back, and she doesn't resist.

"Fine. You don't trust me with your secrets. I'll tell you mine and we won't be able to betray each other." With downcast eyes, Nina tucks her hair behind her ears and folds her forearms over the table. "I slept with him. The baker." Two circles of redness spread from the center of her cheeks.

"What? When?" I say with involuntary glee. But I immediately regret my childishness when my eyes rest on the framed photo on the bookshelf, of Nina and Andryusha on their wedding day. "How did it happen? And what's his name?" I ask more soberly.

"It wasn't planned at all. Yesterday, I was getting out after company class—I had no more rehearsals for the season—and went to treat myself to lunch, since the kids were already gone. I ran into him at the restaurant, and one thing led to another."

"You brought him here?" I ask, and she flutters her chin in assent. "And what's his name again?"

"Let's just call him the baker. I don't want to tell you his name and make him a bigger deal than he is," Nina says. "It was only an accident."

"If you look at it that way, isn't everything?" I say, and Nina's face crumples, as if I've wounded her. "No, I only meant that a lot of things were accidents for me, too. Against my best wishes and efforts."

"You know, this is a hard conversation to be having without anything to drink," Nina says, sniffling slightly. "But I won't have any, since you can't have any."

"Remember how you brought me a bottle of vodka when we were ten? I soaked my feet in it." I laugh, as Nina gets up to ladle stew for us. "Can you imagine Lara getting her little paws on vodka, for any reason?"

"What were we thinking." Nina shakes her head, smiling. She sets down bowls of stew and parsley rice, salad, and cups of fresh-squeezed orange juice. Everything tastes simple, delicious, and nourishing. In fact I've never had anything so wonderful, and say so to Nina. When we're done, we do the dishes together and cut a piece of chocolate cake to finish off our evening.

"I can't believe you stayed here for me, Nina," I say, scraping off the last morsel of cake from my fork.

"That's what friends do," Nina says. "So—do you want to tell me what happened?"

I look up toward the ceiling and then back at her warm and open face.

"This goes back to before Paris—when I debuted *Swan* with Dmitri," I say. Nina leans her head against the back cushion of the sofa, settling in.

"In my second season at Bolshoi, I was cast for the opening night of *Swan Lake* with Sasha. Olga, who had been so honored for the past many seasons with Dmitri, turned off her phone and fled to her dacha. Dmitri brought Sasha and me there and convinced all of us that the only path forward was for Olga and Sasha to dance the opening night, and for Dmitri and me to take the next night. Despite the ongoing enmity between Dmitri and me, I agreed to the plan. I must add that in the country, something was different; I felt less wary of Dmitri and Olga, and we relaxed together like friends. And that was also when Sasha and I became lovers . . ."

—

WE CAME BACK TO MOSCOW and marched into Mikhail Alypov's office. Imagine the general director of Bolshoi Theatre, not just the ballet company but also the opera and symphony, being confronted with four recalcitrant principal dancers. Mikhail Mikhailovich had considered me an ally, and now he looked at me ruefully while Dmitri laid out our terms. But he gave in quickly, because at the end of the day, he had a very wise arts administrator's mindset that artists, especially the most gifted ones, had to be handled with *délicatesse*. "*Le talent, ça n'existe pas—sans égo.*" He sighed, picking up the receiver to announce the casting change to the cascading ranks of the artistic staff.

In the following weeks, I rehearsed Odette and Odile with Dmitri. He surprised me in every way. First, he was not the hardest worker. I'd always been the earliest to arrive and the last to leave. Dmitri usually arrived right on time or a few minutes later, and would need to warm up on his own before getting started. But when he was ready to dance, he was deeply focused. He usually did things perfectly the first time; if, however, there were corrections, he absorbed them immediately. He never had to repeat movements more than twice to get it exactly right, which is something I have not seen in anyone else, before or since. He applied himself to dance the way a savant can pick up an esoteric book, turn to any page, and quickly understand what's going on. On the other hand, I always felt that I had to study every book from cover to cover, regardless of my natural strengths.

Then there was his changed attitude toward me. The Dmitri I'd known until then—vicious, flagrant, arrogant—was replaced by another Dmitri who was calm, knowledgeable, introspective. It now made sense how someone like Olga, who suffered no fools, considered Dmitri one of her close friends. He said some very intelligent things—in fact, he taught me most of what I know about *Swan Lake*. Between our run-throughs, as we both sipped water and caught our breaths, Dmitri told me of Tchaikovsky, Petipa, and Ivanov, the most famous soloists throughout *Swan*'s history, how Plisetskaya danced Odette-Odile for four decades, from the 1940s to 1970s.

Dmitri also knew what every gesture, pose, and movement had to convey, emotionally and metaphorically. This was because at some point in the 1990s, Yuri Grigorovich himself coached Dmitri for his production of *Swan Lake*, which was the version I danced and is still at Bolshoi today. It has many advantages over other productions around the world, but the most important one is replacing Von Rothbart with the Evil Genius. In every other *Swan Lake*, the villain is a fairy-tale sorcerer in a floor-length cape, who destroys Odette and Siegfried for no apparent reason other than his innate evil. In the Bolshoi production, the Evil Genius is clad in a midnight-blue bodice, a jeweled golden chain, and black leggings, with a twisted crown on his head. At the end of Act I, Scene i, the Evil Genius appears behind Prince Siegfried, mimicking his movements like a shadow but with grotesque angles to his body. In this way, the Evil Genius chases Siegfried to the bewitched lake.

"The libretto says the Evil Genius represents Fate," Dmitri once said.

"But isn't he the darkness within the prince himself?" I cut in. "The crown, the gold chain, the mimicry."

Dmitri smiled. "Yuri Nikolaevich would've liked you," he said, in what was the first and only compliment he's ever given me.

This interpretation of the ballet appealed to me and filled me with fresh motivation. It was no longer a fairy tale that presumes good and evil are inherent and absolute, but an allegory about ambivalence in human nature—and our capacity, even *desire*, to destroy what we love. I understood it on a soul level. These realizations brought out new layers to my dancing as I rehearsed Odette, the pure and accursed Swan Queen, and Odile, the beguiling imposter. I was no longer satisfied with dancing so that every gesture, movement, and line was immaculate, or even with inhabiting those roles completely. I was determined to reveal through my dancing what I believed Yuri Grigorovich's choreography wanted to say about being human.

On the night of my performance, I gave everything I had to dance. In the life of an artist, there comes a point when you are presented with a choice to preserve something of yourself, or give everything you have and you are to art. That moment had arrived for me and I said, *Take all of me.* It was wondrous and destructive and dark and luminous, like a star collapsing on itself in the vastness of the universe. Afterward, I shed tears onstage, as flowers rained down from the mezzanine to endless shouts of *Brava!*

So there was nothing that could have prepared me for the way Sasha greeted me the next day. "I'm sorry, Natasha," he said, clutching a newspaper in his hand. "You're going to see this sooner or later, so I thought it's better that I'm the one to bring it to you."

My heart hammered as I snatched the paper and read the review line by line. What was quickly apparent was that the critic saw nothing redeeming about my dancing: everything was horrible, vulgar, and insulting to Russian ballet. My proportions were inelegant, my feet monstrous. Then she finished: "Sources claim that Natalia Leonova's romantic relationship with the company's dashing star, Alexander Nikulin, is responsible for her undeserved casting. It helps to explain the rise of this young prima ballerina, who has no talent, only ambition."

My knees gave out and I sank to the floor. Sasha crouched next to me and said, "You can't let this get under your skin. Protivnaya is a fraud and a hag who was never good enough to dance onstage—as are most critics." He pointed at a small inset photograph, which showed an old woman with a bulbous nose, an evil smile, and a mess of hair sprouting from her scalp in all directions, like the tentacles of an octopus.

"Honestly, based on how completely unjust this is, I would guess someone paid her to pan you. It's known to be done," Sasha said.

"Who do you think paid her? And who are these 'sources'?" I asked. "There are only two people who know we are together."

Sasha fell silent. Ever since returning from the countryside, we'd kept our relationship secret. It was the right thing to do *because* we were serious; we really wanted this to work, safe from gossip, scrutiny, and jealousy. The only people who could suspect otherwise were Dmitri and Olga, who had seen us hold hands on our way back to Moscow.

I didn't have to be suspicious for very long. In his next interview with *Pravda*, conducted by the very same Protivnaya, Dmitri made very clear what he thought of me. "Natalia Leonova is as talented in dance as a pig is talented in hunting truffles. It can be quite miraculous to watch. It's somewhat taught but mostly nature. But does that mean it's art?"

After this, I went into a severe depression. I had trouble eating and sleeping, and already I hadn't been doing enough of those things for years. In class and rehearsals, I kept my eyes fixed on my own reflection and my mouth shut. Above all, I ignored Dmitri and his friends. He had made me a laughingstock of the company—even though I was prima ballerina by rank, I'd let myself get manipulated and trampled by him, and so everyone sneered at me behind my back. I even began to question ballet, no longer able to believe and worship it as a fanatic.

My only solace during the next few seasons was Sasha, who never wavered in his support of me. After Dmitri's interview, Sasha held my hand as we went into company class so that everyone would know that we were together, and that when they attacked me they would face consequences with him. Sasha was so generally liked and indulged that much of the scorn died down, if only to preserve his feelings, not my own. And he did something that I knew cost him artistically as well as socially and professionally—he cut off Dmitri completely. He didn't seem to mind reducing his circle for me. He told me there was divinity in my dancing that he'd never seen in anyone else, and that he wished he could dance with only me for the rest of his life.

When we were not rehearsing or performing, we holed up in my apartment or his, eating, taking baths together. I still remember clearly being enveloped by him in the tub, my feet parenthesized by his feet against the tiled wall. On our day off, we went on a long walk, brought groceries home, and made an extravagant meal. This was the first time in my life that I'd associated food and eating with pleasure, relaxation, and love. Usually, Sasha cooked and I put a dessert in the oven while sewing pointe shoes, and we froze the leftovers for the rest of the week. Afterward we might watch a movie or take a nap in our bed (Sasha and I had finally bought one and carried it up ourselves, standing with it in the elevator and sucking in our stomachs so that the door would close). In these afternoons, my happiness was whole, golden, and miraculous, like an egg yolk inside its shell, basking in the warmth that will transform it into a baby bird.

Thanks to Sasha, I was able to let go of my rage and despair, and to apply myself to dance with cool distance. It wasn't cynicism, exactly, but I became calculating—not so idealistic and naive. I'd thought that all I needed to do was fulfill my duty to art, and that I'd be *protected*. This was true in the space of the dance itself. But that's not how things worked in the real world outside of art.

I still worked hard, but I became shrewd, wary, and self-preserving even in my relationship to ballet. Although I thought this somewhat dishonorable, the directors and critics rewarded me more than when I had offered my whole body and soul—everything that was truly me. Instead I danced to reflect who they wanted me to be. It was actually very easy: they wanted me to be grateful, meek, self-doubting, delicate, sweet, and a bit melancholic. Sasha was allowed to be brash, and people called him spirited and charismatic; I had to be anemic to avoid being called ambitious.

Gradually I perfected embodying these expectations until they said I showed the Russian spirituality of a new Galina Ulanova. My jumps were compared to an angel's—because no ballerina had jumped as high and as weightlessly. My Greek feet became the reason my dance was sublime, a noble triumph over my tragic flaw. Every season, I added new debuts in leading roles. Princess Aurora in *Sleeping Beauty*, Marie in *The Nutcracker*, the title roles in *Raymonda* and *Romeo and Juliet*, and one of my favorites, Nikiya in *La Bayadère*. I danced Aegina in *Spartacus* and Jeanne in *Flames of Paris*, those old Bolshoi warhorses that they trotted out to smash against rival companies. While I wasn't moved by the obvious patriotic themes of these Soviet ballets, I liked their delirium; and they weren't supposed to be effortless and genteel but arduous and sacrificial, which felt closer to the reality of dancing onstage. On those nights the roar of the audience was like a battle cry.

After every performance, I was mobbed by a crowd of fans wanting photos and autographs. Dmitri couldn't poison them against me, because even in my disingenuous state I was sincere to the audience, and the audience recognized it and loved me for it. In a company with an embarrassment of world-class stars, no one drove ticket sales more than I did. Alypov confirmed this with pleasure, since my success was his own in the eyes of the administration. My value went up accordingly, and by my fourth season I was making more money than I'd ever expected to earn in my entire life. More than Olga. More than Dmitri. More than Sasha.

One night, we came home after a performance of *The Legend of Love*. Sasha went straight to the kitchen to warm up the leftovers for our late dinner. I was standing in the bathroom, my mind in that postshow haze, waiting for the hot water to fill the tub. My cell phone rang as I was about to go in. The number started with +33 6 xxx . . . I'd just gotten a smartphone for the first time, and it told me helpfully that this call was from Paris, France.

"Hello, Natalia." It was a man's voice in French-accented English. He pronounced my name *Nataleeah*, the last syllable dissolving softly into silence like an ombré-dyed fabric. "I am Laurent de Balincourt."

I stood up straighter upon hearing his name. Once, Balincourt's biggest claim to fame was that he was one of Sylvie Guillem's two favorite partners. That had recently changed when he was appointed the director of Paris Opéra Ballet. I didn't know how to address him—Monsieur? Laurent?

I settled with, "*Bonsoir*."

"Oh, I didn't know you speak French. You sound very nice," Balincourt said, switching to his own native tongue. I offered a silent prayer for Vera Igorevna, whose iron will had forced me to ace French along with all my general subjects.

"Yes, it must be midnight in Moscow. You must be tired after a show. I won't delay your rest with meaningless chatter. I called to offer you my admiration of your dancing, Natalia. You are sublime. *Vous êtes transcendante.*" He said, with lavish lean into the last *e* of his words—soo-bleeme, trahn-son-donte. "And I want you to come dance in Paris."

"You want me to guest for a show?"

"*Non*. I'm offering you a position as a danseuse étoile à l'Opéra de Paris."

At this point, I found I had to sit on the edge of the bathtub. I listened in silence as Balincourt spoke of my salary—200,000 euros—freedom to guest at any other company or gala without restrictions, and opportunity to work with the most exciting new choreographers. But all I saw was the notoriously closed world of Paris Opéra, a company even more French than Bolshoi is Russian, its hive of dancers who have passed through its own system from day one. And I'd finally found a way to work within Bolshoi. The thought of starting again in a new country, with unfamiliar language and traditions, felt like a very specialized form of masochism. I said this to Balincourt, and he laughed.

"It's not as bad as you think, Natalia," he continued. "And I will be on your side. I assure you that will make a big difference. Do you know why Sylvie loved to work with me?"

"Why?"

"Because I'm not scared of women who are more talented than I am. It turns out this is an extremely rare thing in this world—it might actually be my most valuable quality." Balincourt paused, and I could hear him getting in a car.

"Place des Vosges, *s'il vous plaît*," he said to the driver in a muffled voice. Going home after a show. I was already envisioning how it would feel for me to come out of Opéra Garnier, hail a cab, and watch the Seine out the window until arriving home.

"Pardon," Balincourt said to the receiver. "And most importantly, I will let you be *you*. How many men can promise you that? It sounds rather like the best relationship that a man can offer a woman, *non*?"

Balincourt sighed contentedly, as if easing himself into the backseat. With what I would come to see as Gallic luxuriance, he added, "People think loving someone means letting them be who they are. What a widespread lie that is. Love doesn't set *anyone* free. Art does." He paused, as if to mull over this last pronouncement with due respect.

"Sylvie could choose her partners," I said. "If I can have the same privilege, I will move to Paris."

Silence. Then I heard him take a sharp inhale and slowly blow out through his mouth, and saw a feather of white smoke undulating in the car's darkness.

"You are—how to say—demanding. You must understand, Sylvie was exceptional. She was once in a century," Balincourt said. "But so are you."

A month later, I was on a plane to Paris with my chosen partner, Sasha.

ACT III

L'amour est un oiseau rebelle
Que nul ne peut apprivoiser
Et c'est bien en vain
Qu'on l'appelle
S'il lui convient de refuser . . .

L'amour est enfant de Bohême
Il n'a jamais jamais connu de loi
Si tu ne m'aimes pas, je t'aime
Si je t'aime, prends garde à toi!

Love is a rebellious bird
That none can tame
And it is quite in vain that one calls it
If it suits it to refuse . . .

Love is a gypsy child
It has never, never known a law
If you don't love me, I love you
If I love you, be on your guard!

—Henri Meilhac and Ludovic Halévy, *Carmen*

i

THEY SAY THAT IN 1961, WHEN NUREYEV DEFECTED AND PERFORMED IN Paris for the first time, the audience threw onto the stage all manner of tributes—from rolled-up wads of thousands of francs to many pairs of just-taken-off underwear to sacks of cocaine. And, of course, flowers upon flowers upon flowers that stagehands pushed together into a fragrant monument each night.

But when Sasha and I arrived at Charles de Gaulle Airport exactly fifty years later, I was expecting us to be treated as we always had been—that is to say, ordinary people who are only famous and important onstage. We'd both worked all the time; even during my off-hours, I was sewing pointe shoes, stretching, or preparing meals. So when I saw, beyond the glass doors separating customs from the arrival terminal, hundreds of people waiting anxiously with bouquets and pointe shoes, and photographers with press badges around their necks, I thought that we were on the same flight with some celebrity. Then we crossed the threshold, and their frenzied screaming filled my ears like a waterfall—*Nataleea! Nataleea! Sasha!* We looked at each other, gripping hands wordlessly, struck by the unaccountable sense that this was as much a beginning of something as an *end* of something else.

As a part of my contract, Paris Opéra had given us a second-floor apartment in Le Marais. It was accessed by a beautiful blue-painted door in an ivory-colored nineteenth-century *hôtel*, firm yet ethereal, as if it were made out of buttercream icing. There were two fireplaces, one in the bedroom and another in the living room; as soon as we moved in, Sasha lined up our photos on the mantelpieces, an unexpected gesture that moved me. The living room opened out to a large terrace surrounded by ivy-covered walls. It was so enchanting that I assumed it would have a view of the Eiffel Tower and was immensely disappointed to be proven wrong. Other than that, the apartment was perfect. Around the corner, there was a seventh-century church that still rang its bells three times a day. The rest of the street was lined with a café, a bakery (where Sasha and I would soon develop an addiction to croissants), a contemporary art gallery, and a well-curated boutique with lovely, colorful things in the window.

Within a week of moving in, I went inside the latter and bought myself a green purse that cost more than my monthly wage in Russia. The attendant wrapped the bag in a cloth travel bag, all the while praising my taste; that package was wrapped in scented tissue paper, and then finally placed inside a bigger paper bag. From the moment I picked that off the counter, and as I was carrying it the short distance to my apartment, the rustling of tissues and its delicate perfume and the clear ringing of my heels against the cobblestones made me feel so elegantly alive. It was a fine thing, being rich. For the first time in my life, I had both money and time to spend for my pleasure, because there was a dedicated pointe-shoe sewing staff at the Paris Opéra. That I no longer had to sew three pairs of pointe shoes every week was the greatest gift anyone had ever given me.

Laurent—as I'd been instructed to call Balincourt—also insisted on providing car service and sending a housekeeper twice a week so that I could "just focus on dance." I didn't tell him that I'd completely focused on dance when I didn't have any amenities, when I was sleeping on a mattress on the floor, when everything I owned in the world could fit into two suitcases. It wasn't that I was ashamed of my poverty—I just didn't want Laurent to smile wryly and think I was unsophisticated. He despised those who didn't appreciate beautiful things, who preferred comfortable restaurants to haute cuisine, who said no to free housekeeping out of some poor man's pride. And Sasha accepted our changed station with no resistance, delighting in ordering all the courses at the brasserie and picking up new clothes for both of us on a whim. So for the first time, I allowed my life to take a course toward ease.

This newfound feeling of fortune caused me anxiety. I'd suffered hardships so willingly not just because it was the only option available but also because I believed it was essential to art. The greatest threat to the creative instinct is comfort. No painter picks up a brush after a sumptuous supper, no writer writes anything good while having a high and stable income. Instead, it's hunger, anxiety, sorrow, poverty, illness, and loneliness that lead to art—because the impulse to create begins from a state of tension. That's the underlying condition of every movement in ballet, even simply standing or walking onto the stage. I learned this at an early age; all my life, desperation was my homeostasis. How would I be able to struggle now without hurdles? In one brief moment, I imagined that I missed Dmitri—I had to admit that it was he who forced me to improve more than I ever would've otherwise. But like an urge to cough, the feeling passed after I refused to give in to it. What still drove me mad was not knowing why he wanted to destroy me.

Before I started Vaganova, there was a boy at my school whose father, it was said, was in prison. No one liked this boy or wanted to sit by him. The way he looked at girls, cats, or anyone smaller or weaker than him was exactly how Dmitri looked at me. But Dmitri had no reason to hate or envy anyone—and I'd danced with him and admired him. Sometimes I lay awake at night wondering what was in anyone else's heart, watching the rising and falling of Sasha's chest under the cold light stealing through the windows.

OUR PERFORMANCE OF *GISELLE* WAS scheduled at the end of our first season in Paris. Laurent had made that decision deliberately: Sasha had only danced Albrecht two times in his entire career at Bolshoi. His physicality was generally considered too wild for the role, which is one of the most nuanced male parts in ballet. Sasha was Ali the Slave, Basilio, Solor—the Russian virtuosic male roles heavy on exoticism and sex appeal. He never complained about being typecast, and smirked at the casting sheet before strolling to the rehearsal studio. Getting hurt was as foreign to his nature as it was native to mine.

Unlike Sasha, it pained me physically that I had never danced Giselle. I was almost twenty-eight, and this was the last major part in the classical repertoire that still eluded me, even after every other distinction had been given. Giselle is one of those roles that defy normal expectations: you could be cast as an eighteen-year-old corps member, or you could retire after twenty years as a prima ballerina having never danced it. Katia Reznikova was one such prima who only ever danced Myrtha, despite being a celebrated Odette-Odile—just like the flame-haired Maya Plisetskaya to whom she was often compared. It wasn't a matter of technique or artistry but *emploi*, who they were physically and spiritually.

With each successive season at Bolshoi that had passed by without my name next to Giselle, people increasingly thought that I'd be passed over forever. To play a girl who dies of a broken heart, I was altogether too resilient. No matter how much I tried to seem smaller and softer, no one in Moscow believed I would lose my mind over a man.

Laurent was making a statement by giving me the role after all this time. He also undertook other efforts to help me succeed in Paris. He invited me to parties—intimate dinners of twenty, fashion shows at the Palais-Royal or the Luxembourg Gardens, and movie premieres followed by cocktails on the rooftop of Printemps.

A week before *Giselle*, Sasha and I were asked to attend the opening of an art exhibit at the Fondation Louis Vuitton. Outfits were delivered to our apartment that afternoon. Mine was a long, black-and-gold gown with a low-cut brocade bodice and tulle skirt, and as I put it on I thought of the off-the-rack red dress I'd bought between rehearsals and wore to Nina's wedding, a lifetime ago it seemed. Sasha was loaned a black tuxedo with a dark floral pattern. When we finished dressing, we stood side by side in front of our full-length mirror. The last pink light of a May evening was spilling into the room, making everything inside it—the dresser, the nightstand, the bed, the carved molding—stand out richly as if in an oil painting.

"What do you think of this?" Sasha said, buttoning his jacket. He then took time squeezing some gel onto his palms and slicking his hair back away from his face. Satisfied, he locked eyes with my reflection in the mirror.

"It's a bit flamboyant, but not as much as what you wear onstage every night." I laughed. Truthfully, once Sasha put it on, the suit became him. In fact, he suddenly seemed to have morphed from a dancer—a working man—to a man of the world. By that I mean wealth, but not just. He looked like the kind of person who isn't defined by what they *do* but by what they *have*. By this point I'd had plenty of opportunities to observe such people, who are not only proud to be defined that way but also believe sincerely that they will continue having more and more without necessarily doing more and more.

"I rather like it," Sasha said, twisting around to peer at his back in the mirror. "It's a nice change from tights and a dance belt!" He laughed and moved closer to me. "And I love seeing you like this, Natasha. It's different—new," he said, putting his hands on my waist. Just before his lips met mine, I saw in his eyes the miniaturized reflection of myself like the engraving on a Byzantine coin. It was both familiar and foreign, and a quiet sense of dread seeped into me. Once, I was a challenge and a mystery to him. Did he wish I were something else? I rested my chin over his shoulder and smiled. My reflection in the mirror smiled back, just a second later it seemed.

The sun had set completely but its heat lingered in the atmosphere as our car wound its way through Bois de Boulogne. From the size of the trees to the sound of streams, everything about the woods felt thin. It was hard to believe that this was the remnant of a primordial forest, continually yet never completely cut down for thousands of years. The car turned around a sharp bend; and then against the purple sky, the Fondation came into our view like an exoskeleton left behind by a giant insect, its surfaces of glass and steel crumpled against the darkening grass. Closer up, I could see a reflecting pool directly beneath it. The water was slowly feeding into the mouth of the building, where the entrance was located. The path leading down was edged with glowing white lights like a runway. By the door, guests were arranged in twos and threes, scoping out others in the guise of smoking. The whole scene was brutally ugly and at the same time, undeniably glamorous. Which was precisely the point.

Just outside the door, Sasha stopped to greet an acquaintance, a film producer by the name of Hisham. Underneath his Louis Vuitton cap, he had eyes that didn't seem fully awake even when they were wide-open. His white Louis Vuitton sneakers were as pristine as a rapper's. Next to him, there was a handsome, full-figured Arab woman wearing a strapless ball gown, who had perfectly blown-out dark hair and arched eyebrows. Her name was Behnaz, and she was not a socialite, as I imagined, but an author and a human-rights activist. Hisham and Behnaz greeted Sasha warmly—they'd met at another one of these soirées. They also smiled at me, but the conversation was strained because each person was famous in their own right, yet no one knew exactly what another person was famous for.

Behnaz lifted the cigarette from her mouth just long enough to say, "And your name is? Natalia? A danseuse étoile at l'Opéra de Paris? How impressive." The cigarette returned to its place as if pulled by a magnet. She puffed a few times with obvious relish before continuing. "I danced when I was a little girl. I was quite good—although, of course, not like you. And now I'm just, you know, a writer."

"What is your book about?" I asked helplessly. Just as I expected, she tried in vain to hide her annoyance that I didn't know it already.

"It's a memoir about how I escaped the authoritarian regime of my country, ended up a refugee in England, went to Oxford, and became an international human-rights attorney," Behnaz rattled off before deflecting the conversation toward Hisham. "Hisham has done work with migrant rights. And his films are so—" She exhaled a long, white plume and waved her hand around impatiently. "He's worked with all the biggest actors right now. Right, Hish? Tell us some of their names."

Hisham paused his conversation with Sasha and dropped several names. I didn't know any of them and ended up saying "I will check them out," feeling utterly foolish. It was as pointless and shallow as someone saying to me, "Oh, you're dancing *Giselle*? How fabulous. I'll check it out." Before we could take turns making more meaningless sounds, I excused myself and went inside. Sasha shook hands with Hisham, kissed Behnaz on the cheeks, and followed behind me.

We had timed our entrance stylishly. The evening was already well underway, and guests in finery milled about the cavernous space, drinks in hand. It was the cocktail hour, and all the exhibition halls were specially opened, but no one was paying any attention to the art. Sasha went to get us drinks while I stood in front of a huge sculpture in the shape of a mattress, made of plastic bottles, old clothes, and debris. It would not have looked out of place in the dumpster. But under the tastefully dim light of the hall, the piece resembled a billionaire's next acquisition.

"It's so *raw* and *powerful*, isn't it?" said a voice, and I turned around to find Behnaz. I replied with another one of those universal adjectives for these modern-art situations.

"It's *monumental*," I said.

"Exactly." She nodded. "It's a lifeboat made of ocean trash collected in the Mediterranean. Those are clothes that floated up after some of these unfortunate refugees drowned." She shook her head, and then immediately brightened up. "Ah, here comes Laura. Laura Kent. You know her, I'm sure?"

I did not. In the next few seconds before Laura joined us, Behnaz explained that she was a very celebrated American novelist. The two friends kissed each other on the air above their cheeks, making exaggerated puckering noises.

"You look different today, I almost didn't recognize you," Behnaz said, scanning her friend up and down. Laura, who was a petite ash blonde in a Le Smoking, tapped her thick-rimmed glasses.

"I'm in incognito mode," the American said. "Easier to get around. Where's Jeffrey? Home with the kids?"

Behnaz sighed. "No, he's in New York. The kids are in London with my parents. I'm glad they're not here with me. Kiki is going through her tantrum phase."

"Oh, tell me more. I need a reminder why I shouldn't do another round of IVF." Laura laughed.

"First, you can't drink when you're pregnant. Second, I hated the whole experience—the bloating, the sleeplessness. You know what makes me happy about reaching my goals? I'm rich enough that if Kiki wants to be a mother, she can have the choice to hire a surrogate," Behnaz said, raising her glass. "She should be able to have a career and a family without ruining her body."

Laura arched her eyebrows and toasted, "Hear, hear!"

"By the way, this is Natalia Leonova, the newest and biggest star of the Paris Opéra ballet." Behnaz pointed at me. "I can't wait to see her in *Giselle*."

"How fabulous. I'll have to check it out," Laura chirped, then turned back to her friend. "Hey, do you want to catch up properly over dinner? We made reservations."

"*Avec plaisir*. But before we go, let's take a selfie with Natalia," Behnaz said, leaning in toward me and draping her hair over one shoulder. "Can you take one, Laura?"

Laura stretched out her arm, and the three of us took a photo together. She texted the photo to Behnaz.

"Could I get it, too, Laura?" I asked and told her my number, and she paused, looking troubled.

"Well, let's actually see if I can AirDrop it into your phone." Laura tinkered, wrinkling her forehead and pursing her red lips.

"Oh, well, it's not working," she mumbled in frustration after a minute. "Let's just text then."

I gave her my number again; almost as soon as she sent the photo, they were on their way to an even more beautiful and exclusive scene. I scanned the room and saw Sasha holding court in front of several people. When I waved at him, he excused himself and walked over to me. He handed me a glass of champagne and I drank deeply before telling him what happened.

"As if I would do anything with her phone number if I had it," I said. "Does she think I'm so stupid that I won't notice the slight?"

"Don't take it so personally," Sasha said mildly.

"You don't get it because people never underestimate you. Or you're oblivious."

"And you're judgmental. No one's good enough for you. You think you're better than everybody, Natasha." He rolled his eyes and took a swig of his drink. As I was about to respond I saw someone dazzling walking in our direction. She was taller than I remembered, but as she approached with a smile I recognized her unmistakable blond-and-pink coloring reminiscent of a tea rose. It was Sofiya.

"Natasha, how many summers, how many winters?" She cupped my elbows in her hands and kissed both of my cheeks. When she pulled back, her beauty came into full view. She had always been pretty and was aware of it; but now she had the radiance of someone who had come into her true power. She was wrapped in a sculptural ice-blue column dress. Large teardrop sapphires dangled from her ears as she laughed with her whole body like a golden bell, a mannerism she'd acquired since leaving Vaganova. I was filled with warmth—but also with apprehension.

"You're a vision, Sofiya. Look at you," I said in Russian, and speaking the familiar language to a familiar face brought a burst of happiness despite my confusion. "What are you doing here in Paris?"

"I heard about you joining the Paris Opéra as an étoile. I'm not surprised—you were always destined for greatness," she said, talking over me in haste. "Not like me." She smiled.

"So you didn't keep dancing?" Even as I asked the question, I felt ashamed that I hadn't made any effort to stay in touch. But she pretended not to notice my embarrassment.

"Oh, no. I went to fashion school instead. Now I work here in Paris."

"In design?" I asked, and she shook her head.

"No, I wish. I model. And this must be the celebrated Alexander Nikulin?" She turned toward Sasha, who was waiting patiently to be acknowledged. I introduced them and they carried on immediately, charming each other with ease, trading compliments, questions, and insights like a friendly tennis match. They looked wonderful together, like old friends. Or new lovers.

"I don't feel well," I said to them. "Sasha, you should stay for the dinner. I'm just going to go home and rest."

"Are you sure? I can leave with you." Sasha knitted his brows together. "It must be the stress from the upcoming show," he said apologetically to Sofiya.

I told him he should stay, and he accepted without further argument. Sofiya and I traded numbers and promised to get together soon.

There was no one by the door when I slipped out. The sound of frogs rang clear through the cool night air, and I felt I could breathe again. Our driver, Gabriel, was waiting by the car, recognizable from afar by his mop of curly hair. When he saw me, he quickly saved the game on his phone and held the door open for me. Although I truly didn't feel well, the thought of home didn't appeal to me. And as much as I had been going out, I still didn't know many places in Paris. Then I thought of when Laurent first called me to make an offer. I'd overheard him saying some address to his driver, and for some reason it had remained in my mind—though I'd never found out what it was.

"Gabriel, do you know where Place des Vosges is?" I asked.

"Yes, of course. It's not far from your apartment," he replied. "Should we head down?"

"Yes. Let's go there."

St. Petersburg is elegant, and Moscow is moving. But only Paris is seductive. Here, you come to believe that certain parts of the city—an undulating medieval building clinging to its neighbor several centuries its junior, a cobblestone lane of cottages hiding in the middle of bourgeois Montmartre—have been waiting especially for you to discover it one day. I'd lived nearly a year within ten minutes of walking to Place des Vosges and somehow never stumbled upon this oldest square in Paris, built in the early seventeenth century. It was surrounded on all sides by redbrick *hôtels*, the former residences of the nobility and the current ones of the haute bourgeoisie. The ground level of these town houses were arcaded, so that any passerby could wander into the central square. This was quartered into green lawns anchored by four identical fountains. In the fresh and fragrant darkness, the water streamed out from the stone lions' mouths in the shape of musical notes. Groups of friends were dotted on the grass, surrounded by the linden hedges casting long moon shadows. There were people in the arcades as well—handsomely aged men and women wearing Hermès scarves—eating and drinking with performative flourish under the lanterns casting a baroque glow.

I wandered through the square, searching for a place to sit. The restaurants in the arcades looked ideal for Laurent, who I assumed lived in one of the *hôtels* above. I decided to walk out of the Place and find a quieter street. Just outside the south entrance, there was a bar that was pleasingly simple. It was the kind of place that is suitable neither for people on a first date, nor for couples who have grown tired of each other, but perfect for those who still do each other's laundry with a sense of tenderness and occasionally call each other "lovers." I walked inside, sat at the white marble bar, and ordered a pastis. A few minutes later, the bartender set the drink down in front of me and said, "A lovers' quarrel?"

"How did you know?" I said.

"You're dressed in a stunning couture gown, ordering a drink alone at this time of night," he said. "Your French is very good, but you're not from here."

I explained to him that I learned French at a ballet school in Russia, and that I was now a ballerina at the Paris Opéra.

"I would love to see the ballet sometime. I'm a photographer. I like portraiture, and dancers make great subjects," the bartender said. "So what happened with your *mec*?"

I took a good look at him. He was one of those men who are not handsome but give a strong impression, like a borzoi wearing a bandana. His black hair was striped with a single silver chunk, and his arms were covered in tattoos. He might as well have been an alien to me and my world. So I told him everything. The callousness and hypocrisy of so many that I met in these circles. Pretending to enjoy their company. How Sasha fit in, saw nothing wrong with it, and called me judgmental and proud when I recoiled against the insincere. Meeting my former friend, more beautiful and charming than ever, whom I had deliberately avoided for years.

"So how do all these things make you feel?" the bartender asked.

"I don't know. I can't explain," I said. "My French isn't good enough."

"You should put it into your dance. That's what I would do," he said, making another drink. When it was finished, he set it in front of me and said, "On the house."

"I'm Natalia. My friends call me Natasha," I said. I wasn't flirting with him, but I wanted him to like me. I hadn't wanted anyone to like me for a long time, and that desire alone was refreshing. It also seemed that the bartender reciprocated my strange sentiment exactly: he wasn't seducing me, but a kind of desire nonetheless made itself felt in his mannerisms.

"Léon. *Enchanté.* You can find me here Wednesday through Saturday nights," he said, then wrote down a number on a cocktail napkin. "You can also call me if you ever need someone."

THE NEXT MORNING, I WAS restless through the company class. I had been developing a bunion on my right foot in the past few years, and the pain was finally impossible to ignore. It didn't bother me at performances, with the adrenaline and the ice bucket that I knew was waiting for me in the dressing room as soon as the curtain call ended. During class, however, I found myself saving my feet for the evening in various ways. I realized with a start that I could no longer throw my body around as I had when I was seventeen, eighteen, nineteen. I remembered how that night I danced Gamzatti at Varna, I believed I could touch the sky if I so wanted. Physics didn't exist for me—or it had different rules. If I had to describe that feeling: the purest freedom. I was wild even in the first few seasons at Bolshoi. When Sasha created a new trick, I immediately had to do it—and better. Now, even the thought of doing jumping fouettés made my foot swell up. I could still grand jeté higher than any other ballerina, but I knew not to use all my energy or pain tolerance at once. I saw what would happen from recklessness: falling on stage, being unable to continue into Act II, or perhaps snapping my Achilles like an overstretched cello string.

After the class, I had rehearsal for Giselle's entrance in Act II—one of the most famous scenes in ballet. It is past midnight in the glade in the woods where Giselle has been buried. Myrtha, the Queen of the Wilis, summons Giselle from her grave with her magic. Giselle thus becomes one of the Wilis, spirits of maidens who were betrayed by their lovers. With her wand of asphodel, Myrtha commands Giselle to dance—and she obeys, spinning in place in an attitude derrière by hopping on demi-pointe for eight counts. Then she whirls out of it, usually with bourrées or chaînés on demi-pointe.

Now here was my challenge. I had studied all the videos of the finest ballerinas in this scene. Sylvie Guillem did eight counts of attitude derrière, spinning with a beautiful high leg. She then transitioned to bourrée on pointe, which slowed her down. This created a very French, very Paris Opéra look, too calm and polished for a wraith of a naive and emotionally transparent girl. There were others who spun for nine or ten counts before chaînéing on demi-pointe for a less risky and manic exit. I was determined to do *twelve* counts of attitude derrière hops without slowing down for the chaînés on *full pointe*. This was how I envisioned the lunar delirium of a restless, fleet, bewitched spirit. And this was also pure bravura—in a role normally associated with lyricism rather than bravura. No one had tried this before, and it woke a familiar, irresistible urge to transcend what was expected of me. I thought I could do it—but just six days before the show, I still hadn't managed to achieve it. The dizziness during the rotation, the pain in my bad foot—all of it was maddening. After an hour of struggling by myself, I lay flat on the floor, exhausted.

Sasha walked in, looking tired and worn himself. He'd come home from the party while I was sleeping, and I'd left early in the morning while he was still asleep. Without drinking from his water bottle, adjusting his warm-up pants, or going to the stereo, he came directly to me and sat down.

"I don't think I can do this," I said to him, folding my forearms over my eyes. "I can't dance it the way I want. This is the first time I'm realizing this, Sasha. Almost as soon as I got everything I needed, I've lost the one thing that I've always had."

"Where is it hurting?" he asked. When I pointed and flexed my right foot, he took it into his lap and started massaging it gently. We stayed like that in silence, save for the laughter of corps dancers just getting out of rehearsal from the studio down the hall. As they passed by our open door, they suddenly fell quiet in fear and awe. I could almost hear them whisper, "Sasha and Natasha." Their chatter soon rose back again, and then it was gone.

"It wasn't that long ago that I used to tread softly by Katia Reznikova, as if she were a sleeping lion and not a ballerina in rehearsal," I said, smiling. "I'm already on the other side of my peak. My body isn't what it used to be, and I'm constantly afraid it won't be able to do today something it could do yesterday."

"Natasha, you have just realized this. But remember how I'm a year older than you? I've been feeling this for at least the past year. And to be honest, even longer," Sasha said, still kneading my foot to relax the muscles. "I've been pulling back a little. I'm definitely not what I was when I was nineteen. I can't do some stuff that you and I used to do together, not even to show the audience but just to test our abilities, to joke and laugh, during our first season together at Bolshoi."

"That's not true, I don't agree," I said, but I knew what he was talking about. Sasha was still a glorious dancer, one that most nineteen-year-old soloists couldn't dream of surpassing. But I'd seen him try to push his dancing to the limit and then pull back just before reaching his goal, in order to save himself from disaster. He'd become more believable.

"But aging isn't all bad," Sasha continued. "In some ways, it helps me to have something that pushes back against me—like how you need a hard ground to spring off from in order to jump. Getting older taught me what my limits are and what it feels like to cross them. And that fear that you have of not being the dancer you wish to be—that's what makes the dance more vital. Now it takes so much more guts for me to go for that extra turn or double tour, which is why it's more satisfying when it turns out the way I wanted. I'm not ashamed of any of this."

His hands relaxed around my foot. "Look at me, Natasha."

I did not. I felt him carefully slide my feet off his lap and lift my forearms from my face. I kept my eyes closed.

"You cry a lot more than people think," he said quietly. "And I love you. I love all of you."

I did look at him then. He hadn't shaved in the morning and his cheeks were covered in a mossy beard. He was in his black nylon workout pants with holes in the knees, the pair he wore most often and refused to throw away. I loved him at that moment more than I ever had before—when he was dancing like an immortal, when we were having our first meals together at home, or when we were pulled together that long summer day, his skin against my skin over the hot pebbles, the sky above enlaced with pine trees.

"Will you still be with me even when I'm old and can't dance?" I asked him.

"I promise. Always. Forever," he said.

My days at Nina's apartment unfold peacefully from one to the next, marked by rehearsals, tea, and homemade dinners. After the chocolate cake is finished, Nina serves an apple cake, then a walnut cake, and then a Prague cake until I finally have to say something.

"Stop bringing cake home, or I won't be able to fit into my costume."

"I'm not buying them." Nina presses her temples with her palms. "He just keeps leaving them at the front door."

"It's that guy—the baker? You really only slept with him once?" I say. Without confirming or denying, she pushes herself off the dining chair and stumbles over drunkenly to the couch. She burrows into its corner, hugging her elbows and tucking her feet underneath her. Her face is flushed, yet she is shivering. I slide next to her and pull a blanket over both of us.

"Did you tell him you're married, and so on?"

"Of course I did. He says it doesn't matter. He says Andryusha doesn't love me the way I deserve to be loved. That to Andryusha, I'm just one of many things, whereas *he* doesn't care about anything else above my happiness."

"Do you think that it's good to be with someone who doesn't have anything else in life besides loving you?"

Nina glares darkly at me as if to say: don't be sarcastic. And this lets me know she's in deeper than she may even be aware herself. Then her eyebrows unknit themselves and she sighs.

"I guess the right answer is no. But I can't see why."

"There is no right or wrong answer. Look, I'm not trying to shame you. I don't care what you do." I lean against her, and the couch creaks beneath our weight. "You make a choice, feel what there is to feel, love whichever way you can, and accept the consequences. That's all there is to life."

"I don't love him," Nina says soberly. "It's over."

"So it's definitely over?" I say. "Wait, which one?"

Nina gives me a look of pure anguish and runs away to her room without an answer. It is only revealed the next morning when I find a whole Moscow cake inside the kitchen trash can. But after that, the cakes and the pastries and the bread rolls all disappear. Instead of staying up with me eating dessert and talking, Nina goes to bed early and rises late, sometimes after I've already left for the day's rehearsals.

One evening during a quiet dinner, Nina's phone vibrates on the table and she grabs it in a rush.

"How are you guys? Yes, I miss you all so much. I can't wait for you to come home. Where's Luda? I want to hear her voice," Nina says into the phone while walking away from her half-eaten plate. Before the door of her bedroom closes, I hear her say, "I love you."

AFTER THE SUCCESS OF MY first *Giselle*, Laurent told me to take an injury break. He said I'd more than earned it. My performance had surprised the world, Laurent, Sasha—and honestly, even me. That night, it was not I who was in control but something else far more absolute. I didn't even count the spinning attitude hops, but knew that they'd gone exactly as I'd wanted by the way the audience clapped and roared "*Brava!*" before I'd even finished. I didn't feel any pain in my feet, since my body didn't have any weight; it was only made of music. Then the next day I went to the doctor, who told me that there were five stress fractures in my right foot, two in my left, and that if I'd danced even one more night I could have permanently lost the ability to perform.

So for the first time ever, I stopped dancing completely with no return date in sight. Everyone was tender toward me, the dancers, the staff, Laurent, and of course, Sasha. I'd lived in fear of running into this brick wall all my life, but now that it was finally here, I couldn't help but feel a secret relief. Here was rest, at last, instead of dancing forty hours a week, fifty weeks a year. And I wasn't just physically exhausted. I'd discovered that *Giselle* had changed me. Of course, I was familiar with pouring my humanity into art, which was the only way it could become real. Everything I'd ever done was tearing myself into small pieces and putting it into dance. But I hadn't known that the opposite was also true: That art—if real enough—could lodge itself inside me and become a permanent part of who I am. This new part made me deeply uncomfortable. I no longer recognized myself as simply Natasha. In the mirror I saw someone who looked like me but wasn't entirely me. I was less than a human. All this led me (the original me) to decide that it would be best to do something, anything other than dance until I became whole again.

For the first few months, I stayed in bed while Sasha got ready and had breakfast. After he left for the company class, I made coffee and brought it back to bed. I read books and listened to music, still in my pajamas. I could listen to a Mozart piano concerto or a Tchaikovsky symphony twice in a row and consider that a morning well spent. By then it was two or three in the afternoon. I took a shower and went out dutifully for lunch. The art part of me had replaced the human part of me which contained, among other things, the desire for food. I was never truly hungry anymore, and it took great effort to remember meals, as was socially acceptable. Afterward I sat at a park and stared at things—the quadrangle of blue sky above the carousel, for example—until they seemed to become pure shapes and colors; I repeated this process until the world was filled with pieces of extraordinary beauty. I came home a few hours later when birds were gathering in flocks and people were busy leaving work and meeting friends for drinks. Alone, I lit candles and took a bath while listening to more music.

A couple of sonatas later, Sasha would be home from rehearsals or a photoshoot. It turned out that Sofiya had introduced Sasha to her friend, the most celebrated young fashion designer in Paris, who hired him as the face of his new campaign. Some people who are stunning in real life look average in photos; others who seem captivating on camera are disappointing in real life. Sasha was neither—he always appeared exactly as radiant as he truly was. More modeling offers followed, and as soon as Sasha was home he was already halfway out the door for some gig or a party. A pattern emerged: I would be lying in bed in my pajamas; Sasha would be getting ready in the bathroom, his shadow moving across the bedroom wall. He'd ask, "Are you sure you don't want to come?" I'd say, "I'm sure." He'd kiss me, and as he'd close the door the darkness would fold me in for the night.

One night in February, I was lying in bed reading. Sasha had left for dinner with some friends. It was freezing cold outside; there was no one walking around even in Le Marais. The neon light of the café next door was spreading pink and yellow on the wet pavement. It reminded me of my old friends, people I no longer talked to but missed desperately in certain moments. And just like that, I was tired of being alone. I suddenly wished to talk to someone and have something hot and steaming to eat. It was the human part of me waking up again.

I put on a coat and boots and headed in the direction of Place des Vosges. When Léon saw me walk in, he said, "*Bonsoir, Natalia, un pastis?*" as if we'd met each other only the previous evening.

ii

"MAKE ME SOMETHING DIFFERENT . . ." I SAID. "IT'S LÉON, RIGHT?"

"*Vous avez envie de quoi?*" he asked. What do you feel like?

"*J'ai envie de—d'être amoureuse.*"

He nodded and smiled. "*Je pige.* I will make you something."

Léon started pulling off bottles from the shelf and pouring a bit into a tiny metal funnel. Then he raised the shaker above his shoulder and pumped it up and down with what I would've called performative swagger, if not for his look of calm concentration. He poured the liquid over a strainer into a chilled coupe and set it down in front of me.

"Rosewater, champagne, Cointreau, chocolate bitters for the exquisite pain," he said as I took my first sip.

"It's delicious. And the liquor?"

"Of course vodka! Because you're Russian." Léon laughed. "Couldn't you tell?"

"I have a terrible sense of taste. I confess, I'm not much of a foodie."

Léon sighed and wiped his hands on a dish towel. There was only one other guest in the place, who was talking to another bartender. Léon walked behind him, said something in a low voice, and came out through the small opening in the bar to take a seat next to me.

"I've clocked out for the night. Henri can take care of the closing. There is no one here, with the weather like this." Léon turned to his colleague and ordered a vodka soda and a shot of Fernet. "If we become friends, I hope I get to show you how to enjoy food and drink. I'm half French and half Italian, so this is very much how I grew up—and my partner, Camilla, is Italian."

I hadn't meant to do anything with Léon; nonetheless, I was hurt by this new knowledge that narrowed the possibilities of our acquaintance. From then on, we talked about their visit to Rome, his love of the Eternal City. It was summer when he went, the sun bleeding over the tall black pines. The monuments roared in silence. He walked past the Largo di Torre Argentina—the ruins of temples and the Curia of Pompey. There was an animal shelter inside one of the ancient shrines, and where once Julius Caesar was murdered, feral cats now roamed among the decapitated columns.

"A very Italian way of looking at life. Julius Caesar, feral cats, all the same. Nothing is too sacred or not sacred enough," he said, and signaled for another round of drinks. "Just five blocks away, there is the Pantheon, where you find Raphael's grave. It says: *Ille hic est Raphael. Timuit quo sospite vinci rerum magna parens et moriente mori.* Here lies Raphael. While he was alive, nature feared she would be surpassed by him; when he died, she feared that she, too, would die." He spoke Latin as easily as if it were a prayer he'd learned by heart in Catholic school.

"Quite a eulogy for someone who died so young," I said.

"Because he created sublime art—and because they cared about legacy. When you think about what you leave behind in terms of hundreds or even thousands of years, time takes on different proportions. The past and the future are both so much more present, that they become one. And here are our drinks." Léon raised his glass. "*Ars longa, vita brevis.*"

"Art is long, life is short," I said, raising my own.

THE NEXT MORNING, I WAS seized with a craving to see paintings and sculptures. Soon after Sasha left, I got dressed and walked to the Louvre. I spent the entire day there in the galleries. In the luminous Cour Marly alone, I could have happily rested for hours surrounded by marble statues, potted trees, and clear-eyed art students drawing in their sketchbooks. After the museum, I bought a croissant and brought it to the quai. I sat down on the levee, dangling my legs over the edge like the young couples sitting nearby with a bottle of wine and snacks between them. I couldn't remember the last time Sasha and I had done something for the two of us. Since my injury, all the time we spent together dancing had come to an abrupt end. He didn't insist that I come see his performances—he understood it might be too painful for me to just watch in the audience.

When he wasn't rehearsing or performing, he had photoshoots, parties, and a constant stream of guest invitations that kept him flying around the world. He never stayed still. It occurred to me that we had returned to our natural states in which we found each other all those years ago: I, who was comfortable alone or with one or two people I trusted, and he, who needed to be around many people and countless stimuli. He made friends everywhere he went, although he couldn't possibly know the names of their pets, children, or the number of their siblings. Even his iPhone was full of thousands of songs to which he never listened but once, tapping his feet on the way to the airport. I listened to those songs I loved over and over again. And I liked that about myself, just as he liked being the one who "discovered" new things. Like many couples, we were attracted to our differences when we met. So we tried them on for a while, and ended by becoming critical and returning to our own natures, with possibly more certainty than before. What had really changed was that I wasn't dancing, and therefore I was powerless.

"Excuse me." A woman waved a mittened hand from a short distance away. "Would you mind taking a photo of us?"

"Of course," I said. She squealed a *merci* and passed me her phone before linking arms with her boyfriend. The Seine flowed behind them like cold lava, ashen and slow—but they would remember only its beauty, the white and gray elegance of the mansions on Île Saint-Louis, the faint sound of someone braving the wind to play the guitar near Notre Dame, and the bright red of her mittens standing out in the frosty background. After I bade the couple goodbye, I called Sasha. My spirits lifted when he picked up the phone right away.

"I thought you were in rehearsal," I said. He was starring in *Mayerling* soon, the first ballet in many years he was premiering without me. It was a Kenneth MacMillan ballet, completely English, and therefore not in the repertory of either Bolshoi or Mariinsky.

"I am. We're taking a short break," Sasha said.

"How is it? Is it going well?"

Sasha laughed. "You know how you feel like nothing is going right, the lifts are a nightmare, all the steps and turns are choreographed to the left, and then everything works out in the end? This will be like that."

"Tell me everything over dinner," I said. "Let's go out somewhere nice."

"Ah, I wish you'd told me earlier," Sasha said. "A friend of mine just invited me to dinner at this new restaurant in Pigalle."

"Can I come, too? I'm ready to start meeting people again."

Sasha sighed. "The reservation is for six people, and it's an impossible place to get into. I don't know if they'll allow one more person to join." I could hear him ruffle his hair, trying to come up with a solution. "You know what, I just won't go. I'll cancel."

"Nonsense. You should go," I said, watching the Seine. "If you like it, maybe we can go together next time." Sasha sounded relieved. He had to go back to rehearsal and he loved me.

Afterward I stared at my phone and considered the options. On my contact list I saw Sofiya, whose number I'd saved without clear plans of getting together. I texted and asked her if she was free for dinner. When she didn't respond, I moved on to texting Léon. By this point, the winter sun was hanging low over the river, reflecting heatlessly on the glass facade of the d'Orsay and the stone quai, and making me feel that all of it—not only the dinner but everything—was too late. I just didn't know to which point I would turn back time, if I could. All I knew was that something had to change. As I started going up the stairs, my phone vibrated. It was Léon.

"You move very elegantly," I said to him once. "Most men move with less grace."

"But you're around male dancers all the time. Including your *mec*," he said. We were walking in Le Marais before his shift, as had become our routine once every few weeks. He paused to let a woman with a stroller pass him by, and then continued. "Alexander Nikulin. I looked him up."

"You looked up Sasha?"

"Yes, I became curious. You don't talk about him very much."

"What did you think of him?"

"Sasha is a handsome man. I find him very attractive," Léon said. I started to laugh, and then the way he glanced at me sideways made me stop walking. An old woman nearly bumped into my back and then crossed the street passive-aggressively.

"What about Camilla?" I asked.

"Camilla? She knows I like men. Sometimes we get together with a man we both like." He winked at me. "This seems to shock you. Here, let's go inside this store."

We entered a boutique with dark gray walls and soft, heady music. The mirrored trays held perfumes, candles, and vases filled with peonies that I busily pretended to admire.

"So do you prefer women or men—or is it equal?" I said, picking up and smelling a sandalwood candle.

"I used to be primarily attracted to women. Recently, I find I'm more often attracted to men," he said, folding his arms across his chest and leaning against a wall. I tried to hide my surprise; he had never struck me as particularly feminine.

"And when you're doing your—pas de trois"—I smiled—"does anyone get jealous?"

"Look, it has to be done with caution. It gets very emotional. But for us, it's worth it. And beautiful." Léon reached over and laid his hand on my shoulder, which tensed me up like an invertebrate perceiving a threat.

"For a dancer whose body is her instrument, you seem very out of touch with this part. When is the last time you had sex?"

His stare was frank yet unknowable, like looking through a one-way glass; he put himself out there and didn't care whether I understood him. How very opposite to my own instincts. I held my breath as he placed both his hands on my shoulders and massaged lightly. Just as I was getting used to the pressure of his touch, he walked away to a display shelf. He returned with a bottle of perfume and said, "Here. Try this."

I spritzed it on my wrists and neck. It was a warm, deep, creamy smell, like blooming white flowers at night. Léon pressed his nose against the spot behind my ear and breathed in.

"You smell like a goddess. Also, expensive," he said with a roguish smile. "You smell like an expensive goddess."

On the way out of the boutique, I told Léon about the only time I watched Dmitri from the audience. It was in my last season at Bolshoi, and Dmitri was being given an artistic evening dedicated to him in honor of his twenty years with the company. The program consisted only of pieces chosen by Dmitri, danced solo or with his favorite partners. I wouldn't have gone, but Alypov had stressed to me that several Kremlin officials would be there. During the intermission, they expected to have champagne and caviar with Bolshoi's brightest stars. "Wear a dress, smile, and answer questions. It's a part of your job, and you'd be well advised to keep them happy," Alypov told me, just short of showing his impatience. I was still more stubborn than he was. Ultimately it wasn't Alypov or his superiors that swayed me but Sasha, who insisted that I would miss out on something truly astonishing.

The opening piece was *Carmen*, which was not Alberto Alonso's ballet that had long been in Bolshoi repertoire, but a newly commissioned solo choreographed for Dmitri. It seemed impossible that the drama and spectacle of an entire opera could be reduced to just him, alone onstage against a solid scarlet backdrop. But he began dancing to Habanera and—how shall I say this? If one had only watched his three-minute solo as Don José and no other ballet for an entire year, that would have been enough. Everything one seeks in dance was distilled into it; it was a lightning strike through one's soul. I reminded myself that Dmitri was still capable of weakness and pain by seeing his torso rise and fall as he raised his hands like a gladiator to the hysterical audience. Once they calmed, he returned in a black mesh top and tights, having stripped off his pants and bolero jacket. He was hiding his face behind a red fan. Then he proceeded to dance to Séguedille—not as Don José, but as Carmen. I felt physically nauseated as can happen in the face of true art: He was more sensuous and seductive than any woman I'd ever seen. He was as perfect a Carmen as he was a Don José, which I could never be. Dmitri had won. The evening was an uncontested success.

But in the lobby, as I was waiting for Sasha to retrieve our coats, I heard someone say in a soft but intentionally audible murmur, "*pidoras*."

I turned toward the voice and saw the elf-faced Fedya from the corps, mimicking Carmen's movements in a grotesque way and making vulgar gestures. The other protégés, who had made small distinctions only because of Dmitri's help, burst into laughter saying, "What a *pidoras*."

WHEN I WAS READY TO dance again, Léon asked to take photos of me in rehearsal. I was nervous for him to meet Sasha—I worried both that they would like each other and that they wouldn't get along. But Sasha merely shook hands with Léon and carried on as if no one was there. One of the ways Sasha had changed was that he no longer humored everyone. He could be gregarious or gracious or coolly distant—and it seemed he thought Léon was just another wannabe fashion photographer after his image.

Léon took photos in silence and never mentioned anything like he did that day at the *parfumerie*. I found the results rather bewitching. His black-and-white film photos had a tactile graininess and lasting aftereffect. It reminded me of the silhouette that remains in thin air after every movement and position of a great dancer, or perfume that clings to the wrist of your sweater and surprises you weeks later. I wanted to see more of his photographs and got him admitted backstage when I finally returned to performing in *Swan Lake*.

I still knew relatively little about Léon. I knew that his mother was an Algerian-French linguistics professor and his father an Italian she'd met on vacation. They'd never planned anything lasting, and he was already married. She was older and stylishly opposed to marriage in the manner of French intellectuals. Upon finding out she was pregnant, she decided to have the child alone. Léon saw his father once every four or five years, when he'd come to Grenoble, where his mother taught at the university. On Léon's fourteenth birthday, his father sent him a Canon camera. That was the last Léon heard from him. In Rome, Camilla helped Léon search for his father, but they found no trace of him.

"This happened before everything about a person was online. Back then it was possible to truly and well disappear," he said, pouring me a vodka martini.

"Abandonment used to be much more poetic," I said. To be fair, I was already a few drinks in. Léon, who didn't know about my father, cast his eyes down in displeasure.

"Anytime one acts with such finality it takes an extraordinary amount of will and determination," I said. "To really disappear without a trace, one has to overcome our most fervent desire—to remember and to be remembered."

I picked up the semimatte print in front of me. He'd captured me from the wings as I leaped onto the stage in Act II. My body looked as if it could clear the heads of the swans standing in the back. It was a physical impossibility, but I felt like that while dancing, and the photo showed it.

"You could blow this up into a large print and sell it," I said.

"You want me to sell photos of you?" Léon crossed his arms and regarded me with an amused expression.

"I just think you're talented enough to really go into photography. Maybe turn it into a series and do an exhibit. Haven't you thought about it?"

"I am happy to do this for my own pleasure," Léon said, wiping down the bar with a dish towel. "I have this job, it's relaxed and pays the bills. I go home and spend time with Camilla. And when I have free time, I walk around Paris with my camera and take photos of whatever I want. I'm content where I am." He draped the towel over a rack, excused himself, and disappeared into the kitchen—and did not come out before I paid and left.

I didn't see Léon for a long time after that. Neither of us messaged the other, and life was busy. Having lost a whole season, I didn't want to miss out on anything—and invitations for guest performances poured in from around the world. Sometimes Sasha and I went together to Buenos Aires, New York, London, Sydney, and Stockholm. But more often, I flew on my own to Vail, LA, São Paulo, Hong Kong, Positano, and Berlin, paired up with principals at the local company or another guest artist. Sasha and I each had a suitcase that was filled and ready in the hallway, so we could take off on a moment's notice. Sometimes I only realized that he was in town by seeing his valise there.

Once, we were invited together to Oslo to dance *Giselle*. I had always wanted to see Svalbard in the north, but I was forced to give it up; we had only one free day before we had to fly back to Paris, and it wouldn't have been the right time of year, anyway. I was gloomy, but Sasha convinced me to put on my coat and take a walk in the city.

It was early February and very cold. The sun struggled to break through the dense, bluish clouds. Sasha walked ahead of me, his collar turned up against the wind, hands pushed deep into his pockets. When he noticed me lagging, he turned around and stuck out his hand.

"Come on, we're nearly there."

We held hands until we reached the marina. The opera house, where we'd performed the previous night, glimmered like a glaucous star fallen on the edge of the water. We took a right toward the old fortress, passing through the tree-lined park surrounding the Viking walls. From there we met the wharf again. We walked all the way to the edge of a pier where several sailboats were moored, their black ropes spreading tautly down from masts. The sky was blue-gray and the sea was gray-blue, as if the sky had frozen and chunks of it had crumbled into the sea, and even Sasha's yellow hair had a bluish tint. He let go of my hand and stood facing the ships in silence.

"Don't you think we need a change?" I said then. Sasha turned around with a frown.

"What do you mean?"

"We never see each other unless it's for work. We're never home together."

"Natasha, we only have so long to do what we do. After our best years are done, then we can sit at home and stare at each other." He laughed.

"Do you know why I always wanted to go to Svalbard? There, they have the midnight sun."

"Like in Petersburg?"

"No—I'm talking about the sun never dipping below the horizon. It stays in the sky for four months a year in Svalbard. Do you know, in the North Pole, the sun only rises and sets once a year. One day lasts six months—and one night lasts six months." I put my hands together and blew warm air into them.

"Imagine that you're an arctic fox. Living there in the perpetual night, sleeping, waking, hunting, hiding from polar bears, finding your mate, in complete darkness. And then suddenly, the sun rises and turns everything white. This one long, long day in which you have to do everything in your life before it all disappears again . . ." I was shaking from my head to my toes. Sasha put his hands around mine and rubbed them together.

"That's what it's like for us, isn't it?" I said.

"I have an idea. When you're thirty-five and I'm thirty-six, we'll both feel like slowing down. At that point we will take only the best opportunities. And then we'll get married."

"You want us to get married?" I asked, incredulous. "You never said anything like this before."

"I've always said we'll be together forever. I haven't thought of it exactly as marriage, but I think it's what will make you happy. Make both of us happy." He pulled me into an embrace, but I pushed him away.

"Ask me again properly," I said. Sasha sighed and got down on one knee.

"Natasha, will you marry me?" he said. As soon as I nodded, he rose, took me in his arms, and spun me around. All the seagulls nearby were alarmed and took off at once, and Sasha laughed with that carefree boy-man laughter of his. We were in a snow globe of our own where every snowflake was a gray-and-white bird.

Upon returning to Paris, Sasha took me to Boucheron on Place Vendôme. The employees regarded us with a scarcely veiled look of suspicion: Sasha with his shoulder-grazing blond hair, torn jeans (not intentionally, but due to wear), me in my black knit hat, puffer jacket, and worn boots. Both of us whispering in Russian. Instead of asking us what we would like to see, the men and women in suits followed us with their eyes. With their gaze on our backs, I had a hard time approaching the glass cases—a glittering menagerie of flowers, hummingbirds, snakes, leopards, all captured in gemstones. Finally, Sasha said to a woman in a black wool dress, "We'd like to see some rings."

"Our *haute joaillerie* rings begin around 40,000 euros," she said without a smile. "Perhaps you'd like to see the lower line."

I tugged at Sasha's sleeve, mortified and wanting nothing more in the store. "Let's just go," I said to him. But Sasha took out his phone and called a number.

"*Bonsoir, c'est Sasha.* I'm sorry to interrupt your evening. I'm here at that jeweler you recommended. Boucheron. Yes, yes, exactly." Sasha winked at me and handed the phone to the woman. "This is my friend, who has been a patron of your house for a long time. He wants to speak to you."

The woman frowned as she pressed the phone to her ear. Then her expression changed to that of shock, then capitulation, followed by fawning. "Yes, Monsieur de Balincourt. Of course. Very well. I am so sorry for the misunderstanding." I could almost hear Laurent's impeccably outraged voice, which he reserved not for errant dancers, but for whoever resisted his prerogatives as one of the ruling class of Paris. Even before the woman handed the phone back to Sasha, her colleagues were rushing to pour us flutes of champagne and to arrange jewels in front of a couch. In fifteen minutes, I left with an emerald the size of my thumbnail glittering on my hand.

We got back in our car, shivering from the cold and the excitement. Gabriel turned around, saw the ring, and clapped and cheered. The radio was on some news show, talking placidly about the protests in Kyiv against the elected president.

"Gabriel, turn up the heat please," Sasha said.

"Of course." Gabriel adjusted the heater. "Aren't you from Ukraine, monsieur?"

"From Donbas, but my family's Russian-speaking and I went to school in Moscow." Sasha unbuttoned the top of his coat and settled into his seat. "People are always protesting something, whether in France or Ukraine. I mean, Gabriel, don't you hate the traffic from all the strikes? Let's put on some music—Natasha and I should celebrate."

In the morning, we decided we would throw an engagement party that night. Sasha texted the dancers and his numerous friends from around town; I invited Léon and Sofiya and called my mother to tell her the news. The ringtone continued for a long time before I hung up, deciding against leaving Mama a voicemail. This was how our relationship was; when I was ready, she wasn't, and vice versa. We always managed to repel and circle each other—like the sea and the Big Bear, which can never find rest below the horizon. My hand kept unlocking and locking my phone as I debated calling anyone else. My thoughts drifted to Nina, but she hadn't even called when she had her children. Or maybe *I* was supposed to reach out to offer my congratulations. When my thoughts reached this point, I unlocked my phone, typed a quick message to Nina, and pressed send before I could change my mind. A [. . .] bubble appeared on her side immediately and my stomach churned with anxiety. But the bubble disappeared before turning into an actual word. A minute later, the ellipses tantalizingly appeared and disappeared again.

Feeling nauseated, I went out to get some fresh air, baguettes, and flowers. When I came back, there was a reply from Nina: *Congratulations.* Just one word, no emojis or exclamation point. This wasn't how women friends texted one another—it was cold, bordering on cruel. But perhaps I'd been wrong to expect anything more after years of silence. Maybe for Nina, this was a calm but sincere well-wish. I could even have caught her at a bad time. Of course, the Nina I remembered hadn't been dispassionate or unfriendly, and at one point in our lives we'd shared our joys and sorrows like we had one heart.

I filled my lungs with air and exhaled loudly through my mouth. The important thing was that I was engaged, and there was a party to plan. Sasha procured a case of first-rate champagne and many more cases of white and red wine. Our housekeeper made delicate toasts and laid out little bowls of glistening Spanish olives that guests would pluck with their fingers, first fussily avoiding the oil and then impudently as the night progressed. I draped string lights around the balcony and put vases of English roses on tables.

When that was finished, I got dressed in the bedroom, anxiously wondering if anyone would show up. I perched by the window and looked down to the street. The sky was violet and Paris was orange from the glow of the thousands of lampposts that had suddenly come on in unison. A cat trotted through the ivy-covered alley between our building and the next one. In the summertime, the ivy lushly draped down from our terrace, green and thick enough to shield you from a downpour. Now there were just a few red leaves attached to the vines, through which I saw the first guests walk up to our door. They were dancers—we'd invited almost everyone who wasn't performing that night. Gabriel arrived next, bearing a bouquet of flowers for me, followed by Laurent in a magnificent suit. Another caravan of dancers swelled up our staircase, chatting and laughing loudly. At this point Léon texted back that he couldn't make it because of work. But Sofiya came, balancing a huge display of macarons in her arms. She introduced me to her new beau, a film director and a son of one of the most powerful politicians in France.

Sasha's fashionable friends came in a cluster of colorful fabrics and elegant perfumes. Everyone had many rounds of champagne without worrying about getting up early for the morning class. People were dancing, turning red in the face and sweating, and the windows had to be opened to bring in fresh air. At a point in the evening when drinks began to be spilled and crushes snuck off together, Behnaz, the chic human-rights attorney, arrived late and handed me a wrapped gift.

"It's *The Essential Rumi*. The best love poems in the world," she said, kissing me on both cheeks with real warmth.

"Thank you, this is a beautiful gift! Hang on, excuse me for a moment . . ." I pulled away from her embrace. My phone was ringing, and it was Mama. I hid in my bedroom and picked it up.

"How are you, Mama?" I said. "You sound tired. It's midnight there."

"I'm okay, Natasha. How are you?"

I took a deep breath. "Mama, I'm engaged! Sasha and I are getting married." The end of my sentence became muddled with the beginnings of laughter and tears. I hadn't been so overwhelmed while sharing the news with any of the others.

Mama was quiet on the other side. "Sasha Nikulin?" she finally said.

"Yes, Mama. There's no one else—we've been together a long time now." I laughed, but she remained silent. I imagined her twirling the cord of the landline phone on her finger.

"I rather wished you would get back together with Seryozha," she managed to say.

"Mama, we ended years ago. Seryozha is a great person, of course, but not at all right for me—" I said, suppressing my frustration. "But why aren't you happy for me?"

"I don't think Sasha is right for you."

I threw my head back and stared at the ceiling, taking a deep breath. "Why would you say that? You don't even know him very well."

It was Mama's turn to breathe out a sigh. With long pauses between each word, she said, "He reminds me a lot of your father."

"In what way? My god, Mama, this is ridiculous," I cried out, forgetting that there were guests in the house. "You've never talked about him with me, and now after all these years, you use him to ruin my happiness."

"I have to tell you what I think is true. He won't be there for you in the end."

"Sasha is not my father. And I am not you," I said. Words tumbled out without any pause for breath. "You've kept my father from me my whole life, and now you want to keep me away from Sasha, too."

Mama was silent. I couldn't even hear her breathing on the other end. My eyes were clouding with tears, and I searched for the most hurtful words I could find. "I wish it were otherwise, but sometimes a family just doesn't work. It's better for both of us when we don't try to be in each other's lives. Please don't call me again."

The receiver was silent. I strained to hear the faintest trace of her breathing, and even this drove me mad. As I was pressing end call, she was starting to say my name. But it was too late; I had already hung up on her. That was the last time we spoke. She did what I asked of her.

iii

THE DAY AFTER THE ENGAGEMENT PARTY, I FLEW TO NEW YORK FOR RE-hearsals and a performance at the Metropolitan Opera House. I was dancing Nikiya in *La Bayadère*, staged by a Soviet prima ballerina who defected in the 1970s. Although we'd never met before, we immediately fell into the pattern of a Russian teacher and a student—gruff yet in perfect understanding. The ballet mistress was ethereal and imperious. She looked down at everyone with her heavy-lidded eyes and somehow spoke in immaculate Italian to a boy from Milan, French to the girl from France, Spanish to the girl from Cuba. But to the accompanist Joe, whose provenance was unclear but definitely not Russia, she gravely said "*pozhaluysta*" with the authority of one whose unbroken pedagogical pedigree traced up to Marius Petipa himself. Instead of letting me rest after my variations, the ballet mistress forced me to memorize the rest of the staging. "You will be glad one day when your body is finished and you have to rely on your brain," she said, tapping the side of her head with a long, manicured finger.

While watching the others rehearse, I noticed another Russian speaker among us. He was the soloist dancing the Bronze Idol, and something about his sable skin and Eurasian features was unexpectedly familiar. When the ballet mistress called his name, I finally remembered where I first saw him. I walked up to him after the rehearsal—it seemed a shame to not say anything.

"Hello, Farkhad," I said in Russian.

"Hello, Natalia," he replied politely. "It's been wonderful to see you dance. Thank you for guesting with us."

"I don't know if you remember, but we've actually met before. Well, kind of," I said, and Farkhad raised his eyebrows. "You auditioned at Vaganova, didn't you? I met you and your father that day."

Farkhad seemed a bit embarrassed; whether that was because he didn't remember me, or because he wasn't accepted to the school, I couldn't tell. "Yes. I didn't make it, and I ended up going to the school in Tbilisi—the State Ballet of Georgia."

"But it turned out just fine for you, didn't it?" I said, gesturing at the New York City skyline outside the oversize windows, and that drew a genuine smile from him. We weren't friends, but we might as well have been—the mutual understanding of our struggles and triumphs was so immediate. I could already imagine the multitude of unlikely steps he'd taken and the vast seas he'd crossed to get to this place, just as I had. Through the rest of the week, Farkhad kept offering me coffee and guiding me around the studios. And when we parted after the show, he made a point of exchanging phone numbers. "So we don't stay out of touch for another nineteen years," he said with a grin.

The performance itself had gone well. The artistic director, the ballet mistress, my partner—everyone seemed pleased. I went back to my hotel, took a bath, and immediately fell asleep. The next morning, the ballet mistress called me and asked if I'd read the papers.

"I don't read the reviews," I said, gathering up clothes in one hand and throwing them into the suitcase. "If you could tell me what it was like . . ."

"I'm not talking about reviews, Natasha," she said. "It looks like Sasha is in some kind of scandal."

I finished packing in a hurry and took a cab to the airport. At the terminal, I bought the newspaper in question and thumbed through the pages. Sasha was on the front page of the arts section, glowering at the camera in nothing but nude leggings. Above him was the headline: BALLET'S RENEGADE STAR SUPPORTS RUSSIAN INVASION OF CRIMEA.

On a rainy day in Paris, I met Alexander Nikulin in his apartment in Le Marais. He greeted me in a pair of faded jeans, no shirt, and a charming smile, and proceeded to make us some tea mixed with raspberry jam. "It's Russian thing. My grandmother used to make it. I find it comforting," he said in accented English, rolling his r extravagantly.

It isn't easy to imagine Nikulin seeking comfort in a grandmother's tea. With his long blond hair, six-foot-two frame, and astounding bravura spurred on by innate showmanship, Nikulin has always been ballet's rogue star (or rock star) rather than a typical danseur noble. His forays into modeling and acting have hinted at a restless performer unwilling to be boxed into the classical ballet mold. Asked if he prefers ballet or fashion, he said, "Modeling is fun because it's not art. And I like to have fun sometime."

"Art isn't fun?" I asked, drawing out his laughter.

"Saying art is fun is like saying *love* is fun. Or *life* is fun," he said, lighting a cigarette and leaning back into his seat. "That would be ridiculous. No, art is most serious thing in world. On outside you may look like you're having fun, dancing in *Don Quixote*, for example, but you're on knife's edge inside. It has to be absolute. Like death. 'Art is fun'—only real idiot could think that," he said nonchalantly, unafraid of offending anyone.

More bold answers followed, regarding his past and present companies ("Bolshoi has greater stars, but Paris Opéra has better corps de ballet and overall troupe. Both are legendary and both are dysfunctional, like very ripe and delicious fruits on verge of rotting"), directors, choreographers, and partners.

Of the latter, he turned uncharacteristically mysterious and worshipful. "I had privilege of partnering world's most talented ballerinas. I treasure experience with each of them. But I would give up every single ballerina for one dancer who changed my life. She changed my soul."

That would be the fellow Russian expat dancer Natalia Leonova, with whom he had recently become engaged. Though she was abroad for a performance, traces of her were visible throughout the apartment like a vellum overlay: on the side table, the pin cushion held a threaded needle next to a bundle of leotards, and the mantelpiece was littered with black-and-white photos of her in *Swan Lake.* I murmured at a photograph, "She looks beautiful." Nikulin replied, "Natasha's beauty is the least relevant thing about her."

There is something otherworldly about the way Nikulin reacts to Leonova, which becomes clearer when they dance onstage. Their first *Giselle* together was replete with this quality that's not found in real life, but feels more intensely real. Neither was hitherto known for their ballet blanc, yet the way they shed themselves to become Albrecht and Giselle was sublimely haunting. Nikulin, in particular, seemed to change completely: he is not vulnerable or self-effacing offstage. But as Albrecht, he is penitent and pitiable, on his knees and shielding his face out of shame for Giselle's death.

It is difficult to reconcile the artist Nikulin, who is capable of embodying that transcendent humility, with the man Nikulin, who used the rest of our meeting to commentate about the situation in Ukraine. At the time of this interview, following weeks of protests and overthrow of the pro-Russian government in Kyiv, Russian forces had just invaded Crimea. When asked for his take on the situation, the Ukraine-born Nikulin said, "There are lot of ethnic Russians in Crimea. Their names are Russian, they speak Russian, their families are Russian, and they feel Russian—as do I."

I pressed him to clarify whether he meant that the high number of Russians in Crimea justified the loss of human lives and the oppression of Crimean Tatars and Ukrainians. He pulled long drags of his cigarette in contemplation. "That's not what I said at all, is it? You writers always like to make up answers as you see fit," he said slowly, with a Slavic flatness of inflection. "I hate war. But I also hate riots, killing of police and protesters on both sides. There are Russian people in Ukraine who don't want to be part of it anymore. Isn't it better to let them just be their own country—or part of Russia?"

I pointed out that the Russian majority in Crimea is due to the Russian Empire's annexation of the Crimean Khanate in 1783, led by Prince Grigory Potemkin (better remembered as Catherine the Great's favorite). There followed a period of land seizures, religious and cultural oppression, and enslavement of the Tatar people, who refer to this time of history as the Black Century. The Russian Revolution of 1917 gave Crimean Tatars the opportunity to establish their independent government. The Bolsheviks responded by executing their leader; and Crimea was absorbed into the USSR, first as an autonomous Soviet republic, then as an oblast, and then as a part of Ukrainian SSR. Concomitantly, Soviet-engineered famines and forced deportation of hundreds of thousands of people—a genocide by all modern definitions—decimated most of the Tatars living in Crimea. In their place, Russians (and to a lesser extent, Ukrainians) moved in: today, Russians make up two-thirds of the population in Crimea, while Crimean Tatars only account for around 10 percent.

As I related this, Nikulin's face darkened. "I don't need history lesson. What percentage of population in your country are Indians? U.S. should give back their land to Indians before they say to Russia, give back Crimea to Tatars or Ukrainians." He ended the interview abruptly after this.

Requests to clarify his comments via email or phone went unanswered. In the meantime, Nikulin published and deleted a pro-Russian post on Twitter ("I am Russian. My art is Russian. I stand by Russia"), appearing to praise the Russian president's military invasion of Ukraine. The Paris Opéra management responded to requests with the statement that they take matters of international peace seriously and that they will investigate inflammatory remarks by their artists with due urgency.

Sasha didn't pick up the phone when I tried calling him at the boarding gate. Nor was he home when I arrived there around two in the morning. I took a shower and lay in bed; I was exhausted, but my mind was racing. During my flight, my phone had racked up texts from outraged company dancers demanding an explanation. One of them, who was Ukrainian by birth, said she felt as though she were physically assaulted by Sasha's comments. Laurent had left a cryptic, strangely expressionless voicemail asking me to call him back. All my calls to Sasha immediately went to voicemail.

For the second time in recent memory I thought of Nina and yearned to talk to her. I remembered us not as we last parted—her smugness as a newlywed and my coldness upon rising beyond where she could follow—but as children, when we'd trusted each other above anyone else. Back then, she could soothe me just by listening on the other end of the call. But I didn't deceive myself that this young Nina still existed. What I missed and wanted was someone long gone, not the adult Nina who was, by all accounts, efficiently carrying on her own life with her family.

The garbage truck went by, breaking apart the silence. In an hour or so, the street below would fill with the smell of fresh bread and the footsteps of early-morning joggers. I heard the lock turn and Sasha enter on unsteady feet. He paused at the entryway, and I imagined him taking a look at my suitcase and registering my presence. He went to the kitchen, drank a glass of water, and sank into the couch.

"Where have you been?" I said, walking out to the living room. He was lying on his stomach, hair draped over his face. Raising an arm toward me, he said, "Come here."

"What were you thinking, Sasha?" I said, standing with my arms crossed over my chest.

He repeated, "Come here, Natasha." When I didn't move, he sighed and turned to lie on his back. "You have always been such a hard woman."

"This isn't about me! This is about you saying crazy things—and for what? To sound contrarian? To show you're different?"

"I hardly need to *say* anything to show I'm *different*." He slurred his words, waving his arm around. "There are thousands of people who believe what I said. They're good people. You just don't get it. Now come here. I need you right now. Come hug me."

"No! Do you know what our colleagues are saying to us right now? To *me*? Laurent left a voicemail when I was on my flight. What did he say to you?"

Sasha seemed to sober up at Laurent's name. "He said I should take a leave of absence. He said it will be announced as voluntary. A break of about four months, or until the press cools down and moves on."

"Bravo! You've really done it. Supported a war, taken yourself off stage, and drunk while at it," I yelled.

"Look who's talking. You drink a lot, little bird. You think I don't notice? That's going to take *you* off stage, if you're not careful. Now, come here—this is the last time." When I didn't speak or move, he lowered his arm and said, "You cold-hearted bitch."

This was only the second time I'd ever heard him call someone a bitch. The first time was when we were driving to Olga's dacha that summer and he got into a fight with Dmitri. The image of Dmitri's contorted face flashed before my eyes. The shock and the pain. Without thinking, I rushed toward Sasha and slapped him hard across the head.

For a second, we both held our breaths, unable to believe what I'd done. Then things happened in a blur: he stood up and grabbed my wrist, and I pushed him away calling him vile names. He slapped me and I punched and kicked him wherever I could. He pinned me down to the floor, tore off my pants, and put his hand over my mouth. He buried his face between my legs but with a kind of vindictiveness, as if giving pleasure was a power he held over me. He moved up and thrust inside me until I came with involuntary release. At the same time, he shuddered and squeezed his eyes shut. He pressed himself away immediately and stumbled over to the couch, leaving me on the floor. After a while, I got up and went to bed alone.

When I opened my eyes, it was already afternoon. I listened for the sound of Sasha and realized that he'd left. From the bed I could see the first clear sky of the year, vivid blue with an underpaint of gold. The color of spring. But the sight deepend rather than consoled my hurt. I limped to the bathroom and forced myself to examine my body. There was a large purple bruise on my shoulder blade from Sasha shoving me onto the floor. It would take only a week to heal; it would be easy to hide in the meantime. But he'd broken some part of me beyond repair. To be fair, I wasn't just a victim. He had lost something since we met, a kind of wholeness. I didn't know the exact nature of this change, but I knew I was the catalyst. And I pushed him as hard as I pushed myself, even if I saw how ugly that made us. Just as we brought out the best in each other, we also brought out the worst in each other—we had turned each other into monsters.

I took a hot bath until pain stopped vibrating throughout my body. It was replaced with the calm certainty that I would leave Sasha. I would have to give him back the ring. I would stay at the apartment; Laurent would help Sasha find a new place. It would be awkward at first at work, but breakups were not uncommon within the same company, and it was fortunate that Sasha was taking a leave of absence. By the time he returned, the change would hardly draw notice. Yes, it was a shame that we'd announced the engagement and had our friends over to congratulate us—but as I became older, I no longer felt quite as embarrassed as I had before about any sort of mistake. Life was such that everything was a mistake; at the same time, nothing was a mistake.

I put on a coat and jeans and walked to Place des Vosges. It was sunny but still cold and damp in the shade. I sat near a fountain for a long time, and then meandered to the bar. When he saw me, Léon's eyes brightened.

"*Bonsoir*, Natasha. What do you feel like?" he said, wiping his hands on a towel.

"I feel like leaving Sasha. I feel . . ." I sat down on a stool and cradled my face in both hands. My cheeks tingled and my tongue was heavy and hot. It was one thing to decide this inside my head, and another to speak it out loud.

Léon walked around the bar to my side and wrapped me in his arms. He smelled like the woods after a rain—moss and mushrooms on a log, campfire smoke.

"What happened? Do you want to talk about it?" he asked. I shook my head, cradled in his arms.

"Do you still love him?"

"I don't know." I was remembering when I first saw Sasha in Varna, our teenaged energy barely contained by our skins. Then the overwhelming rush of our early years at Bolshoi flashed before my eyes. I thought of how he'd changed. How I'd changed.

"There isn't the same feeling I had when we fell in love. It's not that we're bored because we've been together too long. I think we broke each other," I said. "I do love him, but I didn't know it was such a base emotion."

Léon pulled a little away from me and met my eyes. "Let's go. I will show you something." At the same time, he waved at Henri at the other end of the bar. Henri was a Senegalese grad student with a penchant for white shirts and black glasses. He had just been promoted to manager, but still had no control over Léon as if they were equals. "I'm leaving early. Cover for me?" Léon said, unwrapping the apron from his waist. The manager threw his hands in the air, half frustrated and half resigned.

"Where are we going?" I asked as Léon led me out of the bar, a hand lightly placed on my back.

"I'm going to show you Paris."

"I have seen Paris—I've been living here for three years."

"You have not seen the Paris I see. The other side of the telescope." He smiled and pulled me by the arm to the curb, where a taupe Vespa was parked.

"Is this a scooter?" I asked.

"It's a motorcycle," he said.

"I'm pretty sure it's a scooter."

"It's an Italian motorcycle," he said, straddling the seat. "And I'm half Italian. Sit down and hold me close."

I swung my leg over the seat and locked my arms around his waist. And then we were off, weaving around Le Marais and passing by the glass-and-steel Centre Pompidou. We crossed the bridge in front of Notre Dame as the sun slipped softly below the skyline and twilight bloomed. At once, the sound of bells and flocks of pigeons rose up and dissolved into the atmosphere. The whole world looked submerged in a glass of rosé wine. We threaded our way through the throng of cars and pedestrians on the crosswalk, turning right on Quai Voltaire. Léon drove around the slow-moving cars and gained speed, whipping past the green stalls selling vintage books. As usual, a youthful crowd was gathered by the Latin Quarter. We pressed on to Saint-Germain-des-Près, to the soigné publishing houses, boutiques, and cafés. Within a few turns, the Eiffel Tower suddenly loomed large, glittering gold in the fast-falling night. Léon zoomed straight toward it and made a large circle at its base so that everything looked like a blur of light. We crossed a bridge back to the Right Bank and headed for the Arc de Triomphe, dodging the tangle of cars at the rotary. We passed more slowly next to a quiet park, a bit more English garden than the typical French, with dirty ponds and pale cherry blossoms shining in the darkness. "This is Parc Monceau. My first girlfriend lived near here," Léon said, turning his face slightly. He took a right and sped up steep inclines into Montmartre; the streets here were lined with extremely long stairs, and musicians played and sang on landings, as if to encourage out-of-breath climbers. A miniature cobblestone plaza with a carousel came into view, and he slowed the Vespa to a stop next to a bistro.

"We're here," he said, hopping off and giving me a hand. It burned a little memory into my palm; not a lot, not like Sasha did once—but it felt significant in its own way. I expected him to hold on, but as we walked away from the well-lit bars and restaurants, he let my hand drop.

"It's over here," he said as we entered a gated area with trees. There were some beaten-down benches here and there and people in jogging pants walking their dogs. Spring didn't seem to have reached this hidden park, and the shrubs were covered in damp brown leaves.

"*C'est joli*," I said.

"Just wait," he said, quickening his pace. "Here, this is what I wanted to show you."

It was a black tiled wall inscribed with hundreds of handwritten messages. Amid the white writing, there were little red pieces scattered about like confetti.

"Do you see Russian?" he asked me, and I pointed at one corner.

"This is called *Le mur des je t'aime. I love you* in languages from around the world."

"What are those red splashes?"

"Pieces of a broken heart. Evidently, they can be gathered to form a whole one."

"How fitting."

"I like finding the languages I know. It feels like someone is saying it to me," he said, meeting my eyes. "I never once heard my father say that to me. And I never said it to him."

"Me, too." I took a deep breath. I'd never wondered if Nikolai had said those words to me when I was a baby; I believed it ultimately wasn't worth brooding over an externality. Most people lived the life they were given, and very few people created their own lives. But I created my own *world.*

"You know, it's not true that men say *I love you* to deceive. Most people can't outright lie about it," I continued. "If you don't love someone, it's very difficult to say *I love you*. And if you do love someone, it's just as painful to remain silent. A heart can break into pieces trying to hold love in."

"Stay still," Léon said. He reached out a finger and gently tilted my head toward him. "Look at me."

I looked at him. He grabbed his camera from his messenger bag and took just a single shot. "That was the end of the roll," he muttered.

"I thought you were only going to take photos of me dancing," I said, flustered. I was always a little embarrassed to see my face in photos. I wasn't like Sasha and I didn't always feel beautiful.

"Just now when you were talking—you looked the way you do when you dance," he said, putting the camera back inside the bag. "Who were you thinking of?"

"Sasha. Of course, Sasha," I said, and I knew I wasn't going to leave him.

I'VE BEEN STAYING WITH NINA for a month, and it's that wistful time of year in late August, early September when everything attains a transparency. The summer holidays are over and Nina's family is returning. She implores me to stay as long as I like, but we both know there is no room for me. I agree to a last dinner together with everyone before returning to the Grand Korsakov. We cook together side by side in peaceful silence, our faces flushing from the steam. Nina puts extra care into every dish and makes an apple cake from scratch.

"Are you going to be okay?" she asks me while taking the cake out of the oven.

"I feel much better now. Are *you* going to be okay?"

She wipes her hands on her apron and looks at me square in the face. "Trying to be okay is ninety-five percent of life." She casts her eyes down and starts whipping up powdered sugar in a bowl. "You can't stay at a hotel forever. You need to get an apartment."

"I'm going to go back to France after *Giselle*. That's just around the corner," I say, chopping fresh dill. "I'll be fine."

After dinner, Nina stays with the kids and Andryusha volunteers to drop me off at the Grand Korsakov. I resist as much as possible; he has just gotten home from a long trip and I can easily take a cab. Nevertheless, Andryusha insists that it is the least he can do. He remains quiet while we drive. But when we stop in front of the hotel entrance, he clears his throat.

"Natasha, I know you're friends with Nina, but you're friends with me, too. Right?" He says.

"Of course, Andryusha," I say. "You're one of my oldest and dearest friends."

"So please tell me!" he shouts, then shuts his eyes and exhales. "Sorry, it would just mean a lot to me if you could tell me truthfully." He plows through my silence. "Is there something wrong with Nina? Has she told you about anything? Or about anyone?"

"What? No. Of course not." My voice quakes, and I wonder if that makes me sound outraged or guilty. "Nina? Never."

"Because you know, Natasha, I know things haven't been great lately, and she doesn't seem happy. But I still love her to death." Andryusha's voice trembles to match my own.

"And she loves you"—seeing Andryusha's eyes hungry for more, I continue—"to death. She hasn't used those exact words but I know her. Don't I?"

"Three children. Been together since we were sixteen. That's *life.*"

"I don't disagree! Andryusha, dear, I know you two will be okay. Nina loves you very much. I'll talk to her about it tomorrow if you want."

"You'll do that for me?" Andryusha looks up hopefully from under his brows, more like a sad bear than a principal dancer.

"Of course. Now go home—you must be exhausted."

As autumn flows, I settle into a quietly hopeful routine. I have fruit juice and kasha at the breakfast room before heading early to the studio. I work with my teachers starting at 11:00 a.m. In the early afternoon I take a lunch break—Nina's cooking has awakened my appetite—and head to the canteen to eat soup or a big salad. We resume rehearsing until 5:00 p.m. I sleep more or less well and haven't had any episodes of confusion, time slips, or delusion. The inflammation in my feet is now almost unnoticeable, and my ankles feel stable. And I'm pushing myself at every jump and turn and getting past the line of fear. Pointe work, which had been one of my strengths, has returned quickly, impressing even Vera Igorevna. Tae and I breeze through our duets with the connection and warmth of partners who have danced together for years.

Mid-October, I realize one morning that I haven't brought any coats in my suitcase. I think that I need to borrow one from Nina. The leaves have all decided overnight to turn gold and orange. It is suddenly freezing in the streets, the dressing room, and the hallway. Somehow the studio has managed to stay warm, as I note gratefully. After I've stretched and conditioned on my own for an hour, Sveta joins me for a barre and center. Later, Vera Igorevna walks in alone; TaeHyung is sick with a cold. We spend the rest of the afternoon rehearsing the Act I variation until even Vera Igorevna can't find fault with my toe hops. While we work, Dmitri stands by the open door for about fifteen minutes. He's known to shout corrections in any rehearsal, even the ones he's not leading—but he glares at me and moves on without a word.

At six in the evening, I pull on warm-up pants and jacket over my clothes and leave the studio. The sun is already below the skyline; just a few months ago, it was purple and mysterious outside at midnight. The air is chilly, dry, slightly peppery. I zip my jacket all the way up to my chin and walk to the curb to find a cab. Then I see a man walking briskly in my direction, which sends a shiver down my spine. I'm not sure if he's real—or if he's one of my imagined threats. From a distance, I can only tell that he has a slight build and is wearing a long coat. I turn around and rush back toward the artist entrance. I hear him call out, "Natalia!" I pick up my pace, and so does he.

"Natalia Nikolaevna, please wait," he shouts at my back. It occurs to me that he's unusually polite for a real or imagined threat. The voice is diffuse and reedy for a man's; if his throat were an instrument, it would be a recorder. I halt and turn around to face him.

"Who are you?" I ask the man, who is catching his breath with a hand around his waist. He's about sixty years old with gently thinned hair at the crown. His worn gabardine coat looks a little too big on his short frame, but his shoes and plaid scarf are of a nice quality. On one hand he holds a briefcase, and he extends the other toward me.

"I'm a friend of your parents." There are beads of sweat along his hairline, which transects the North Pole of his head like that of Renaissance ladies. When I don't accept his hand, it falls back bashfully by his side.

"My parents didn't have friends," I say—but even as the words leave my mouth, I feel as though I know his answer.

"My name is Pavel Golubev. I worked with your father in Sakhalin back in the day. We met your mother on vacation . . . I was very sorry to hear about her passing." He shifts his weight between his feet and grasps the handle of his briefcase with both hands. "I also wanted to tell you some things about your father."

Pavel sits with his hands on his knees, eyes skimming the white-draped table at the Grand Korsakov. On his high forehead, there is a large birthmark the color of dried blood. As he sips his tea his Adam's apple rolls up and down on his neck; it is so thin that the collar of his shirt hangs loose like a necklace despite being buttoned all the way to the top.

The more I stare at his every detail, the more Pavel hesitates. I'm beginning to think that I've scared him, the way he'll do everything in his power to look anywhere but at my eyes. I try a gentle tactic of asking Pavel about his own life. This works: he talks for a while about his wife—a nurse, who was widowed with a little son when they met. They didn't manage to have children of their own, but his stepson is like his own blood. That stepson recently had a baby girl, so Pavel is a grandfather—he explains, eyes still darting around the room but warming up nonetheless.

"So did Nikolai come to your wedding?" I ask, and Pavel shakes his head nervously.

"No, by that point we weren't really friends. I'd seen how he treated Anna, and it upset me."

And so Pavel begins telling his story. He met Nikolai at a logging camp in Sakhalin in the 1970s. Pavel was not made for the excruciating and dangerous labor of harnessing, sawing, felling, and transporting timber. But Nikolai took a liking to Pavel for some reason and protected him as much as possible. More than once, Pavel was standing in the way of a log that was rolling out of its harness and would have been instantly killed, had Nikolai not risked his own life and pushed him to safety. Nikolai was in every way Pavel's opposite. Pavel was city-born, short, soft-spoken and soft-handed; he didn't know how to do things that Nikolai handled efficiently, like tying a knot that never slipped or clearing the underbrush with an electric saw. In physical appearance Nikolai resembled a spruce, with blond hair and mossy beard that fluttered in the wind like lacy lichen on treetops.

Nikolai was sometimes charming and often generous, but he was also moody and difficult. ("I was definitely never moody and difficult, because someone like me couldn't afford to be," Pavel added.) Nikolai vacillated between believing that he was a nobody and that he was gifted and destined for greatness. The difference between these two states—perhaps even the paradoxical moments when he fervently believed *both*—drove Nikolai to the edge of sanity. He tried to hide that internal storm and act as if he accepted his position in life. It was what all the other men at the camp did—feeling some bitterness, of course, but also pride at their manly, Russian resignation. They were pleased to be martyred by fate among such dignified, barrel-chested compatriots. The men sensed that Nikolai wasn't quite like them—moreover, that Nikolai secretly felt *superior* to them. This earned their distrust and disdain, and they laughed at him behind his back. Nikolai was a loner, even compared to other loggers who had sought out this island at the end of the earth for a reason.

The one person who didn't scorn him was Pavel. They became friends, although calling it that would have made both of them uncomfortable and embarrassed: they were two men who watched out for each other in a precarious ecosystem, like the symbiotic relationship between a wolf and a bear who hunted together. They ate their meals in companionable silence, only broken when either one was unusually cheerful or mournful. Perhaps once or twice, Nikolai told Pavel about his father, who began his day with a shot of vodka and ended it by beating his son. One night, his father hit Nikolai so badly that he passed out. When he awakened, he discovered that the hearing in his right ear was permanently diminished. His stepmother, an unhappy woman with deep grooves along her forehead and the sides of her mouth, did everything to protect her own children and nothing to protect Nikolai.

When Nikolai was just old enough to pass for a youth of seventeen or so, he ran away and took a train going east. He had no money, no family, and little schooling, which qualified him for coal mines, slaughterhouses, or logging camps. This isolated and perilous place was not as bad as other ones where he could have ended up. Although the loggers didn't remark on it or even truly notice it, there was beauty in the forest shrouded in sea fog. The coast was not visible from the camp, but they smelled its expansive scent rolling inland. Unable to see that there was something better out there, they were nonetheless touched by it in a molecular way. On good days, when the work flowed without a hitch and the weather was clear, Nikolai sat on a tree stump and wiped his brow with a faint smile on his face. But when there was a downpour, or the wheels of a truck got stuck in the mud, or someone made a costly mistake that sent a good tree crashing into pieces, his eyes glazed over and lost their brilliance as if his soul was receding deep into him.

If there was something that brought Nikolai out of that abyss, it was music. He had the knowledge and love of music that someone of much more education and wealth would have; Pavel never discovered how exactly, but it seemed that Nikolai had a capacious mind for certain things that interested him. A particular passion was Maria Callas, who had just perished alone in her Paris apartment at age fifty-three. When the news of her death reached Nikolai in his room on the other side of the earth, he listened to his LP of Callas for weeks on end. He only had a handful of records, but that did not frustrate him—he seemed to relish the flavor of obsession. When he wasn't listening to music, he read books, for he rarely did both at the same time.

Nikolai and Pavel had been working at the camp for many years when they flew out to Petersburg on a holiday. Without speaking these thoughts aloud, they tacitly knew their first priority was to meet women, the rarest resource that couldn't be found at the camp's general store. As soon as they left Sakhalin, female presence overwhelmed and intoxicated them. The flight attendant smelled extraordinary with not only her powdery perfume but also her not-unpleasant sweat and hair oils and even the mustiness of her pantyhose. Her odor was so sharp in their nostrils, they battled the cognitive illusion that she was the most beautiful woman in the world, which belied clear visual evidence. Once in Petersburg, they checked into a modest hotel and went for a walk. They decided they would need some new, decent clothes to present a respectable appearance in front of these city women. So they walked into a store, and there they met Anna.

Anna was one of those barefaced, penniless twenty-year-olds who looked as plain as black bread in certain moments and glorious in others. She had wide-set eyebrows and large, gentle eyes, and a short and straight Greek nose, encircled by the smooth, rather generous semicircle of a jawline. She wore wispy, rounded bangs and an expression of limpid melancholy, like clear little raindrops clinging to leaves and the windowpane. In some angles she appeared artless to the point of gullibility. In others, she looked as poetic as the young Zhanna Prokhorenko in *Ballad of a Soldier*, that Cannes winner about a Russian hero on leave from World War II. Like Shura in that film, Anna would fall in love at the slightest provocation from fate. She had openheartedness, sweetness, and even ardor—a robust combination that struck Nikolai not like an arrow but like a club. ("So he truly loved her?" I ask, and Pavel takes a gulp from his fourth cup of tea. "Let me put it this way," he says slowly. "Anna transformed Nikolai like water changed into wine. And that is not something that can be faked.")

Naturally, Pavel made himself rare during the rest of the vacation. He met other women and courted them ineffectually. By the end of the leave, he was surprised by his yearning to return to the camp. While he wasn't fully competent there, he didn't feel as inadequate as he did in the city. His loneliness was more bitter when surrounded by the vivid proof of everything he lacked. Soon, the camp with its familiar evergreen scent, the sea fog, and routine dangers welcomed him home, and he sighed in relief. When the next leave rolled around eighteen months later, Pavel went to visit his aunt in Khabarovsk, only 610 kilometers away. It took two days by bus, ferry, and train to get there, and he caught a stomach flu immediately upon arrival. Nonetheless, it was a profitable trip, since at the emergency clinic he met a nice nurse. Nikolai, of course, went to visit Anna and his baby daughter in Petersburg. He flew to the old capital in high spirits, and returned looking suitably downcast. This depression lasted for weeks on end. Even when he was talking to Anna, he seemed withdrawn into his familiar abyss.

At first, Pavel thought his friend simply missed his sweetheart and daughter. But as time passed, it became clear to Pavel that Nikolai was deeply anxious. He kept avoiding calls from Anna, and Pavel was often in the awkward position of having to explain to her that he was unavailable. Anna hung up sounding increasingly forlorn. Her suffering touched Pavel: he told Nikolai that he would no longer lie or smooth things over. Anna was the mother of Nikolai's child; she deserved honesty and respect. When Pavel announced this, his friend was lying long on his bunk bed, fidgeting with a length of thin rope. He held it up and looked sideways at Pavel.

"You see what this is?" Nikolai asked. Pavel saw that it was a knot, possibly one that Nikolai had taught him patiently once, although it was hard to tell from a distance.

"I don't know what it is, Nikolai. Some sort of figure eight knot? Anyway, stop changing the subject," Pavel said, sitting down on an unpainted wooden chair.

"Guess again," Nikolai said.

"A variation of a butterfly knot?" Pavel answered. Nikolai shook his head and fixed his gaze back on the rope.

"It's a Gordian knot," he said. "Do you know what that means?"

Pavel shook his head, irritated and clearly wanting this knot lesson to end. But Nikolai carried on as if he didn't notice.

"Thousands of years ago in Greece, there was a poor peasant named Gordius. One day, he traveled to a city on an ox cart. He didn't know that there had been a prophecy in this place that their new king would arrive on an ox cart. So the people of the city made him their king. In gratitude, Gordius dedicated his cart to the god Zeus and tied it up with a knot so intricate that no one could untie it. It was the greatest mathematical problem in the known world. Then there was another prophecy, that whoever could untie that knot would rule Asia. Hundreds of years later, Alexander the Great passed through the city. He heard the prophecy—and rather than trying to untie the knot he just cut through it with his sword. And so, he came to rule Asia," Nikolai said. "A Gordian knot is one that cannot be untied. It's irreversible."

"That's all well and good, my fellow," Pavel said, shaking his head and crossing his elbows over his chest. "So don't try to solve a problem, just cut it off? That's the important lesson?"

"No. The really important lesson is"—Nikolai got up from the bed—"that *every* knot eventually becomes a Gordian knot. At some point, you can't untie it—you have to cut it off." He tossed the rope onto his bed and walked out of the room.

After that day, Nikolai no longer made any pretenses to hide that he was leaving Anna. Without hearing a clear explanation, Pavel intuited that his friend did not and could not feel up to the task of being a father. Nikolai had learned nothing of love or warmth from his family. Everything he knew of tenderness, he'd felt instinctively toward Anna. But like a male animal that gets along with its mate only until the litter is born, Nikolai was deeply agitated. Some of these males turn violent toward their own young; this was what Nikolai was afraid of becoming himself. He chose the other path of running away.

A few months later, Pavel arrived at work and discovered that Nikolai had quit. He'd left nothing behind—no note, no token, no new address or phone number. Although their friendship had noticeably cooled for a while, Pavel was nonetheless hurt by this severance. After all that time—watching out for each other, eating their lunches on tree stumps, listening to records, borrowing each other's equipment or tobacco or other small comforts—didn't that merit some sort of farewell or leave-taking? Then he realized that Anna had had a much higher claim on Nikolai. Having been raised by people without duty, Nikolai thought he also didn't owe anything to anyone. Only later did he hear, through the foreman of his team, that Nikolai had gone to a camp near Vladivostok on the mainland.

Although Nikolai had made no effort to sustain their friendship, Pavel felt his absence greatly. There was an emptiness to the daily motions of the camp, and Pavel sensed himself slipping, as though walking through mud after a rain. He remembered the widowed nurse in Khabarovsk, with whom he'd gone on a few dates. Most women of Pavel's own age did not find him an attractive partner. The widowed nurse, a little older but shapely in a full-figured way, didn't turn her nose up at him. It was not that she didn't see him clearly, or that she thought herself past her prime. It was that she had experienced loss and became kinder toward others as a result. But when Pavel called her and said he was thinking about moving to Khabarovsk, she said she was soon transferring to a hospital in Petersburg.

Pavel said, "Oh." A bit of moisture rose to his eyes against his will. "I wish you all the best."

"Thank you," she said softly. Then the line went quiet, and Pavel pressed his ear into the phone to hear her calm breathing on the other end. So that would be the end of that, and he would go on alone—only slightly more so than before. Then the nurse spoke again.

"Why don't you move to Petersburg also?"

And so, Pavel took a leap of faith and moved to Peter's old city at the end of his contract. He had been logging for years, and since there wasn't an abundance of opportunities to spend money in Sakhalin, he had saved up a tidy sum. He bought a small apartment for him, his now wife, and his stepson. His wife got him a job working as the facilities manager for the hospital, which was essentially a glorified handyman, but also significant because in less than ten years he was overseeing all the maintenance of this government-funded medical center. In a relatively short time, he had gone from a lonely logger on a wild eastern island to a husband and a father with a secure job that many would envy. Sometimes Pavel lay in bed at night and the images of the trees and the sea fog flashed before his closed eyes, and he thought that it all felt like a long dream.

There was just once when this distant memory abruptly collided into his reality. It was early into his marriage and he was walking to work after an off-site lunch. Across a nearly empty plaza, he saw the outline of someone familiar—which was odd, because he still knew so few people in Petersburg. As she came into focus, he recognized the plain yet sometimes beatific face of Anna Leonova. She was pushing a stroller with an empty, soulless expression caused by profound and ceaseless sorrow. Although none of this was his fault, Pavel felt accountable for her pain. He had been there when Nikolai and Anna met. He had sometimes covered up for Nikolai's avoidance and weaknesses.

Pavel's wife happened to have a good friend who was a makeup artist at Mariinsky, a young woman named Tanya. This makeup artist happened to tell Madame Golubeva that there was some difficulty in the costume department due to an unexpected departure of a seamstress. When Pavel heard this over the dinner table, he arranged for Anna, "a talented seamstress and a young mother in need of aid," to secure this position. Anna thanked him sincerely and then disappeared into work and childrearing. After that, Pavel did not hear from Anna or Nikolai for many years. It wasn't as deliberate as one might think, at least on Pavel's part. He felt that he'd done his best to help the former lover of his former friend, and life continued to hurtle forward for them in different directions, as if they were two trains that ran on parallel tracks near a country station for a very brief spell.

Three decades passed. Pavel now had time to read with his breakfast and tea before heading to work. Usually it would be a novel or a book of poetry, since he wasn't all that fond of newspapers. At the hospital, his colleagues respectfully addressed him as Pavel Ivanovich, almost as if he were a doctor. Afterward, his wife prepared him a hot meal and a hotter water bottle against his frequent indigestion. One evening as they sat lingering over the last remains of dinner (Pavel suffered from severe acid reflux, and she had forbidden him to do anything except remain absolutely upright for a few hours after eating), Madame Golubeva said, "There was a strange patient at work today. Someone crazy."

Pavel's wife and even Pavel himself encountered many insane patients over the years. So he'd had the chance to observe that the line between sanity and insanity was so thin as to be invisible: like lines in certain mathematical formulas, it definitely helped to explain the world, but was not actually real. Thus Pavel felt mostly compassion for these poor souls. Besides, they reminded him of what he now took for granted (safe home, relative health, loving wife); and sometimes they were even entertaining, not in the way of truly funny things but at least like a good, solid feud between famous people. Pavel sipped his tea, asking, "Well, what is it this time?"

"This man, who rambled and couldn't say anything that made sense, didn't know what city he was in or who the president was . . ." she said somewhat nervously. "We made him sign his name for the discharge papers, and he scribbled *Pavel Ivanovich Golubev.*"

iv

A SILENCE FALLS BETWEEN PAVEL AND ME AND INTERRUPTS HIS STORY, like a waiter pointedly clearing the table to rush the last guests. The candle between us has long burned out. I scan the room and see that we're the only patrons remaining; at the bar area, servers in their white shirts and black bow ties are whispering sullenly. It's a few minutes to midnight, the closing hour. I'm certain that Igor Petrenko has instructed his staff not to disturb me under any circumstances, and I'm briefly warmed by gratitude and fondness for the manager.

"I'm afraid I've talked too much and exhausted you," Pavel says, although it is *he* who looks in need of rest.

"I am so sorry." I clasp my hands over my mouth. "I lost track of time and didn't even suggest we order food."

"Not to worry. I'm sure my wife left some dinner for me at home," Pavel says weakly. "It is a lot for you to take in."

"I want to hear the rest of the story. But you're right." I motion at the bar, and one of the waiters dashes over. I write down my room number on the check and he bows, grateful to be finishing his shift. "It is so much for one day. I feel quite dizzy, Pavel Ivanovich."

"I could come back here tomorrow evening at six."

"Will you please? I would be so thankful." I rise, gathering my things, and Pavel also grabs his briefcase and his coat. We shake hands again, and I watch him disappear into the revolving door before going up to my room.

I have to force myself to take a hot bath before collapsing onto the bed. I fall asleep like someone losing consciousness, dreaming of black birds swirling around in an amethyst sky. Then that tornado turns into a dark waterfall as the birds drop in unison. I also lose the ground beneath my feet and fall into the depths of the earth.

Morning slips through my window and I wake up with a start. I lie in bed for twenty minutes, unable to move. I will myself to move just a finger first. After that, I test my strength by lifting an eyelid. One by one, my body clicks into place until I can crab walk to the shower. The blast of hot water yet again performs a small miracle. I towel off with more energy, moisturize, put on a clean leotard and warm-up clothes, and eat a little breakfast before heading to the theater. Dancers learn early on how to compartmentalize. If the teacher criticizes you in front of everyone and then asks you to do something perfectly without your usual mistakes, you compartmentalize. If you fall during dress rehearsal and have to go onstage for the performance, you compartmentalize. If you're dancing with a partner you loathe, you compartmentalize. Those who can't steel their nerves, who put their feelings before their dance, cannot succeed in this world. I always put dance before my feelings because without dance, no emotions in my life would have been worth anything. At least, that's what I believed until now.

But as I go through barre and center with Sveta, I find myself waning. The energy it takes to not think of Pavel's story last night is robbing my body of its strength. After petit allegro, I ask for a water break and crumple down on the floor as Sveta gazes down worriedly. Then Vera Igorevna marches in with a disturbing expression, which I haven't seen since Nina struck out at the second round of the Varna competition. She has the look of a parent whose twenty-year-old cat had to be put down yet cannot sob in front of the children, who think it's at a farm or some kind of feline resort.

"Tae cannot come to rehearsal," she announces sharply. "He just called and it turns out he has *pneumonia*." She pronounces the last word as if, instead of a common respiratory illness, Tae has something alternative and ignominious like a pet boa constrictor or a foot fetish.

Sveta's mouth falls open. I say what we're both thinking. "Forget about rehearsal! The premiere is six days away. He'll be bedridden for at least two weeks—more realistically he'll be out for a month."

Vera Igorevna pauses to take the biggest breath I've ever seen anyone take. Then she says, "True. Dmitri Anatolievich is aware of this and is finding a replacement as we speak."

Most of the time, medical emergencies don't create this much of a rupture. There are alternates who have been practicing the role silently like mimes in the corners of studios; also, most of the in-house dancers have partnered one another for many seasons, so switching out for another partner isn't going to shake anyone to the core. But I was out for two years, and this was supposed to be a big comeback performance. I have been avoiding the posters around the city but know that they have been advertising my return with the words *Natalia Leonova Is Giselle*. This pressure upon pressure, a hundred-kilometers-under-the-earth's-crust pressure, makes Tae's unavailability so troublesome.

But aside from simply being taken off guard, I'm now forced to reckon with the more pragmatic reason for my pairing with Tae. Although I have made strides in regaining my technique and stamina, the truth is that I'm still far from my best self. Sveta has assured me that my not-best towers over most dancers' absolute best, but I find even this answer revealing. To not disappoint fans, I need an exceptionally strong partner who can make up for my weaknesses with stable lifts and supported turns in pas de deux, and who can even offload some pressure on me with dazzling solos of his own. And among Mariinsky's ranks, Tae is the only dancer with comparable star quality as well as selfless partnering. Dropping in another male dancer with me now, one slightly less virtuosic or even physically strong, can result in a hundred different things going wrong.

When I beg to be excused from rehearsing alone, Vera Igorevna gives a curt nod. I make my way back to the hotel and lie in bed for a few hours. So I won't be able to dance again, after all. Tears start to pool in my eyes and I realize I'd believed that this was going to work out, even when I was sick in mind and body. Deep inside, I had begun preparing for *Giselle* the moment Dmitri sat next to me in the Summer Garden and offered me the role.

At a quarter to six, I take the elevator down to the hotel restaurant. I'm a little surprised and touched to see Pavel waiting for me already, his coat and briefcase stacked neatly by his side. I make sure to order food and drinks as soon as I take a seat.

"How are you feeling?" Pavel asks shyly.

"I'm well," I say, and then quickly shake my head. "Actually, it's been difficult. But I would be grateful if you could finish your story—about the patient who signed your name."

Pavel nods and picks up the story from yesterday.

PAVEL WAS STUNNED WHEN HIS wife told him about this strange patient, an imposter. He asked her if she'd found out anything else about him. She said she couldn't; it was a busy day, and she had patients with life-threatening conditions all around. And she was only handling his discharge, glancing at his form for a split second. Perhaps the deranged patient just happened to have the exact same name as her husband.

The next day at work, Pavel used his connections (the hospital's systems engineer had owed him a favor for a reason that both men had already forgotten) to pull up information about a patient who was possibly named Pavel Ivanovich Golubev. It returned zero results. He tried using his own birthdate—and that came up blank, too. Finally, he tried looking up all the male patients discharged from the hospital the previous day and found an entry for one Nikolai Konstantinov. Pavel's heart was pounding in his ears as he clicked open his record. No photo. There was a birthdate—but Pavel couldn't remember his friend Nikolai's. A long list of treatments over the course of almost twenty years. It was only the next page, with the doctor's notes from the very first visit, that confirmed who this man was: patient (31) with right lower leg amputation following workplace accident where patient attempted to save another logger from a runaway log. (See transferred records from Naval Clinical Hospital, Vladivostok.) Patient experiencing severe pain in amputated leg suggesting central sensitization and somatosensory cortex damage. Symptoms of other specified and unspecified bipolar disorders and paranoia present. Family status unknown. Address unknown.

Pavel clicked open the transferred records, which showed that Nikolai's accident happened only a year after he moved to the camp near Vladivostok. He shut down the record and thanked the systems engineer, trying to hide that he was dizzy and nauseated from shock.

Nikolai was living on the streets, evidently only admitted to the hospital when he was having an especially bad episode. Unless he was sick again, there would be no way to find him. Even if there was a way, what could Pavel do? Nevertheless, Pavel found himself staring intently at older men whenever he was outside, looking for the swish of now-gray beard and wild eyes.

One evening, Pavel came out of the Metro at Vosstaniya Square, on the way to see a contractor for the hospital's ventilation repair. The thick, slate-colored cloud cover, which had oppressed the city all day, was rolling up slightly at the horizon so that a burst of pink twilight silhouetted the two-story rotunda of the Metro station. That lifted Pavel's eyes a little higher, which so often naturally found their resting place somewhere near the pavement. To the east, Nevsky Prospekt turned cheap and unsavory, but to the west stretched the fashionable part of the boulevard, which he hadn't much visited in the past thirty-odd years. Beautiful cafés and restaurants were overflowing with *zapadniki* and wealthy young Russians in slim-fitting clothes and designer belts. There was the Grand Korsakov Hotel with its magnificent Art Nouveau facade and bellhops dressed in stiff red costumes. Several blocks farther out, shining in the sorbet light, would be Passage, the celebrated pre-Revolution department store. There in the glass-roofed galleries, Pavel had once spent half a month's wages on a new winter coat alongside his former friend. He'd then inwardly wondered whether this coat was too expensive. Now he thought that it was as costly as anything else in his life, but not because of the money.

As Pavel lowered his eyes and picked up his pace to get out of the chaotic area in front of the station, he noticed a large, gray heap of a man in a wheelchair. Under normal circumstances, Pavel would not have been able to recognize him. It was only that he had just been thinking of that first day in the city, and those remembrances of youth allowed him to see that this vagabond was his old friend Nikolai.

Pavel ran to him. "Nikolai! It's me!" he cried out. Nikolai's eyes were distant and unfocused, as if Pavel weren't standing right in front of him. "It's me," Pavel said again, his voice quiet and shaking. The truth was that he was afraid of Nikolai, the baggy leg of his pants where his right calf should have been, and the prodigious smell. But despite his fear, Pavel laid a hand on his friend's elbow. Nikolai shuddered. His pupils opened and narrowed like the aperture of a camera, focusing on Pavel.

"Pavel Ivanovich Golubev," Nikolai said slowly, sounding as though his mouth were full of rusted steel marbles. "Sakhalin."

Pavel nodded and clasped both his hands around Nikolai's. "That's exactly right, Nikolai. I didn't know you were here in Piter, my fellow . . ." There was so much that they needed to say that there really wasn't anything they could say. At the same time, Pavel remembered that he was already late to the meeting with the contractor.

"Nikolai, I have to run to a meeting. Will you be here in an hour? Please wait for me and we'll have dinner together and talk," he said.

Nikolai shook his head. The eyes had already become unfocused, as if the effort of recognizing Pavel exhausted him.

"My friend, just stay here. I will be quick—it's just that we have to fix the ventilation at the hospital—quite an urgent project . . ."

Nikolai said something a little odd that sounded like "blame birds." Pavel realized that his friend's once brilliant mind was flickering out like those fluorescent lamps at the hospital with several fat flies trapped in the frosted glass case. He glanced at his watch, the one given to him by his wife for their twenty-fifth anniversary.

"I'm sorry, Nikolai. Please, please stay here, okay?" Pavel said, backing away toward Ligovsky Prospekt. He kept his eyes on Nikolai as long as he possibly could without bumping into the Romani fortune-tellers and teenage hooligans milling around the station. When he finally crossed the street to Ligovsky, Nikolai shouted in his direction: "Anna!" A second later, Pavel thought he heard, "Natasha!" Before Pavel could turn back, the evening crowd obscured the man in the wheelchair like a rock being submerged by a rising tide.

"SO THAT WAS THE LAST time you saw Nikolai?" I ask, and Pavel nods with downcast eyes. "By the time I ran back to the Metro station, he was gone. I've been keeping an eye out on the hospital admissions, and asked friends in the area. No one has seen him," he says. "I tried to reach out to your mother. We had lost touch for many years, but I thought she deserved to know about him. My wife contacted her old friend Tanya, who let us know she'd sadly passed just days before."

I say nothing, and Pavel sniffles a bit. It is past 9:00 p.m., and I feel desperate to process everything alone in my room. I signal the waitstaff, and one of them hurries to put the check on the table. As I jot down my room number, Pavel gathers up his things and rises.

"Pavel Ivanovich, whatever I can say to thank you would be inadequate," I murmur, also standing up and leading the way to the exit.

"May I ask just one last question?" I say, and Pavel nods.

"That coat you're wearing. Is that the coat you bought with Nikolai? And the one Anna tailored for you?"

Pavel nods, flushing and pulling self-consciously on the lapel. That's how I know that it isn't just Nikolai he is mourning: it is also Anna, with whom he fell in love, and the life he may have had with her.

After saying goodbye to Pavel, I lie in bed, thinking of the man in the wheelchair. I saw him after Nina's wedding, in front of the Metro station in Vosstaniya Square. But I don't think that could've been Nikolai: if his lower leg had been missing, I think I would have remembered that detail. Making this problem immeasurably difficult is the fact that I've never seen a picture of Nikolai.

Pavel said that Nikolai muttered something strange—blame birds. *Korit' ptits*. It reminds me of those dreams I have of the swirling tower of birds. Did he also see them—and did they make him lose his mind?

The dawn arrives before I have slept an hour straight, but I don't feel tired. It's as if my body knows I need it to not fail me this day—indeed, for most of my life, this was my secret and rare gift. As soon as it's decent enough for a phone call, I ring Sveta. She picks up quickly, as if she, too, had trouble sleeping.

"Sveta, let's not do class this morning," I say. She begins to protest that the performance must continue; Dmitri will find an alternate partner for me; we've come too far to give it all up now. I tell her that there's something more important I must do today, and that I need her to come with me.

"It's been a rough couple of days. Are you sure you want to do this right now?" Sveta asks, standing in her prim black outfit of turtleneck sweater, slim trousers, and a hip-length cape. Her hands sheathed in elbow-length gloves grasp the top handle of her purse like an armored knight holding the reins of his horse.

"I used to spy on you from upstairs as you walked in here," I say as we cross the ancient courtyard. "I thought you looked so beautiful and glamorous. You were the first representation of that world for me."

The concrete slabs of the walkway are broken in places, and the apple trees that had lined each side have been cut down. Even though the day is not cold, I reflexively cup my elbows.

"These buildings were never anything to look at, but they've really not maintained them at all," I say accusingly as we slip through the entrance—but I feel my hypocrisy as someone who has only returned after more than a decade.

"Well, they're going to demolish it in spring. Most of these *khrushchevka* have been torn down already. Not a lot of these left in the city."

We climb the stairs to the fifth floor in silence. Once we stand in front of the door, Sveta fishes out a key from her purse and unlocks it. Without saying so, we both wait for fresh air to penetrate the apartment for a few minutes. I have to fight the urge to say to Sveta "I'm afraid." She understands me and slips into the open door so that I can simply follow her.

Everything is exactly as I remember except older and in worse shape. The lace curtains in the kitchen have become stiff and yellow like plaque. I grimly recognize their companions, the matching eyelet covers on the TV and the sideboard—frilly bonnets on sheepishly aged furnishings. I'm amazed to still encounter the sofa that was at home for as long as I could remember, the same one that I slept on those first months of entering the corps de ballet of Mariinsky. Originally a vivid but lifeless green of billiard tables, it has faded to a brown of rotten pears. Once I've become accustomed to the sameness, I also realize that someone has taken care to put away the little things that would have been left lying around—the cups of half-drunk tea, a sweater taken off in the middle of the day, her sewing kit.

"Thank you for straightening it up, Sveta," I say, and she nods.

"I don't know why she didn't use the money I sent her. I always took care." I sit on the sofa and fold my arms around me. "Even after we stopped talking. I made sure she had plenty."

"Your mother was a lot like you," Sveta says dryly. "Prideful." She goes to the window and cracks it open, and a gust of autumn air rushes inside. She comes back and sits next to me.

"Did she tell you what happened?" I ask.

Sveta nods. Then she says, "God, you're making me want to smoke, and I quit forty years ago."

We sit in silence for a few more minutes before she speaks again. "You probably felt that your mother was unfair to you—and to Sasha. But as it turns out, she was right. That Sasha was a terrible man. Honestly, I'm not surprised. He always had the look of *those* men who destroy lives, either their own or others'. It's not a matter of ego or talent. Nina's husband, Andrei, was never like that."

"Sveta, please." I moan, and she softens.

"Okay, I will stop." She gets up with sudden vigor and starts rooting around in the kitchen. "Do you want some tea?"

"Sveta." I come up next to her as she flies open the pantry doors. "Who cares about Andrei. I mean, I do generally . . . But right now I want to know—what was Nikolai like?"

It takes a moment for Sveta to realize to whom I'm referring. She sighs and slowly closes the pantry. "I never met him, as you can probably guess. He'd already left by the time your mother and I became friends. All I know is what Annoushka told me."

"You've never seen a photo?"

She shakes her head. "Why would your mother show me a photo if you've never even seen it? I'm sorry for not being very helpful. But my dear girl, why are you asking these questions about your father all of a sudden?"

So I tell Sveta about how Pavel came to meet me the other day and told me about Nikolai, and how I want to find him. For that, I would need to know what he looks like, and this apartment is probably the only place in the world to have a photo of Nikolai, if such a thing even exists. Sveta's face goes through all the phases of shock, fascination, doubt, and determination that I've gone through, only in a few minutes instead of a few days. She suggests that she tackle the living room and the kitchen (perhaps an odd place for a memento, but basically Mama's office).

I take the bedroom with its heavy wardrobe and chest of drawers, both of which I find promising. They are packed with old, faded T-shirts and pants that have lost their shape after many washes. I don't recognize most of them; I haven't seen her much since leaving home. What feels most familiar is their scent. I run my fingers over the fabric and close my eyes, and I feel as though Mama and I are lying in bed together, her hand stroking my head. I'm flooded with the deep fear of her and the equally deep desire to please her. And love that is so absolute that it's crushing—from me to Mama, then from Mama to me, like the light that passes back and forth between stars. I bury my face in her moth-eaten sweaters and let them soak up my tears. Memories that I haven't thought of in years suddenly fill my mind. After Sveta announced I got accepted to Vaganova, I ran outside the building. Mama was standing there in the sun, short and soft and round, with a certain dark look, even though she was dressed in light blue—like a black bear. Her face was red and damp, and even at a young age my heart ached, wondering how long she'd been waiting for me in the heat. I locked my arms around her middle and shouted, "I made it, I did it for you!" Then we went to get *stakanchik* ice cream, which we ate standing at a kiosk. We didn't have money for such treats back then, and the rich, expansive creaminess, slightly softened from the heat, was nothing short of a miracle. What I felt then was the purest happiness I've ever known. And the purest love I've ever known or will know.

Then crushing guilt like a tsunami knocks the breath out of my lungs. I don't understand how I could've thought I had any right to blame her. Animal cries escape my throat before I get a chance to muffle my mouth. I weep calling for her, twisting fistfuls of fabric in my hands, until Sveta finally steps in and envelops me in her arms. She suggests we leave and come back at a later point, but I insist I can calm down and do this. If there's anything I've learned, it's that life is so short and death so permanent—and I want to find out everything I can about Nikolai.

We resume the search, pulling out all of Mama's belongings one by one. Yet I discover nothing of Nikolai's, no threadbare men's shirt or an old Soviet passport, let alone a photo. I didn't think of Mama as a sentimental type, so this is not entirely shocking, but I'm nonetheless disappointed. I look under the bed one last time and discover only kitten-size balls of dust.

"I didn't find anything, did you?" I ask hopefully, walking into the living room. Sveta is sitting on the floor in front of the sideboard, putting a mountain of things back one at a time.

"No, nothing to do with him, although I did find this cute photo of you from your first *Nutcracker* at Vaganova." She sighs, handing me a picture frame. I didn't even know that Mama took this photo from that performance. I'm in arabesque wearing my Little Masha costume, holding the hand of a boy who played the Nutcracker Prince.

"I was so mad I was cast B and Nina was cast A," I say, sitting down next to her. "Unbelievable."

"Here, I also found these." Sveta passes me a thick black dossier that looks something like a decade's worth of tax documents. I open it, imagining old bank statements, medical records, maybe even letters from Nikolai or my mother's parents. Instead, the file contains clippings of every interview, review, or profile that's ever been written about me, starting from when I first entered Mariinsky. The last piece about my retirement from Paris Opéra is dated just a week before she passed away. Inexplicably, there is a frowny face doodled in blue ink next to that headline. Mama hadn't notated any of the other articles—the good ones announcing my Moscow Grand Prix or promotion to prima ballerina, for example—with an equivalent smiley face. I imagine her studying the accompanying photo of my last performance before the injury, carefully cutting out the article, and drawing in that frowny face.

"Let me help you put stuff back," I say, wiping away tears. Sveta pretends to be busy storing away some old LP records. There are not many, and one of them catches my eyes. It is indeed a picture—and although it's not of Nikolai, I recognize his presence like a detective recognizes fingerprints. I pick up the 1964 recording of the Paris Opéra's *Carmen*, Maria Callas staring resolutely out of the cover.

MARIA CALLAS, LA DIVINA, PRIMA donna assoluta. When she made her Paris Opéra debut in 1958 (singing her signature "Casta Diva" from Bellini's *Norma*), she wore couture and a million dollars' worth of jewelry. In certain high registers, she could make the audience members' shirts tremble as if from the tremor of an earthquake. But her extraordinary voice declined unusually early—when she had barely passed thirty. By the time she reached forty, her career was effectively finished. No one could figure out why, although there were many guesses: her drastic slimming, or the overuse of her voice at the beginning of her career, or improper technique. Then her lover Aristotle Onassis left her to marry Jacqueline Kennedy, in plain view of the world. Callas broke off contact with her family, too, so that she eventually became quite alone and without the biggest love of her life: singing. At the time of her death, it was reported that the cause of it was a heart attack. Only decades later, it became known that Callas had a rare disease that attacked the connective tissues, muscles, and ligaments, including her heart—and the vocal cords.

Recorded at age forty, the 1964 studio album of *Carmen* is the only time she sang the opera in its entirety. She never got to perform it onstage.

THERE WAS A TIME WHEN I listened to only *Carmen* obsessively for weeks. It was because of Dmitri's one-man performance, in which he danced Carmen, Don José, and all the other roles himself. If I had a choice in the matter, I would have resisted being so enraptured by him, but I couldn't help being drawn. That evening—the music, dance, stage lights, the audience sitting in the dark, and everything—had been perfection; it was truly one of the few hours in a lifetime that made all the other hundreds of thousands of hours meaningful. And maddeningly, I hadn't even been the one dancing.

Soon after that, Laurent called me to Paris and I forgot about Dmitri. My world expanded even beyond his reach, and I had plenty of other things to occupy my mind. There was my bone-fracture injury, which forced me to sit out most of my second season in Paris. Piecing myself back together psychologically and physically was a long and unpredictable process. And when I returned, I was changed. I danced both better and worse than before. I knew what part was better: I was dancing less to *please* others, so my presence was free and genuinely my own. Young children are like this before formal instruction both refines and ruins them. Among professionals, only very few dancers are so self-possessed. Sylvie Guillem was like this. Among the men, Vladimir Vasiliev comes to mind. Maybe such an attitude is vanity, but it's also a kind of extreme artistic integrity. Maybe it is both—but whatever it really is, it gives the dancer a singular and irreducible character. This was what I'd acquired in those hectic years after my return to the stage.

But I also danced worse than before, and for far less mysterious reasons. Like a platinum ring that has been cut and rewelded together, my fractured bones had completely healed on the outside—but were immeasurably weaker. My jumps no longer had the same buoyancy and quality of disbelief. From a technical standpoint, my virtuosity that had set me apart had faded to gray. I didn't like to speak of it; Laurent didn't point out what he knew I knew; besides, I still sold tickets like nobody else, especially since Sasha went through his own breakdown.

After his disastrous interview and media fallout, Sasha took a leave of absence of seven months. Laurent had initially proposed a break of only four months, and if Sasha had been silent, it would have worked. Within a few weeks of his infamous interview, the furor had already died down; Americans didn't particularly know or care about Crimea. But in April, separatists in Donetsk and Luhansk broke away, declaring their own republics, and Sasha saw fit to say in another interview something about "standing by his Donbas brothers." By August, tens of thousands of Russian troops moved into those territories and the real business of war began. Europeans and particularly

Americans, who nine out of ten couldn't point to Crimea on the world map, sounded the alarm over mainland Ukraine on another level. And the response was similar for the Russian and Ukrainian dancers in our circles, who were initially too shocked to register other emotions. No one expected this situation to last long—it was irrational and bizarre. We had always been friends, relatives, going to schools across the border and working in each other's companies. Then, as it became clear that the conflict would last more than a few weeks, the battle lines were drawn among the artists, too.

On the Russian side, the Bolshoi general director, Mikhail Alypov, came out in full support of the administration, to no one's surprise. More startlingly, Olga Zelenko—a Bolshoi prima ballerina, but a graduate of the Kyiv Choreographic School with Ukrainian ancestry and a Ukrainian name—signed a public letter endorsing the Russian annexation of Crimea. I immediately recalled the summer weekend when Sasha, Dmitri, and I had driven to her dacha: drinking kvass on her porch, her arrogant gray cat, Alexey Arkadyevich and his rosebushes, and the breakfast served in painted Polish bowls. After the trip, the slight warmth between Olga and me had cooled again; we were never meant to be friends. But I no longer disliked her, since it's significantly harder to dislike someone after they feed you things they've grown and shelter you for a night. Or after you see them vulnerable. I doubted that Alexey Arkadyevich agreed with his wife; I couldn't imagine a Tolstoy scholar falling for political slogans. But Olga was said to have powerful supporters in the administration, and I guessed that she didn't want to lose her place at the top.

My mind drifted to the other major Ukrainian figure in my life—Seryozha. I hadn't thought of him in so long and never looked him up—not because he hurt me, but because I hurt him, and that knowledge shamed me the older I got. I still didn't have courage to call or text him to ask how he was doing, what he thought of all this. I didn't even have access to Nina. We hadn't messaged each other since my engagement. The one time I dared to check her Instagram, I glimpsed a few tasteful photos of her performances and children but nothing about the war. It didn't surprise me, as it would cost her a great deal to make even careful allusions—and Nina, though perfectly sensible and peace-loving, never liked to stand up to authority. The idea itself wouldn't have entered her head—just as it wouldn't have entered mine.

We'd never talked about politics as students or as professionals. Most dancers were content to stay out of it, and some elite soloists said vague "stabilizing" words for the benefit of the TV camera in election years. If things didn't seem altogether right, they also didn't seem wholly wrong, either. Russia—not her politics, but her language, woodlands and meadows, rivers and lakes, centuries-old capitals, her poetry, her prayers, Tolstoy, Gogol, Bulgakov, Tchaikovsky, Prokofiev, Akhmatova, Mayakovsky, Pasternak, the White Nights, summers and winters, families, dachas, and above everything else, her ballet—birthed us and gave us a reason for life. I loved this land, and my place in it was at the theater. And if some things weren't as they should be, that was also the case in every other country. It hadn't seemed necessary for me to engage with politics at all—until now.

As casualties mounted on both Ukrainian and separatist-Russian sides, the viciousness and death threats to Sasha started in earnest. At first, he seemed bewildered: he'd never been openly hated before in his life. Moreover, he didn't believe he'd said anything morally wrong.

"If people actually bothered to read what I said, or understand that I'm a quarter Ukrainian on my mother's side, they wouldn't make me out to be some murderer," he said. "Wasn't the West supposed to be all about freedom of speech?"

"In Russia there is only one person who knows if you're guilty or innocent. In the West, it's millions of people—anyone with the internet," I replied.

Even I wasn't free from criticism. Like Sasha, I left the apartment wearing sunglasses and hats and directed all mail to the Paris Opéra office. The other dancers—colleagues I'd always liked and respected—smiled at me tightly or suddenly stopped talking when I appeared. Kindhearted Farkhad sent me a long text saying how Sasha's statements had personally wounded him. As a Tatar, he watched with horror as the Russian occupiers kidnapped Crimean Tatars suspected of resistance. Some never came home, and others returned in body bags. Sasha's endorsement of the occupation was an endorsement of crimes against humanity; and as Sasha's fiancée, I'd forever lost his respect and friendship. My frantic messages to Farkhad were unanswered, and I guessed that he'd already blocked my number. This affected me in a more real way than reading the news. I didn't know how I could've acted any better, but I nonetheless felt guilty.

"Look what you've done," I said to Sasha, waving my phone in his face. He said he couldn't care less what my "Tatar American friend" thought about his morals. He was utterly intractable, and I was shaken by his shamelessness. But this changed when I walked in on Sasha taking a phone call from home.

"Almost everyone in the village is gone." I could hear the muffled voice of his grandfather. "The younger men have joined the separs, and most of the women and children moved where it's safer."

"They wouldn't attack their own people, would they?" Sasha asked anxiously.

"The post office was shelled, wouldn't you know. And the electric grid's been destroyed," his grandfather said. "Do you remember stingy old Vadim? Well, he made a couple of trades with the Ukrainian soldiers who were passing through. He didn't think much of it—wasn't for friendship, just common sense. Needed some petrol for his generator and those guys wanted some fresh foods. Not to mention, he charged them too much. And then a week later, he got on his tractor and it exploded. A mine."

"The separs did that?"

"Maybe, or maybe it's the Russians—they don't care about people living here, now do they?"

"Dedushka, you have to get out of there," Sasha pleaded. "Do you need money? I'll wire you."

"Who is going to work in the field? What about the orchard? Masha is fifteen and on her last legs—the vet saw her one last time before evacuating, and told us not to move her. And there's the bees . . . I'm not abandoning any of them," his grandfather said. "I have enough petrol for now, so I can power my phone and drive out if we really need to. But we are too old to leave our home."

After this conversation, Sasha finally stopped trying to vindicate himself. When I came into the apartment, he went to the bedroom. If I suggested dinner, he replied he'd already eaten. Neither of us mentioned splitting up. I wanted us to work, but I sometimes wondered if Sasha was actively trying to get me to break up with him first. When I'd talk, he wasn't listening half the time; and the other half of the time, he would be aloof or acerbic. He even put me down for getting excited or distraught about a role: I was too "intense" and "emotional" and "too much, all the time." I remembered how at our first dinner together at that Georgian restaurant, Sasha said that everyone was accusing me of exactly the sort of things he was now calling me. He'd told me then, "Don't ever change." He'd loved me once for who I am, and now hated me for the same reasons.

After his reinstatement, we both understood without saying so that we would no longer partner each other almost exclusively. Like Nureyev and Fonteyn, we had danced all the important ballets together unless one of us was injured or sick. That tacit agreement was one of the highest honors in an art form in which performers themselves held little autonomy. It meant: these two dancers together are more than the sum of their parts, more than bureaucracy; they must be treated as something a bit apart and precious, like the last remaining pair of an endangered species. But now, for his comeback performance, Laurent put Sasha in *Swan Lake* with a twenty-year-old sujet named Théa. The director felt the need to explain that it was better for Sasha to return quietly, and that it's less provocative than putting two Russians as leads given the current tensions.

One afternoon, as I was practicing on my own before a *Don Q* rehearsal, I suddenly found I couldn't move. Sometimes this happened to dancers—I knew of a celebrated American ballerina who once woke up perfectly healthy but mysteriously unable to twist her neck sideways. The neck, of course, is everything, especially if you're a turner, and I carefully shook my head until it was clear this was still in my power. But as Minkus played on, my feet still refused to jump. It was an overcast day and the windows let in only the dregs of cloudy gray light. I turned off the music, and the buzz of the fluorescent lamp filled my ears. The mirrors were smudged, the floor scuffed and sticky. Everything that had once held romance and history looked terribly ordinary.

I finally lay down on the floor, breathing deeply until sensation returned to my toes. I stared at the domed ceiling and thought about how in everyone's eyes, I was only slightly less reprehensible than Sasha. I agreed with them—not because I was Russian or because I was his fiancée, but because I truly was complicit. It wasn't about just Ukraine but also the state of humanity; it was the famine, violence, oppression, and crushing poverty on every continent. I began to doubt for the first time whether art had any relevance in this world. My greatest achievements were laughably inconsequential—and no matter how I danced, the world would still burn. Amid the ashes and the fire, I was taking class, rehearsing, and going onstage as if nothing was wrong. In this epoch it was impossible to honestly practice art, the highest form of which was selflessness. *That* was the true nature of art, yet I was no closer to attaining it than if I weren't even aware of it. But what alternative did I have?

I didn't share these thoughts with anyone, especially Sasha. We hardly spoke at all, let alone about the reason for his disciplinary action. But to his credit, the continued violence had a sobering effect. The thousands of casualties on both sides disillusioned and devastated him. Although he refrained from speaking this out loud, I knew he worried about his grandparents constantly—and that he paid a great deal of money to finally smuggle them out to west Ukraine. He no longer said incendiary things about the war, publicly or privately. Instead, he closed off and turned into himself, something I'd never seen him do before. Even after his comeback performance, which had gone as well as he could have hoped for, Sasha seemed sullen and cold. And then I realized that he wasn't just a terrible person. He was depressed.

When his birthday came around in December, I made an elaborate dinner for us—wild mushrooms cooked in wine and fresh pasta. He was performing in *The Nutcracker* that night, and as the clock kept ticking away, I worried that he somehow wasn't going to come home.

I kept taking the food out of the oven and putting it back in at the lowest setting. After a while, I blew out the candles so they wouldn't burn all the way. Close to midnight, I took off my dress and changed into my pajamas, fighting back tears. Then I heard the lock turn, and Sasha walked in. He looked at the table set for two.

"What's all this?" he said, as if I had made a mess.

"I made dinner for your birthday. It's in the oven if you want it." I walked away and threw myself on the bed. I heard him shuffling around and expected him to undress and take a shower. Instead, he opened the door and sat down next to me with a bowl of pasta.

"It's delicious," he said, taking a bite.

"It's cold."

"No, it's still warm." He twirled some pasta on his fork. "Here, try it."

I lay still for a long time. He hadn't acted so tender toward me in months—and the same was true of my dinner-making. We were at a point in a relationship where we could hold on or drift apart for good. We'd been together a long time—perhaps too long—and were both tired of each other. But underneath the fatigue, there was also something more indestructible, like a safe discovered in the rubble of an earthquake. It was just that neither of us knew what was inside the safe.

I pressed myself up and took a bite from his fork.

"It's good," I said. He smiled at me, crinkling the outer corners of his eyes. His golden hair fell like corn silk around his face. I put my head on his chest and he held me there without saying anything. It was like a film I once saw, late at night in a hotel room when I was performing at a gala in Madrid. It was about a man who had to cross a chasm hundreds of meters above ground. But the only way to get to the other side was to step on the thin air, believing that the bridge would then appear. And that's what happened: he walked over an invisible bridge. I felt like that man just then—except that Sasha from the opposite side also had to take a step over the emptiness to meet me. Love was an illusion for the most part, but it became real if both people risked themselves to believe in it.

One fall morning before class, I realized that Sasha was gone. After I got out of the shower, I stood by the window and saw his tall shape disappear into the ivy drape below our entrance. A few minutes later, he burst in through the door, bearing a white bag of croissants and two cappuccinos; a gust of clean, vigorous air followed him in.

"What's all this? A special treat?" I sat at the table. Sasha put the cups down, pulled out two perfectly bronzed pastries, and laid them on the paper bag like a couple of sunbathers on a beach towel.

"Is there something you have to tell me?" I teased, taking a bite from a croissant and dusting off my mouth. Sasha smiled a little nervously.

"I do. You won't like it."

I stopped chewing and looked at him. "Well, go on."

"You know there is *Romeo and Juliet* next spring."

"Oh, that—" I sighed, waving a hand. "I talked to Laurent about it. I know I'm not dancing Juliet. I'm debuting Tatiana in *Onegin* just before *Romeo*, and it didn't seem wise to divide my energy."

"It's not that." Sasha fidgeted with his pastry, breaking it apart into pieces. "Laurent invited a guest artist to dance Mercutio."

"Why Mercutio and not Romeo? Oh." My mouth dropped open, and Sasha took a sip of his cappuccino.

"Yes. It's Dmitri. You know he's never danced Romeo. But he's the best Mercutio in the world."

"I gotta go." I grabbed my cup and swept up my dance bag. "Sorry, I know you're not ready. Gabriel can come back to pick you up in thirty minutes."

When I found Laurent in his office, he was seated at his desk and talking to his assistant about dinner with a composer from Mexico. Seeing my flushed face, he dismissed the young woman, walked around his desk, and sat down at its edge next to the Hermès paperweight in the shape of a horse's head. He gestured at the chair in the middle of the room, and I sat down.

"You invited Dmitri Ostrovsky to dance here?" I said without formalities. Laurent narrowed his eyes.

"How did you . . . ? I haven't even made the announcement yet." He dragged his palm down his face and blinked several times. "Well, in any case, the answer is yes."

"You know the history between Dmitri and me. He's vile, dishonest, and unethical. You agreed with me several times."

"Natalia," he said slowly, as if to a wayward child. "Of course I agree Dmitri is a snake. When he dances, I bet he sweats poison. But that's personal and this is business."

"I don't want him to come to Paris. You promised you would let me be the way I am."

"I promised you would get to choose who you dance with. I didn't promise you would get to choose who dances at the Paris Opéra, period." Laurent stood up, frowning. I also rose from the chair, my cheeks burning.

"I don't care if Dmitri once spat on your face or swore at your mother. Put it behind you," he said, somewhat extravagantly for his taste. He seemed to realize this as well and shook his head. "You're not even dancing in *Romeo*. Also, it's been years since you left Bolshoi, which breeds politics and backstabbing almost as a matter of principle. Now you're not bound to the same place. He's only here for one week, and then you never have to see him again. He's forty-two, for god's sakes. Frankly—I shouldn't tell you this—but Dmitri told me he's planning to retire next summer."

There was nothing I could do except wait for the inevitable. I'd forgotten about Dmitri, but once I was reminded of him, I realized that my hatred of him had not abated at all in the past five years. This surprised me. I didn't know I was capable of hating someone so much that I would wish this person were dead. But I honestly thought that would appease me—and I didn't like discovering how raw and beastly I was at the deepest level of my soul. What was equally disturbing was that this was the same place from which I drew upon to dance. Sometimes in my life, I'd been more frightened by myself than by anyone else, and this was one of those times. I decided to chain up my hatred and not let it out or look at it in the face.

I struggled through the class and afternoon rehearsal and went to the only place I could think of, which was the bar at Place des Vosges. When I walked in, Henri was manning the bar alone. I asked him where Léon was, and he wiped his hands on a towel.

"We had to let him go. Too many absences, taking off in the middle of the shift." Henri looked at me accusingly, and I thought about leaving. Instead, I sat down and ordered a negroni. Henri made it for me without any love, as if afraid that I might get close to him and infect him with the same laziness that Léon caught.

"Do you know where he's working now?" I asked. Henri shrugged.

"You know Léon lacks focus. He's always doing this and that," he said. "I think someone saw him working at a tattoo parlor in Pigalle that advertises 'free student tattoos.'" He snickered; and then, as if remembering some important appointment, he excused himself and got busy making sure all the liquor labels were positioned perfectly en face.

As I left the bar, I texted Léon without any expectations. I wasn't surprised when he didn't respond—not just right away, but ever. Léon could spend time with me, talk to me as if he truly cared, and then disappear for months. When we next saw each other, he acted as if he hadn't ignored my messages. Normally, I loathed this type of behavior. I didn't judge Léon with the same harshness because I found he was somehow being true to himself. It was as though he could only live for the moment, not just when it came to his career (a word that fundamentally didn't suit him) but with regard to every part of his life. As long as I was in front of him, I mattered; when I went out of his sight, he forgot about me. His inconsistency was his consistency. But a relationship could only deepen with fulfillment of expectations, so ours remained shallow no matter how many years had passed.

Over the next months, I focused on interpreting new roles. I'd been dancing more neoclassical, modern, and contemporary works, which not only breathed freshness to my classical-heavy repertoire but were sometimes less taxing to my body. These were mostly Balanchine, Robbins, Petit, Alonso, Forsythe, Cunningham, Preljocaj, Ratmansky, Dawson. I became frustrated after a while—where were the women? I marched into Laurent's office, made some phone calls, and negotiated my contracts at other companies. I managed to dance Graham, Tharp, De Mille, Childs, and a new work in the manner of Isadora Duncan. Laurent seemed pleased I'd found an outlet and supported my call to elevate female choreographers. Without saying so, Laurent thought that this was a fair exchange for inviting Dmitri.

In the weeks leading up to *Romeo and Juliet*, I anxiously fantasized about running into Dmitri—on the streets, in the hallway of Palais Garnier, Laurent's office. When it did finally happen, however, neither of us was in the position to snarl or make offensive remarks, as we were separated by several barres and dozens of dancers in class. From far away, it looked like he hadn't aged a day since I last saw him. His hair was still velvety black, and his body still coltish with high and narrow hips. When the pianist stopped warming up and the dancers' chatter died down, Sasha came and stood behind me at the barre. Dmitri glanced in our direction and raised his eyebrows in a not-quite greeting. I turned my eyes away. But after the class—during which Dmitri effortlessly sailed through the rapid-fire petit allegro of the French—he walked over to our side.

"Sasha. Natasha," he said, panting a little. "How many summers, how many winters?"

"Dima, hope you've been well," Sasha said carefully. "You've danced here before, right? How does it feel to be back?"

"Well, as I always say, there are only three schools of ballet in the world. Moscow, Petersburg, and Paris." Dmitri pulled up the hem of his damp T-shirt and used it to wipe his forehead, exposing his bare abs. "I happen to like some of the things here. And the food is much better in Paris."

"Tell me about it." Sasha grinned. "I'll see you in rehearsal then."

Dmitri gave a slight jerk of the chin to me and a half smile to Sasha before walking away.

The next day, I was on my way out of a rehearsal for *Onegin* when I passed by an open door of another studio. Some soloists were spilling out of it, folding their hands together over their waist or their hearts, staring reverentially at the center of the room. I approached, and a few of them scooted in farther to make room for me. The corps de ballet was lining the perimeter of the space with no less rapt attention. And in the center, Dmitri was dancing his Mercutio variation. *Romeo and Juliet* is the toughest ballet for the male dancer, and while onstage for less time than the title role, Mercutio is no less tricky. It has all those en dehors to en dedans turns, and then countless gestures and acting on top of it. The choreography lends itself to looking jerky at worst, or technically proficient yet effortful. But interpreted by the right dancer, it is hypnotizing and seamless from one movement to the next. Mercutio is an ion: charged, unpredictable, devilish, delightful. Not only that, the best dancer will even foretell through the merry dance the sign of Mercutio's imminent death. Ironic, Prokofiev! This was exactly how Dmitri played it—a whirlwind of *leggerezza*, that luscious Italian quality of ballon plus speed—so that when he ended the solo with a triple pirouette landing on his knee and blowing a kiss, you thought of humor, sex, death, and life as a single one-minute-and-twenty-second dance.

Everyone watching him broke into an involuntary roar and applause. Out of the corner of my eyes, I saw Sasha clapping and whispering something to Théa, the sujet who was debuting as Juliet. I knew he flirted with nearly all his partners. Sasha almost couldn't help himself; this was how he naturally was, although I thought he should show more restraint in front of me. Yet I couldn't find it in myself to be angry, because Dmitri had moved me once again.

I came home alone, and Sasha returned an hour later in a pleasantly exhausted state. I could see that rehearsal had gone well for him and nothing more was necessary for his happiness. We were too absorbed in our thoughts to chat and ate dinner in near silence. Afterward, I showered and lay in bed, facing the wall where Sasha's shadow was washing his face and flossing.

"Théa is just twenty-one, but she's intelligent and has the right instincts," he said, gargling and spitting out foam. I pictured her wide eyes, olive skin inherited from Provençal ancestors, and perfectly even, small white teeth. She was young and eager, which made her dance everything "at the top," like a marionette pulled by strings. She didn't know how to not just be airy but *spatial*, trusting the gravity and the body.

"She's talented," I said.

"Well, it's too bad for Théa." He climbed into bed. "Her debut as Juliet will be completely overshadowed by Dmitri. Sorry, I know you hate hearing about him."

"Yes and no. Thank you for being sensitive. But he's . . ." I paused, searching for the right words. "Unique. I get why you feel the need to talk about him." Sasha smiled, gave me a kiss on the cheek, and turned off the bedside lamp.

Of course Dmitri had won over everyone, just as he had in Moscow. But I blocked out his image so I could focus on my own debut in *Onegin*. My competitiveness had softened over time, and I no longer measured my success in terms of how I outperformed others. I didn't care about being the toast of the town that week, eclipsing Dmitri's triumphant return to the Paris stage. But I always had something to prove to myself, and that wasn't going to change until the day I died. Going onstage always took the same amount of sacrifice, and overcoming the fear of the certain sacrifice. I gave myself like someone pawning everything she owns for a small chance of perfection for a few hours. It didn't win over everyone, but those who noticed what I did loved me for it. The real price of this was that I couldn't dance for several days after many shows. I couldn't continue to ignore the cumulative wear and tear of my body, and recuperation took increasingly longer. I knew that one day, the recuperation would be indefinite and I would not return to the stage.

The day before Sasha's performance, I stayed home from the morning class. I'd had a terrible dream. Once I shook it off, I realized I was physically well enough to go to class, but my mind was still unsettled. The dream was this. I was in a huge house that evidently belonged to my father, Nikolai. I was going through his things and keeping, selling, or donating them, including a stack of LPs. Then I woke up out of that dream and into another one where Sasha and I were in our apartment. He was very cold to me, and I reacted in anger. Then he started pulling out my clothes from the closet and throwing them away. Everything had to be discarded, he said. When I turned, he was pushing out the front door someone who resembled him, who was in fact, a double of himself. This second Sasha looked sad, pale, and fragile, as I had never seen him in real life. I didn't know which was the real Sasha and which was the imposter. That was when I woke up with a start.

Slowly, I returned to my body and listened to the sounds outside. The birds were singing and the cars purred by in the narrow street, signifying a balmy morning that would soon turn into an impetuous July day. Everything was as it should be. I got up cautiously, thinking that a complete time-off would help me recover. I would take the rest of the day easy, not even doing light stretching. Once or twice a year I enjoyed this ultimate luxury, twenty-four hours spent in bed as if I were sick. I got out only for a few minutes to go to the kitchen to boil water, which I was craving even in the heat.

Around noon, I asked Gabriel to bring me a soup and ate it under the covers. I read several chapters from a book I'd been carrying around in my suitcase for months.

As the sun descended and the heat rose from the ground like mist, I decided I was well enough to go out for dinner. I would surprise Sasha as he was getting out of the final rehearsal. The next day, his mind and body would be elsewhere, shared by his dance partner and two thousand spectators. That night, I wanted him for myself.

Gabriel dropped me off at the Palais Garnier and idled by the curb while I went up to fetch Sasha. Half the corps de ballet exited through the artist entrance as I walked in, talking about their upcoming vacations in Spain and Italy. I passed by ballet mistresses in their black sneakers and apprentices bobbing to their headphones, but saw no sign of Sasha. The empty hallway smelled of sweat and nostalgia, like a school after the last day of the year. I took the elevator up to the rotunda floor. Only the door to Studio Noureev was open, and Mozart Piano Concerto no. 23 poured out of it like twilight. Although dancers barely noticed this during rehearsals, the round windows of the Bailleau rotunda gave way to a sweeping vista of Paris. Through the grimy glass, the city sparkled with the quick pulse of

July. I walked inside to take a better look, almost forgetting why I was there in the first place.

There was heavy breathing in the room. The sound of the piano had muffled it, but I heard it clearly now. Lips searching and meeting, skin against skin. A groan of pleasure, not shrill and performative as in one's youth, but deep and grounded and exquisite. Of course I knew who that had to be, even before my eyes found the pair of linked bodies on the floor. The golden one was Sasha. Entwined with him, olive skin shiny with a film of sweat, was Dmitri.

With the music turned up, they didn't notice that I was there. I slipped out before they could see me. Now nothing made sense and at the same time, everything made sense.

V

AS SOON AS I EXITED THE BUILDING, I RAN TO THE CURB AND VOMITED. I watched the long strings of saliva stretching from my lips to the sewer grate. It was a relief to be curled up six inches from the ground littered with cigarette butts, which closely mirrored my own state of mind.

"Natalia! Are you okay?" Gabriel shouted, rushing to raise me up by the arms.

"I'm not well. Please take me home," I said. Since I'd told Gabriel that I was sick that morning, he thought he should take me to the hospital. At my insistence, he drove me home and walked me up the stairs, completely forgetting about my plan to have dinner with Sasha.

Once I lay on our bed in the darkness, all the distasteful thoughts of the wronged partner besieged me. These consisted of the signs I should have seen and missed, even from the very beginning of our relationship. Sasha had been close to Dmitri—had even said "he likes me." Dmitri had blessed Sasha's career like he helped other, select young men. The closer Sasha and I became, the more he and Dmitri drifted. It now occurred to me that the trip to Olga's dacha was probably the turning point of their relationship. I replayed the scene in the car when, after much passive-aggression from Dmitri, Sasha called him a *suka*. Dmitri's violent rage made sense now, but not his refusal to out Sasha in front of me. Why didn't he? Perhaps their relationship wasn't physical. But then, Sasha said he'd been to Dmitri's home, which was where he invited only very few close friends. Even the way Dmitri readily tossed the keys of his Ferrari to Sasha spoke to their intimacy. And after so many years, I finally realized that Dmitri hated me because I took Sasha from him. Now I supposed that he meant to take Sasha back.

All that was something I could think about, overcoming the vertigo that appeared along with the image of their bodies on the studio floor. I couldn't even begin to process the fact that Sasha was involved with not another woman, but a man. It might have been easier to be told that I was actually Anastasia Romanova or that there was a comet about to collide with Earth.

A few hours later, Sasha came home. He brushed his teeth in the bathroom and sat down on the bed next to me, typing something on his phone.

"Hey," I said to him, and he laid the phone facedown on the nightstand.

"I thought you were asleep. How are you feeling? Still sick?"

"Yes," I said, my voice trembling. "Will you kiss me?"

Sasha looked at me with sympathy and perhaps guilt. "Of course, little bird." He leaned down and kissed me softly on the lips, enveloping me in the fragrance of an unfamiliar shampoo. My eyes leaked long, streaky tears over my cheeks.

"Are you crying?" Sasha asked, alarmed. "You really don't feel well. Should we go to the hospital?"

I shook my head. Sasha laid his palm over my forehead, taking my temperature.

"No, I'll be fine. But I probably can't go to your show tomorrow night."

"You've danced *Romeo and Juliet* with me about a hundred times, anyway. It won't be anything you haven't seen before," Sasha said. He put his arm around me so that my head rested in the nook of his shoulder. "I'm sorry I left you alone today. Our summer break is coming up. Let's go where we don't have to think or do anything."

I nodded and pretended to fall asleep. After a while, Sasha carefully uncoiled his arm and turned to his side of the bed.

When I woke up, Sasha was in the living room. I went straight to the shower. The night before, I'd been too freshly wounded to get angry or confront Sasha. I'd wanted to shut everything out and just be comforted. After sleep, I was quickly recovering my senses as if I got a shot of rage straight to my veins. But I didn't want to lash out at him without a plan, and for that it was better if he could tactfully remove himself while I was in the shower.

But he was still in the apartment when I finished. I put on a robe and crawled back into bed, and Sasha walked in, carrying a tray of coffee and oatmeal with blueberries.

"You should eat something even if you don't have much of an appetite," he said, laying down the tray next to me. "How are you feeling?"

Instead of answering, I stared at him out of the corner of my eyes. It angered me how he looked so genuinely concerned—and how he looked the *same* as before. I considered saying to him, You're a liar. Everything you've shown me and said to me is false. You've ruined my life.

"Better," I muttered dryly. Sasha smiled, as if a huge weight had been lifted from his chest.

"Good. Stay in bed. I'll be home late obviously, but I'll spend all day with you tomorrow." He took a sip from my coffee and then rose. "I'll call you when I'm on the way home."

Once Sasha left I went straight to the kitchen, poured the coffee down the drain, and dumped the oatmeal in the trash. Then I sprawled out on the bed, torn between the opposite desires to obsess over Sasha and to block him from my mind. I now understood why some people experience complete memory loss over their traumas: those events broke down their entire world, so it was much easier to just pretend it never happened, like cutting out some parts of a film reel and piecing the rest back together with tape. I imagined doing that with what I saw and keeping Sasha. If I were being honest, I always knew deep down that our relationship wasn't meant to last; but it had been something worth holding on to as long as possible, like an especially breathtaking sunset. That was something I actually thought of, and that childish naivete disgusted me.

No, I couldn't pretend it never happened. So the other option was to find out the truth from Sasha. Not today, since I couldn't distract him on performance day, even under these circumstances. But no matter: it wasn't his words that told the most truthful story.

With my mind thus made up, I spent the rest of the day in bed watching mind-numbing shows. In the late afternoon, I dragged myself to the bathroom and carefully did my hair and makeup. I rarely put on an evening dress when going to see performances on my off-nights, but this time I chose a raw-edged black tulle gown from Chanel that was both very simple and diabolically expensive. In full regalia, my reflection gazed back at me like a frozen diamond: anyone who knew me would think I was newly in love or more likely, exceptionally angry.

I took a moment to regret my lack of interest in collecting luxuries. The Chanel had been a gift following a costume collaboration. After I bought my green handbag in my first week in Paris, I'd lost interest in proving myself through beautiful things. But objects could hold you up like scaffolding if your reality was crumbling down. Sometimes objects—even a simple mug or a couch—were much more steadfast, loyal, and accountable than a human heart. If I'd been wiser, I would have pulled a Callas and stacked on every piece of jewelry I owned for a public appearance in a wounded state: that was what the singer did on the night when the director of the Metropolitan Opera canceled her contract. But the only valuable jewel I had was my engagement ring. I slipped it on and off my finger for a few minutes before finally deciding to wear it.

Gabriel dropped me off at Palais Garnier and I found my way into Laurent's box, where he took in every performance from the best vantage point in the 1,900-seat theater. Laurent stood up as I entered and pulled out my chair for me with his old-fashioned chivalry, for which I was grateful this night. Once we were both seated, he said, "You look ravishing. Black becomes you, even though you're a brunette." I thanked him without a smile, and he turned his attention to the stage, crossing his legs and interlacing his hands together. He was taking detailed mental notes of every role, which he would deliver backstage right after the curtain call—or if he deemed necessary, even during intermission.

But Act I was going smoothly even by Laurent's standards. Romeo wasn't Sasha's most celebrated role. His style of dancing—

big, explosive, bravura, pure Bolshoi—was less suited to nimble and mellifluous choreography. But once you let go of the expectations of how Romeo should be acted, Sasha's interpretation made sense. He wasn't ever going to convincingly play an impressionable adolescent boy besotted with a thirteen-year-old girl. Instead, he was a youth possessed by passions that would have driven him to destruction, whether or not he met Juliet. Their first pas de deux ended, and Laurent smiled.

"What do you think of the new Juliet?" he whispered, pointing his chin at the pink-chiffon figure on the stage. Théa's quality of dancing at the top was on full display, as if she were determined to prick the entire stage with her toes for the next two and a half hours.

"She looks like a hyperactive flamingo," I said coldly. Normally, I would not have said something so cruel about another dancer; it was ungracious and unbecoming of my position as étoile. But the reserve of my self-discipline and civility had run out over the course of the past two days. Laurent smirked.

"*Ne sois pas jalouse*," he said, lightly tapping my knee. The idea that I could be jealous of Théa was so absurd that I snorted. Laurent opened his mouth again, and I shushed him with a finger to my lips so I could pay my full attention to Dmitri's solo. I'd forgotten how stunning he was onstage with his dark features and long legs. Some performers were exciting to watch even when they were simply standing; but, of course, Dmitri did so much more than that. Somehow I was able to take my eyes off of him for a second to look at Sasha. It told me what I needed to know, what I most feared.

The show ended. During the repeated curtain calls, when Dmitri, Sasha, and Théa each received standing ovations and air-splitting whistles, Laurent suggested we go backstage together. By the time we arrived, the curtains had closed for the last time. Finally hidden from the eyes of the audience, Sasha embraced Théa, who stood up on her toes to hook her arms around his neck. Dmitri was shaking hands with Tybalt and undoing the bodice of his costume. When he saw me, he nodded and said, "Natasha. You made it." This caused Sasha to turn around, letting his arms fall away from Théa's body. Laurent kissed Théa on both cheeks murmuring his congratulations, and Sasha dutifully replicated those moves on me. I closed my eyes and received those kisses like a cancer patient receiving chemotherapy.

"Beautiful dress," Sasha said. "We're going to an after-party. At your friend Leo's bar, I think. You should come."

"It's Léon. You mean where he used to work?" I asked, and Sasha nodded.

"Yes, I suggested it. It's nice, intimate, never too busy. Most of the dancers are going, and of course Dima and Théa. Laurent, what about you?" Sasha turned to the director, who flashed me a handsome smile. I nodded; it would have been awkward to feign illness and excuse myself, and I wanted to keep observing Sasha, who was now being pulled away for congratulations from other dancers and the rest of the staff. When Théa joined the circle of winners with Sasha, I unlocked my phone and impulsively texted Léon. Our message history showed that he hadn't even replied the last few times I reached out with a quick *how are you*. Nonetheless, I explained briefly what had happened with Sasha and asked him to come to the after-party. It made me feel worse to be so clingy and open with someone who clearly didn't need me that much. But I had so rarely been as relieved as when Léon texted back immediately, *I'll be there.*

Twenty minutes later, some forty postshow dancers, Laurent, and I descended upon the bar, which was nearly empty and tended only by Henri. The manager was instantly beleaguered by drink orders, sweat beading his temple and soaking the back of his shirt. Everyone took pity on him and switched to the easiest drink order: champagne.

"Thanks to Laurent de Balincourt, our extraordinary director!" Sasha shouted, passing the flutes down a line of dancers. Laurent bowed lightly, and dancers clapped and cheered. Before everyone had a glass and the first toast could be made, Léon walked inside and slid into my booth.

"Natasha, you look splendid," he said, as if we had seen each other only recently. Before tonight, I hadn't heard from him in over a year. But no matter: now that he was here, he would be my friend for the night. That was the deal with someone like Léon.

"Here, take this." I handed him a glass of champagne. "They're about to do a lot of toasts."

"Okay, I see Sasha. Which one is Juliet, and which one is his secret?"

I took a long swig of champagne just as Laurent cleared his throat for a speech and dancers quieted around the room. Laurent was congratulating every dancer of the troupe, but especially the honored guest artist Dmitri Ostrovsky, who showed the true meaning of the role of Mercutio with meteoric clarity. (Dmitri bowed his head lightly, and Léon raised his eyebrows at me.) Laurent took a moment to acknowledge those who sublimely played the two title roles, and Sasha and Théa traded meaningful glances.

By this point, the director was becoming moved by the power and poetry of his own speech. Now he was mixing in the salacious anecdotes of the ballet legends behind this production, enjoying the gleeful gasps and squeals; and then he was reciting a paean to the art of ballet, the magic of creation and tradition, conceived in genius and passed down from master to dancer, ever new, inviolable, eternal. The dancers were touched by the passionately unfurling speech, but also visibly restless and thirsty. Finally, to their great relief, Laurent raised his glass and said, "To our incredible soloists and guest artist, to *Romeo and Juliet* and the great tradition of ballet that made it, and above all, to each and every one of you."

As one, the room toasted, kissed, and drank from their glass in shared euphoria. Then the organized appearance of the party broke down, replaced by a cheerfully anarchic ambiance. The music was turned up and people started dancing with loose hips. Heavier drinks than champagne were being ordered at the bar. Sasha was talking to a circle of friends and admirers. Théa was doing the mambo without any hint of fatigue, as if she'd just arrived from taking a long nap instead of performing a three-act ballet. Léon was going around the room, taking photos with his boxy camera. Small explosions of bright white flash lingered in his wake. Besides myself, the only person at the party who was adrift in their own thoughts was Dmitri, sitting by himself in a corner with a drink.

"I brought you another one," Léon said, holding out a classic daiquiri. He sat down next to me with his own drink. "We should do a toast as well. How do you do it in Russian?"

"We do it a few different ways. *Vashe zrodovye*, which means the same as the French *santé*—to good health." I said, my hand cradling the coupe's frosty surface. "But my favorite one is *budem*."

"What does that mean?"

"It just means, 'We will.' We will go on."

"There's nothing better," Léon said. "*Budem!*"

We clinked our glasses together and took a sip. Léon patted my shoulder for a moment. "Oh, Natalia. Today is hard for you and I'm sorry. It will pass."

"It's not nearly as hard because you're here," I said, eyeing the opposite corner of the room. Sasha had taken a seat next to Dmitri and they were talking quietly to each other. "I'm not just hurt by the cheating. It's the fact that Dmitri is—"

"A man?" Léon said. "You don't have to take that as meaning something about *you*. A man, a woman. Does that really make a difference? You don't have to assume that Sasha was never attracted to you, for example, or that your entire relationship was a lie."

"But it was."

Léon regarded me with a strange expression. "I'm going to get another one," he said, making his way toward the throng of revelers. Once there, he somehow was sucked behind the bar mixing drinks next to Henri, who seemed to have forgotten how inconvenient Léon was most of the time. I stood up and realized how much I'd drunk without eating any food for more than a day. I felt like collapsing right then and there. Instead, I forced myself to walk out without saying goodbye to anyone, just as Dmitri had once told me to do when leaving a party.

Fresh air and darkness greeted me like my true friends. Place des Vosges was empty at this time of the night. It was quiet except for the fountains and someone playing the guitar, somewhere in one of the yellow windows.

Four days to the scheduled performance of *Giselle*, I wake up to a string of text messages from Sveta, Vera Igorevna, and Nina. I open Nina's first. She says it would mean a lot to her if I could come see her in *La Bayadère* that night, although she heard about Tae's illness, and it would be fine if I'd rather stay away from the theater for a while. Both Sveta and Vera Igorevna want me to call them immediately upon waking—our rehearsal must resume, they've figured out some work-arounds, and they will explain everything when I get there. After taking a shower and eating breakfast downstairs, I only reply to Nina. *Of course I will be there.*

Once I finish the last drop of porridge, my mind draws a complete blank. I'd only gone downstairs because I was starving. Now I have nowhere to go. Though I regret ignoring my well-intentioned teachers, the rehearsal studio is the last place I want to be in right now. Nor do I particularly wish to go upstairs and spend the rest of the day in bed. Going on a walk has lost its charm a long time ago. I zip up my jacket and venture out the entrance anyway, nodding at the doorman's salute. I stand on the curb and hail a cab. When the driver asks where I'm going, I say the first address that comes into my mind, which is Nina's apartment. She'd given me a key while I was staying with her, and Andryusha might be there, doing whatever he does while he's on an injury break. Sure enough, when I ring their bell, Andryusha opens the door in a gray T-shirt and sweatpants.

"Natasha! A surprise visit?" he says brightly, although I've surely caught him off guard.

"Is it okay that I'm here? I needed somewhere to go."

"I heard. Nina told me that Tae is out. I'm sure Dmitri will find a replacement—maybe even has one already. Anyway, don't just stand there. Come in," he says, holding the door wide and stepping aside. I walk into the hallway, picking my way around children's shoes and clothes.

"Sorry, the house is kind of a mess right now. I was just doing my workout before cleaning and grocery shopping," he says, picking up the bundles of mess behind me. "But if I don't exercise before the chores, I don't get it in."

"I don't mind. No, please, don't even bother making tea," I protest as the sound of Andryusha opening and closing cabinets wafts from the kitchen. "Come sit down and talk with me."

Andryusha pads back into the living room and sits diagonally from me on a chair. "So tell me what's going on. Why aren't you in rehearsal right now? If you ask my opinion, this is too premature to give up." Andryusha leans forward and starts counting on his hand the premiers and first soloists at Mariinsky who could pick up where Tae left off.

"It's not just that, Andryusha." I shake my head. After a pause, I start telling him about Pavel and what I only recently found out about my father and mother for the first time in my life—and that my father might be alive somewhere on the streets of Petersburg. It takes an hour of ceaseless talking, and by the time I'm finished, I say, "Actually, some tea would be great."

Andryusha has been listening with his mouth half open the whole time. "Yes! Tea!" He gets up like punching the ceiling with his head and brings back two hot mugs and a plate of cake. This reminds me of Nina's paramour, and I hope he doesn't catch my changed expression.

"Nina likes sweets. She always keeps these things in the house. But she eats so little and the kids and I end up eating most of it," he says with a laugh. "Anyway, yes. Families are complicated. Even mine."

"Yours cannot be that complicated." My voice is mostly exasperated, but also reassuring. Seizing this opening, Andryusha launches into his own tale of woe. I can tell he's been needing an audience for this. Men—even "nice" men like Andryusha—don't easily open up to a friend, unless it is a very old friend or they are very desperate.

"Nina probably told you how she thinks my parents look down on her?"

"No, she hasn't," I say honestly. Unlike me, Nina always acts with tasteful reserve when it comes to airing out grievances.

"Well, she does. Because my parents have supported us over the years—kept us safe, especially during our early twenties, being newly married and in the corps. And, of course, her parents were never in a position to do that. So she claims they think that she's not good enough—and even that she married me for money!"

The only time I remember meeting Andryusha's parents was at their wedding at the Grand Korsakov, which was unspeakably lavish by our early-twenties standards.

"But that's absurd. Nina would never marry anyone for money. Not even you, Prince Andrei," I say with a smile. Andryusha tries to return it and fails miserably.

"Wait for it, that's not all. Nina thinks *I* think she's not good enough, that *I* think I'm better than her. Better parent, better dancer."

"Well, do you?" I ask, and Andryusha blows the air out of his cheeks in frustration.

"No, of course not. Everyone knows I'm not the smartest. Yes, I know that's what people think! I don't even know why I'm good at ballet. It takes me a little longer to get the choreo, but I had the lines, the jump, a natural turnout for a male. It's the one thing that came more easily to me than to others, and if I didn't find this gift when I was young, who knows what I'd be doing right now?"

"Working at your father's company?" I suggest, and he glares at me.

"My point is that Nina is the intelligent one who always knows what to do. And she's just as gifted as I am as a dancer. Who cares if I outrank her? I don't."

"Tell her, just like how you told me."

"I've tried, Natasha. Maybe we've reached a point where talking doesn't solve anything," Andryusha mutters. "I don't think she loves me anymore."

No matter how much I care for both of these people, this is a point where I can no longer speak for one of them to the other. I remain silent, pretending to take long gulps of the lukewarm tea.

"Andryusha, I was wondering if I could ask you a favor," I say, when it feels safe to respectfully change the subject. "Will you please come with me to my mother's apartment? I need to start organizing her things, store them or give them away, and it will be better if I have a friend with me."

"Of course. I have three hours until I have to go pick up Luda at her school. Let's go."

ANDRYUSHA'S PRESENCE MAKES ENTERING MAMA'S apartment feel almost safe. Andryusha is a very real person, robust of body and mind, tangible, and mostly problem-free (despite his insistence otherwise). I don't mean this to slight him, but he is what a German-engineered luxury sedan would be if it were turned into a human being. So while Andryusha is in the room building boxes and taping them up with me, I am protected from ghosts and uncomfortable truths. He helps me sort out what's important to keep for memory's sake (some clothes, photos) and what can be given away or discarded (pantry items, most of the unremarkable dishes, plenty of loose paper and mail, most of the old furniture). In just a few hours, we clear out many boxes—and with each one, I feel relieved rather than heartbroken, simply because Andryusha is doing it with me.

"Okay, that was a good start, don't you think?" He looks at me and then at his watch. "Now's about time to wrap things for today and pick up Luda."

"Go! I'll do maybe an hour more by myself. I can't thank you enough."

"Natasha, how long have we been friends?" Andryusha envelops me in a hug. "Don't mention it."

"Thank you. I'll see you later."

After Andryusha leaves, I reorganize the place until dusk. Finally, I turn off the lights and lock the door. Just as I exit onto the courtyard, a strangely familiar voice calls me from behind.

"Natasha!"

Trotting out of the building after me is someone I haven't seen in years, but whose voice instantly awakens all the memories of the past.

"What are you doing here, Seryozha?" I ask, overlapping his words of surprise and joy. We both laugh and pull in for an awkward hug.

"I was dropping off some things for my parents. And you? What are you doing here? Aren't you supposed to be getting ready for *Giselle*? I've seen the posters around town. You look great, by the way."

"They still live in the same place? Oh, thank you. You seem to be doing great, as well." After the first gushing exchange, we take each other in quietly. His skin is still youthfully smooth; but he wears his pants a bit looser and his middle is rounded, so that he looks a little shorter and stouter. Overall, he has an air of being older—not resigned, but more accepting of himself.

"I want to know what you've been up to, Seryozha. But I have to go back to my hotel and get ready for Nina's show tonight."

"I'm not doing anything right now. I mean, I don't have any plans tonight," Seryozha says.

"Well, would you want to come with me? We can talk at the hotel and I won't take long to get ready. And I'm sure we can both watch from backstage. Less complicated than trying to get into the Duke's box at the last minute."

Seryozha accepts my invitation and we ride together to the hotel. When we arrive, he offers to stay in the lobby while I get ready. I go upstairs alone to put on makeup and zip into the only dress I packed in my suitcase, a black sheath that I thought I'd wear for Mama's funeral. Even though I am not trying to impress Seryozha, the dress is frustratingly dour with or without a black cardigan on top. I hope that the copious amount of red lipstick brightens my face instead of making me look even more like the bride of Dracula.

"Sorry, this outfit is horrible," I say, tucking my hair behind my ears and sliding into a chair in front of him at the lobby café. "I meant to wear it for my mother's . . ."

"I know. My parents told me. I'm incredibly sorry. She was wonderful." Seryozha gazes down at his lap, which emphasizes the deeper contours under his eyes and cheekbones.

"How are you doing? What have you been up to?" I say, changing the subject.

"Didn't you ask Nina about me?" he asks, and an embarrassed pause falls between us. Finding out Seryozha's updates just hasn't been a priority in the past few months. He pretends not to notice the lapse and says, "Well, you've been to company class. I quit five years ago already. They were never going to promote me beyond coryphée. It wasn't only that, though. I just lost the—joy of it."

"What are you doing now?"

"You remember Ambrosi Simonovich, the Vaganova rector?" Seryozha says, and I picture the kindly, petite, thin-voiced headmaster of our school years. "He invited me to teach at the school."

"He always had a soft spot for you, even when we were students. Doted on you like he never doted on me," I say with a hint of envy.

"You never needed his doting because you were going to be a superstar no matter what. He paid me special attention because I reminded him of himself." Seryozha smiles. "Apparently I don't have enough gravitas to be a danseur noble. But I danced the Blue Bird a number of times, just like Ambrosi Simonovich."

"And what about family? Are you married?" I ask without embarrassment. Although we are exes, we are also very old friends.

"No, not yet," he admits shyly. "I've been dating someone. Almost six months. She's a teacher, too—kindergarten. I have to tell you, it is *most* refreshing not to be in a relationship with a dancer."

We both laugh, at first carefully and then as if nothing funnier has ever crossed our minds. "A lot healthier, I bet," I say with a snort.

"So tell me what's going on. I heard about your retirement from Paris Opéra. It made me sad to think you were leaving the stage so early. I mean, I'd reached the end of my limits. But you were supposed to keep dancing until at least forty-two. That's what I expected of you," he says, and then sits back in his chair, as if afraid of my reaction. "Sorry if what I said is triggering."

"No. It's what I expected of me, too."

He regards me quietly, waiting for me to tell him what happened. The news coverage had been breathless, ubiquitous, and vague. A flurry of articles merely revealed that after a career-ending injury, I was bowing out permanently from ballet. Only Laurent and Sasha know what happened, but neither of them have the complete story. I didn't feel I owed anyone a more detailed explanation.

"It's too much to get into just now. We've got to get going!" I rise, and Seryozha follows my lead.

WE MAKE OUR WAY TO the theater and pass easily through the security. Under the harsh fluorescent light of the corridors, dancers are warming up and taking photos with each other in full costume. One of the girls is telling her friend, "I dropped a glob of adhesive right into my eye. Had to reglue the lash about ten times."

"It is awful when your lashes don't stick on the first time," the friend sympathizes.

"Oh no, for me this means I'll dance well tonight. It's lucky," the first girl says. They both giggle, linking arm and arm on their way to backstage. A pair of young corps men follow them, laughing at each other's fake facial hair. Seryozha and I trade glances, smiling.

"We're so old," we say at the same time. Then Seryozha shakes his head. "I just miss this place. It's okay to be nostalgic once in a while—doesn't mean we're old."

The backstage is as usual filled with not only dancers standing by but also pedagogues, former dancers and well-wishers, and company members on their night off. Resplendent in a beaded blue chiffon costume, Nina is warming up her feet by herself in a corner. She waves at me, a smile lighting up her anxious face.

"*Toi toi toi.*" I wish her luck, kissing both her cheeks. When that's done, she turns and cups her hands around Seryozha's shoulders.

"Seryozha! How good to see you—it's been so long," she says, kissing him in turn. "How did you two meet up?"

"We ran into each other at our old building. Let us get out of your way so you can warm up in peace," he says.

Nina smiles, and Seryozha and I tuck ourselves in a corner where we won't be disruptive. Nina has danced Nikiya four times over just as many seasons. She's already told me that she hasn't danced it once to her satisfaction. One of Mariinsky's most beloved lyrical ballerinas, she is cast because she has the right spirit for it: she is the tragic heroine rather than the jealous antiheroine of Gamzatti (which was my first principal role). But her weakness is the loss of stamina that has always plagued her as a dancer—and feels worse now at age thirty-five. Sure enough, she is beautiful in Act I. She bravely dances Nikiya's famous elegiac solo in Act II, and gets unexpectedly spicy for the "snake dance."

Because I know Nina's dancing as well as I do my own, I know the real challenge for her will be the Act III pas de deux. As she walks out holding the long sheet of white chiffon for the scarf dance, my heart migrates to my throat. She starts doing the fouetté arabesque balances; the maestro is setting the tempo much too slowly to be helpful, and I get an urge to throttle him. Her face is visibly red from the effort, even under the blue light of this ghostly scene.

Then comes the part that throws off even bravura dancers who do thirty-two fouettés in their sleep: three rounds of three arabesque turns into en dedans pirouettes, all while twisting one end of the scarf that's held by your partner on the other end. Music is still self-indulgently slow. The violinist is luxuriating in the solo without any regard to what the dancer needs, and Nina falls out of her pirouette in the first round. After this, it's a mental game even more than a physical one, and I shoot out reinforcement beams of focus and strength in her direction. Another, smaller hiccup in the second pirouette landing is met with a single person's encouraging clapping in the audience, which quickly dies. But it seems to have done the trick. The third round of this cursed turn sequence is accomplished with more cleanness, and the scarf is rolled away and out of the stage.

I sigh: there won't be any major mishaps in the rest of the ballet, because the worst has already happened. Nina propels herself through the coda by mustering a fresh burst of energy. Her unfaithful lover, Solor, redeems himself through their union in the Kingdom of Shades. The ovation begins even before the dancers assume their final positions and swells at the fermata. The curtains are lowered. More applause like the sound of a rainstorm. The soloists run out to the wings, backdrops are pushed upstage, and the corps de ballet array themselves in rows. The curtains open again, and the audience bestows their honors upon them. Hidden in the shadows on the other side of the stage, Nina is biting her lip. I can tell she's angry at herself for making two mistakes—just two out of hundreds of steps she performed this evening.

After the Three Shades, it is Nikiya's turn to take a bow. Solor leads her by the arm, and the applause is warm and affectionate. The audience has always loved and protected Nina. She curtsies, is presented with a huge bouquet of flowers, curtsies again, and then leads the smug maestro by the hand so he can take his bow. (Older and gray-haired, he is different from the one Katia Reznikova married a few years after I left Mariinsky.) The audience, knowing this is only the beginning, stay put respectfully and increase the volume of their applause. The Three Shades each receive a single-stem white rose, and Solor kisses Nina's hand again. After that is done, something less usual happens when Dmitri walks onto the stage carrying a mic.

"Ladies and gentlemen," Dmitri says, standing tall under the spotlight in his crisp, tie-less black suit. "Created for this very same company in 1877 by Marius Petipa, *La Bayadère* is a crown jewel of Mariinsky and Russian ballet itself. Each night we present this ballet is a uniquely shining moment in its centuries-long history, showing a timeless classic as it has never been seen before or will ever again. Tonight is even more special because it showcased the profound artistry of Nina Berezina, someone whose dedication to this company is unparalleled, whose beauty and humility astound me, whom I'm proud to call my colleague and fellow artist, and now, beginning this moment, a principal dancer of Mariinsky Ballet."

Before the last syllable of Dmitri's word fades, an avalanche of applause shakes the theater. I'm sobbing uncontrollably in the wings, but Nina smiles calmly and kisses Dmitri on both cheeks. Spectators are rising to their feet, chanting "Brava! Nina! Brava! Nina!" Now that is uncommon, much more so than being named principal dancer on stage. Under the roof of this theater, the story goes that the only dancer to ever get applauded by his name was Angel Corella.

Behind me, a jumble of different-size people push past the corps de ballet. They emerge on the edge of the stage as Andryusha, Petya, Lara, and tiny Luda, who is carrying a bouquet about the size of her own body. Nina hugs them each in turn and lifts Luda up for a kiss. The curtains close on them while the crowd is still clapping, hoping for another glimpse of the extraordinarily rare moment when someone good and deserving realizes her lifelong dream.

ONCE THE AUDITORIUM IS SCREENED off, Nina finds her pedagogue and gives her a deep curtsy. The ancient teacher whispers something inaudible to others, but probably some mixture of doting congratulations and constructive criticism. Meanwhile, Andryusha sidles up to kiss me and pat Seryozha's back. The children divide themselves between their parents, Petya and Lara flanking Andryusha and Luda acting as her mother's shadow.

"Nina was incredible. You saw how gracefully she handled that devil of a conductor," Andryusha says. I realize it must have been Andryusha who clapped in the middle of the scarf dance to encourage her along.

"I can't think of anyone who deserves the promotion more," I say, and Seryozha basically repeats what I said, just in slightly different words.

Once Nina is done thanking her teachers, she returns to us red-faced and breathless. When she hugs me, she finally lets a sob escape her mouth—but her eyes are still dry, as if so much emotion can't even be cried out easily.

"I love you, Nina. I couldn't be prouder even if it were me," I whisper in her ear, and she nods.

All of us are taking turns embracing heartily when Dmitri inserts himself into the circle.

"Isn't this like a village wedding. Nina, congratulations again. Natasha, I need to talk to you," he says, snapping his fingers at me. On either side of him stand Sveta and Vera Igorevna like his backup officers about to apprehend me.

"Can't you just let me be happy with my friends for once?" I say, walking away with Dmitri.

"Happy? You sound like a *zapadniki*." He makes a ridiculous scoffing sound. "I tried to call you. I have found Tae's replacement. But I want to know if you're still up for it."

It is Dmitri's dark and meaningful expression that tells me who it is. "This is crazy," I finally answer.

"Not crazy. Your most frequent partner. Together you're the most celebrated partnership in the world since Fonteyn and Nureyev. The two of you have danced *Giselle* more memorably than any others currently active."

"We did not part on good terms."

"According to *you*. Funny he didn't mention that," Dmitri smirks.

"What did he say?" I can't resist asking him, and he rolls his eyes dramatically.

"He said that he would dance with you always."

"Can I have some time to think?"

"Fine. You have until tomorrow morning at nine to decide. After that, we're either going forward with Sasha or canceling your show."

THE LAST TIME I SAW Sasha was a week after Dmitri left Paris. The company was finally on summer break. Sasha had wanted us to go to Corsica or someplace where we could float and snorkel in the shallow water all day, getting tan on our backs and pale on the stomach like some species of fish. I refused, hiding behind vague excuses; I hadn't confronted Sasha about Dmitri, but I had to draw the line at pretending to be happy. At first, Sasha was frustrated—and then he seemed relieved to not have to put in more effort. So we stayed in Paris, which was being submerged in a heatwave that eventually became known as Lucifer. All the surfaces inside the apartment were warm to the touch, including silverware and plates in the cupboard and the tiled floor of the bathroom. As soon as you walked outside, hot air blasted your body like the jet engine of an airplane. The Seine evaporated to a thick, syrupy drizzle. Even the Louvre closed when its air-conditioning failed. Corsica, the news said, was swept up in wildfires.

On the eleventh morning, the heatwave finally broke. Everyone who'd remained in the city the entire time felt they'd successfully defended something from attackers. That first refreshing day, hopeful and sweet blue threading through the usual golden smog like Venetian glass, took on a sloppy, delirious quality. People received the wrong orders at restaurants, parked in no-parking zones, and wore dresses without a bra. Music played loudly and drinking started around three in the afternoon. Sasha, who had been applying himself more fastidiously ever since returning from his leave, went to his gym to do conditioning exercises. He had a gala concert in Oman coming up. I don't remember what we said or how he looked as he left. Somehow we'd come to an unspoken agreement to manage our schedules so as to best avoid each other, like polite roommates with nothing in common.

I lay in bed, thinking about the same thing that had been driving me insane for the past few weeks. But every time I mulled over this, the edges of theories and memories were blunted. I felt a need to chew on this and suck on the flavor of pain until it was completely gone. Finally I was nearing the conclusion: I had to detach from reality as much as possible. Tuck the real me away so it doesn't get hurt. I'd been told that my soul radiated beyond the surface of my skin and filled the stage, even the whole auditorium. Now I wished the exact opposite to happen, for my soul to retract to the most hidden part of my body, shrinking into nothingness.

My phone vibrated and I lolled to the other side of the bed to pick it up. *We haven't chatted in a while*, Léon texted. *Come to the new bar where I work.* In all the years we'd known each other, he had never messaged me first. I double-checked the name and the address of the bar and started getting ready. After some debating, I put on jeans and a sheer black top with a light blazer. The outfit was a bit warm in the late afternoon but just right for when it would get colder at night.

I skipped downstairs and realized that Gabriel was taking his holiday, too. Only a few cars were on the road, presumably on their way to the countryside. Even the tourists seemed to have ebbed from the city, frightened by the record-breaking heat. I started walking northward, hoping to catch a cab.

A couple blocks away, in front of a lively wine bar, a man and a woman got off from their Vélib city bikes and parked them at the stand. I asked them how to check out a bike; they started to respond in an offhand way until the woman squealed, "You're Natalia Leonova?" She happened to be a ballet fan, and for the next ten minutes she both explained everything there was to know about riding bikes in Paris and peppered me with questions. After taking several photos together, I rode up to Montmartre, playing hide-and-seek with the white domes of Sacré-Cœur that loomed in and out of my view. I realized that the distance wasn't a problem, but the incline was. Montmartre was on a geological formation shaped essentially like a top hat, and the way up was not at all as refreshing as I remembered from the back of Léon's scooter. I hopped off the bike and climbed past Le Moulin de la Galette. I continued to the top of the stairs, where there was a little theater, its limestone wall dripping with ivy. At the inconspicuous plaza to my right sat a quintet of friends, a mix of boys and girls, an overflow from the steps in front of Sacré-Cœur that were always overrun by nodding, posing, swaggering teens. I observed, once again, that the young everywhere were never afraid of being too loud. Their laughing voices carried clear through the cool and sepulchrous air.

I turned left at the corner of the theater and stood at the top of a serpentine, wide but somehow discreet avenue. Either side of the road was lined with pale Art Deco mansions, graceful, dignified, reminiscent of a row of swans. As I stood there, all the lamps on the street turned on at once. It made me feel very excited, sad, and alone.

About halfway down the cobblestone pavement, I found the address that Léon had given me. It was tucked away from the avenue and hidden by a black metal gate. I punched in a password. The door opened with a beep, leading to a gravel path surrounded by fragrant jasmine bushes with their dark, glossy leaves. The path ended at a garden where guests were seated at café tables. A tapestry of city lights was unrolled at their feet, and the Eiffel Tower rose high above the rest to glitter against the crimson night sky. I gazed at the view for a moment, then found my way to the patio doors.

The bar was situated inside, which was the basement level of a boutique hotel. I searched and spotted Léon in his short-sleeved shirt, making a drink. I waited for the chic revelers in front of me to receive their orders. Even after they did, they lingered at the bar to banter with Léon, who hadn't yet given me a glance or a wave. I was warm and could feel my blazer lining sticking to my bare underarms. Surely, he would have seen me by now, standing just a few meters away. I kept tucking my hair behind my ear and making it fall just so in case he would turn around, and felt ashamed that I cared. Finally, the group meandered away to the corner booth, scattering laughter in their wake like cigarette smoke. I stepped up to the bar and Léon met my eyes as if just then noticing me.

"Great to see you, Natasha," he said, as though he hadn't been the one to invite me just a few hours ago. "What would you like?"

I glanced at the menu and picked one. He turned his back to me to start making it.

"I need to talk to you," I said when he handed me the cocktail. He looked surprised.

"Okay, now I'm a little busy," said Léon, pointing his chin at a group of friends headed in this direction. "Go and sit down in the garden. I'll come find you."

I paid and obediently went with my drink to the terrace. It really was the most magical view of Paris I had ever seen, yet savoring it alone was like watching Earth from space: it was beautiful but you wished you were less lonely. When I finished my cocktail, I was too embarrassed to go up to the bar and get another. So I sat there silently without any drink or a friend, as the rusty light-polluted sky deepend to maroon. I realized how much time had passed because the Eiffel Tower shimmered twice, each time on the hour, as I waited in the garden. After the second time, I got up and left without saying goodbye.

I retraced my steps back from the butte and got on the Vélib bike. I sailed downhill, the gentle night air brushing my hair back. It *was* colder now and I was shivering in my blazer; but every time my feet barely pressed down on the pedal and the wheels gained their own momentum, I got a strange, thrilling premonition. I had already experienced certain moments of ecstatic clarity in life, like the night I performed the Gamzatti variation at Varna and discovered I wanted Sasha. Gliding through the streets, I realized that the sense of premonition came from *weightlessness* defying gravity. That was why I loved to jump. And this time I discovered that I was free—of Sasha, of Léon, of all the things that had caused me pain and fury. I finally knew who I was and felt tenderness and compassion for everything that led me here.

I passed by the Cemetery of Montmartre and then Parc Monceau, gaining speed along the empty lanes. As I turned onto one of the avenues that became a spoke of the rotary around the Arc de Triomphe, someone's wheels skidded on the asphalt like a scream. Then the last thing I remember is a pair of headlights merging into one circular light, erasing the entire city and swallowing me whole. And like Icarus just moments after he gained his wings, I charged smiling into the sun.

CODA

> I want to dance because I feel and not because people are waiting for me.
>
> I wanted to dance more, but God said to me, "Enough." I stopped.
>
> I am life, and life is love for people.
>
> Beauty is not a relative thing. Beauty is god. God is beauty with feeling.
>
> —Vaslav Nijinsky

AS I SAID: EVEN THE MOST FAR-VOYAGING BIRDS WILL ALWAYS RETURN home. An albatross, which flies alone in the ocean for up to several years without ever touching land, sleeping midair and never seeing one of its kind, eventually comes back to its colony—the exact place of its birth.

I have no memory of arriving at the hospital following the accident. Because of a concussion, I was unable to remember my own address or the date. I don't even recollect drinking water and talking, as the nurses said I did—although I apparently asked for Mama several times.

The scans showed that I had broken a rib, my lower right leg, and multiple places in both feet. After an orthopedic surgery, I wasn't lucid for forty-eight hours. When I finally regained full consciousness, a nurse was in the middle of measuring my stats.

"Oh, you missed your partner," she said with a smile. "He stayed by your side night and day, and only just went home to rest."

"I don't want to see him," I said. She lowered her chart and regarded me suspiciously, as if I were still confused by the head trauma. I closed my eyes and heard her scribble down my stats in silence, as if she were annoyed with herself for momentarily getting too personal. But Sasha was not admitted to my room again.

When we did speak, it was over the phone. Before I even said a word, he already knew what I knew. He didn't try to deny anything. He listened in silence while I attacked him as cruelly as possible. But it was useless, and I felt like Polyphemus, the blinded Cyclops, hurling boulders at the quick-departing ship of Odysseus. I was already defeated, and he was already gone.

He only became agitated once, when I accused him of never loving me.

"You can't possibly believe that," Sasha said in a distressed tone. "My god, I loved you. And I still love you." He sniffled and gasped, and I pictured him shutting his eyes and pinching the bridge of his nose with two fingers.

"Is this what you do to people you love?" I asked.

"No, I know it isn't," he said weakly. "Sometimes in life, it's not possible to match up what you think, what you say, and what you do. Not for lack of trying though, Natasha. Because by god, I tried."

"Apparently not hard enough, Sasha." I shook my head, as if he could see me. "Tell me, do you love Dmitri?"

Sasha held his breath for a moment. "No," he said finally.

"Don't say no because he's a man. You coward."

"That has nothing to do with it. I just don't."

"You slept with him."

"I was attracted to him."

I took a deep breath and stopped myself from asking why. There was no reason anyone had for feeling love or an inclination or intimacy. It had simply happened to Sasha, the way it happened to anyone.

I told him to move out of the apartment before I left the hospital. A week later, I came home and saw that all his things had been dutifully removed. I was disappointed that he hadn't left anything for me—no letter, no flowers in a vase to wish me a quick recovery. There was just his key at the center of our table. Sasha wasn't a romantic. His only farewell gesture had been paying off my medical bills, which I realized upon returning to the hospital for my first follow-up appointment.

The doctor pronounced me lucky to be alive and my surgery successful, but neither felt true. I applied myself to daily physical therapy for hours, yet it was a year before I could even walk normally. I was mortified by my condition and responded with silence to everyone who reached out—a group conspicuously missing Léon, who never checked in with me once. After some weeks, even these messages from friends dwindled down until I was utterly alone.

Because I wasn't dancing, I found out Sasha's whereabouts after everyone else. It was Gabriel—who'd always been more loyal to me—who told me that Sasha had gone on a dating rampage, laid waste to half the corps de ballet, and finally settled upon moving in with Théa. Gabriel also said that Sasha was partying and drinking heavily; that he had bags under his eyes; that he missed half the company classes; that in one evening of *Don Quixote* he twisted his ankle coming down from a saut de basque and fell on his ass, and an alternate had to finish the rest of the performance in his stead. Gabriel seemed to think this news would cheer me up. I thanked Gabriel and asked him not to bring up Sasha again.

For the first time in my life, seasons passed without meaning anything to me. At a doctor's appointment, it was pointed out to me that I was depressed. I had no social interactions and ate only when hunger pangs kept me awake. An antidepressant was added to my pain medication regimen; and always a good student, I took these religiously until the world receded from me with pleasing gentleness. Sharp edges and contours blurred, noises and light softened, and the air hugged me like a warm bath. I skipped physical therapy. I didn't think there was a point to putting all the broken pieces of my body back together. Whoever said you're beautiful where you are broken was not a dancer.

Laurent called me to ask about my progress and I told him I wanted to retire. He only resisted me a little so as not to be rude; I could hear that his sigh had a tinge of relief in it. He did have affection for me, but he always thought first of the good of the company. Truthfully, what he had been fond of wasn't *me* but my dancing, and he regretted losing the dance not the dancer.

Almost two years to the day of the accident, my retirement was announced with the utmost gravitas and pomp. Laurent, my esteemed teachers, and other dance stars around the world paid me tribute as if I had just died. Some dance fans were interviewed shedding tears at the news. The Paris Opéra delivered a huge mound of flowers and gifts that had been sent to me via their offices.

By the time those flowers died, it seemed everyone had already moved on. This was when I received a call from Sveta in the middle of the night. I hadn't spoken to her or, indeed, anyone in Petersburg in years, but she cut off my pleasantries and got straight to the point. Mama had gone to the hospital because of abdominal pain. She thought she had ulcers, and the doctor agreed. They did an X-ray just to be certain, and discovered that she had endometrial cancer instead. The doctor wanted to hospitalize her immediately, but she insisted on coming home. One week later, she was dead.

My first thought was that I didn't believe this. My second was that it had to be true, but that I couldn't panic and lose my head. I didn't cry or get knocked off my feet. Within hours of the phone call, I bought the first flight out to Petersburg and dashed to the airport. When I went to the airline counter, the clerk said that there was a problem checking me in. I thought at first that they had oversold their seats and offered to buy first class, or the next flight, anything to get me back home. My mother just passed away, I explained. She apologized and signaled to a more senior clerk; the senior clerk didn't meet my eyes while sifting through their system. Even in my foggy state, I was becoming irate, raising my voice. A GTA—airport gendarmerie—officer in a light-blue uniform came over and I quieted down. The gendarme said that I had to come with him.

"I apologize for getting upset, but as you can see, I bought a ticket that's leaving in less than an hour, and these clerks are refusing to check me in for my flight," I said as calmly as possible without budging from the counter. "My mother has just passed away. I need to go home."

"Your name is Natalia Leonova?" the gendarme asked, and I nodded. "You're on the DGSI no-fly list. Please follow me."

What I found out inside the detention room at Charles de Gaulle's own police station: I was barred from flying in and out of France as a national security risk; it was to do with Sasha's rant about the war and his known pro-Russia stance. The gendarme asked, *What did you know about Sasha's position on the war?* Tearing off the ends of my nails, I explained that this had happened a long time ago. Five years had passed since Sasha's outburst, and he had been punished accordingly. As the war spread to Donbas and the death toll rose, he regretted his impulsive statement and worked hard to rebuild his reputation. And besides—this was the most important thing—I was no longer in any way related to Sasha, as we had broken off our engagement and were no longer in contact. I opposed the war and was friends with both Ukrainians and Russians, individuals who could not be judged by their nationalities or place of birth.

The gendarme recorded my answers and took notes with no interjections. I'd already missed my flight, but neither he nor I were concerned with that now. Humming a little tune, the gendarme rose from his seat; then he raised his visored hat with one hand, smoothed the thinning crown of his head with the other, and repositioned the hat in its place.

"I will be back. Do you need anything? Water?" he asked cordially.

"I want to speak to my attorney," I replied.

The gendarme raised his eyebrows and gave a nod. After he left the room, I called the only person I could think of.

"Hello? Natasha?" I couldn't believe she picked up the phone in a few rings.

"Behnaz, I'm so sorry to bother you this early in the morning. I need your help," I said, looking at the bleeding ends of my nails. Over the next ten minutes, Behnaz listened in silence as I explained what had happened.

"I'm really sorry, Natasha," she finally said. "I wish I could help. But this isn't really my area of expertise. Most importantly, I don't practice law in France—I'm only called to the bar of England and Wales. Let me see if I can find you some references."

"Thank you. I really appreciate it," I said.

Behnaz hung up and never sent me any contacts during the rest of my time in France.

Next I called Laurent, who was in his car on the way to the theater. He listened attentively and said he would let me know after making some calls. About two hours later, he rang me back.

"I spoke with the Minister of Culture, who's calling the airport gendarmerie himself as we speak. We can get you out of Charles de Gaulle, that's easy," Laurent said without characteristically relishing his power and influence. "The trouble is, it's harder to get you on a flight to St. Petersburg, because you're still on the no-flight list."

"All this because of Sasha's outburst? This is absurd." I could barely string words together at this point. I felt as though days had passed since I'd been trapped inside that room with its steel door; it was impossible to recollect when I'd last slept, drunk water, or eaten anything.

"No. Sasha caused the investigation, but it seems our intelligence found out more things about you from back in Russia. It appears your employment at Bolshoi was sponsored by the highest levels in the Kremlin." Laurent rattled off names that more frequently ran with international conflict news than the ballet. "They don't just think you're an ex-fiancée of some moody male dancer. They think you might be connected to the Russian state."

I laughed dryly, and Laurent let it pass before speaking again. "So, what the Minister and I can do is vouch for you as an artist of the Paris Opéra and bring you back to your apartment. But clearing you for flight is beyond even my abilities." He paused, and I heard the click of his lighter followed by a long exhale. "It's terrible about your mother. I know you wanted to go home for her."

When we hung up, the gendarme opened the door and told me I was free to go home. I dragged my suitcase out of the terminal, dazed, unsure about the date or the time. Gabriel brought me home and forced me to eat a takeout meal he picked up on the way. After that, I spent days unable to move out of bed. I missed my mother's funeral but was too sick to even know it. I thought I'd hit bottom before, but that was nothing compared to the bottom I hit now. On the ocean floor, there are mountain ranges and valleys, and I'd fallen from a sea cliff and plunged to the bottom of the bottom. I took my meds and drank until I lost consciousness.

THE PHONE WAS RINGING. I didn't pick up. Later, I heard noise from just outside the door. More calls ensued, and I could no longer ignore the ruckus. I tried to walk out of bed and found my legs couldn't carry out the task. I threw myself off the mattress, crashed on the floor, and crawled to the front door. I opened it. And the person I least expected walked in and held me by the arms.

"Natasha," said Sofiya, carrying me to the sofa. She seemed to be in shock, looking around at the appalling mess, the thick layer of dust. "Behnaz told me what happened. I can help. But first, let's get you cleaned up."

She filled the bathtub, undressed me, and placed me in it as if I were a ragdoll. I didn't resist or pretend at modesty. We had circled each other warily in Paris and I had seen her only a handful of times in the past several years. But we'd been very close when we were young, and she seemed to think it natural that she should take care of me.

"Do you remember," she said as I lay in the hot water, "the night we went to see *Swan Lake* with Seryozha, Nina, and Andryusha? I didn't want to go, but you kept convincing me and dragging me by the arm. The heater was broken again, so I took a thirty-second shower. You were waiting for me next to the stall, holding my knit hat so I could put it on right away. I did the same for you."

"Just thinking about it makes me shiver," I said. "Sasha always made fun of my hot baths and said I couldn't even bear to brush my teeth with cold water. It's because I hated how freezing it was all the time, when we were young."

After the bath, Sofiya put me in a robe to rest on the couch while she changed the sheets and picked up the mess. Her assistant dropped off some soup, bread, and fruit juice. Once we had some food, Sofiya told me that her boyfriend's father, the powerful politician, was going to take me off the no-fly list. She would let me know when I could buy my next flight out to Petersburg.

"You didn't have to do all this for me," I said. I was ashamed that I always focused on her flaws and never gave her enough credit. "You know, I was terribly envious of you."

"I was terribly envious of you, too, Natasha. Sometimes I knew what you wanted from me and I'd hold back from giving that to you." Sofiya pulled her legs up and hugged her knees to her chest. "I saw what that did to you. You became furious. But I think you also—at the end of the day—you cared about me, because I felt the same way."

Sofiya came to me every evening until I was cleared to fly. A week later, she dropped me off at the airport. The plane made a large U in the air, orienting itself toward the east. Below my window, Paris passed like a puddle of light after a heavy rain.

It is the morning after Nina's promotion. I've been slipping in and out of dreams all night. Still in bed at 8:45 a.m., I call Nina.

"Hello?" she whispers.

"Congratulations again. How does it feel?"

"Like I'm dreaming," she murmurs *sotto voce*. "It's surreal. I keep thinking someone could just take it away from me." There's a discreet shuffling sound, and I envision her turning away from sleeping Andryusha on the other side of the bed. It is a blessing to have friends who will pick up the phone even while lying next to their spouse.

"You should relax and enjoy it, Nina."

"Did you decide what to do about Sasha?" she asks, changing the subject.

"No, I haven't," I say, checking the clock on my nightstand. It is twelve minutes to nine. "I've only just moved on from Sasha. I don't want to see him and reopen the wound."

"I agree," Nina says easily.

"But?"

"I feel like if you really wanted to give up on performing, you wouldn't have called me. It's like you want to be convinced otherwise." I hear Nina rise from the bed and start her morning in the kitchen.

"I marvel at how well you know me." I shake my head, also getting a glass of water from the bathroom sink. "Giving up would be easier if I didn't see your performance last night."

"You know, last night wasn't my best," she confides. So this is why she's mired in doubt—because she was rewarded when she faltered, not when she was truly self-satisfied. "But we can talk about that later. Call Dmitri. Tell him you'll dance with Sasha."

I then realize something that had nagged at me the first few days in Petersburg before everything else consumed me. "*You* told Dmitri I came back, didn't you?"

Nina sighs. "Are you going to be angry at me? He knew you'd be returning at some point and told me you'll want to dance again. Please don't be mad."

She sounds so upset with herself that I have to joke that she should henceforth call Dmitri and all my old enemies when I show up in town. Finally, I hang up with Nina and call his number. When I tell him I've decided to partner with Sasha, he laughs and says, "Good, because he flew in last night."

THREE DAYS TO THE SEASON premiere of *Giselle* and two days to the first stage run-through, I walk into the studio an hour before class. I haven't danced in three days, which is reckless in performance week. Skip one class a week, and you notice the difference; skip two classes, your teacher notices; and skip three classes, the audience knows. I sew my pointe shoes, stretch, roll out, condition, and plank until Sveta and Vera Igorevna enter together amicably. In the past few months, they seem to have bonded over my waywardness. They lay down their things by the mirrors, passing meaningful glances like comrades in arms.

When we're about to start the warm-up tendus, my heart just about stops when I see the tall silhouette of Sasha framed by the open door.

"Sorry I'm late. I got into town a few hours ago," he says to the room. The ladies perk up unconsciously at this sight—even Vera Igorevna, who is usually as grumpy to charming young men as she is to everyone else, being an equal-opportunity grouch. Whereas she would have scolded me like a child for tardiness, she now steps forward with an outstretched hand.

"It's great to finally meet you, Alexander," Vera Igorevna says, eagerly shaking Sasha's hand. "Here's my colleague, Svetlana Timurevna."

Sveta spends some time cooing over Sasha, listing her favorite roles he's danced and spreading gossip about Bolshoi and Mariinsky dancers. This effectively takes so much time that Vera Igorevna finally puts her foot down barking, "Well, we have a lot of work to do today. Let's begin." Music is restarted for warm-up tendus. And Sasha and I are saved from an awkward reunion in front of the teachers. I almost suspect that Vera Igorevna and Sveta planned the whole thing beforehand and feel renewed reverence toward their infinite wisdom.

While we go through the barre, I reacquaint myself with Sasha sans words. My first impression is that he hasn't changed at all since I last saw him two years ago. His golden hair still falls nearly to his shoulders. His body is lean and taut with its muscular contours, tendons, and shapely dimples. But dance always tells the truth. During tendus, I see someone who puts great care into basic steps because these become more pleasurable—and less painful—as one gets older. During adagio, I notice how gingerly he positions himself around the wear and tear on his spine and hips. And grand battements: his raw strength is past its prime, but he's not ready to give up. Sasha is thirty-five and just entering the five-year twilight of the male dancer. It's something he and I talked about often. He'd always been prepared for it—but when it happens, it is still surprising and disheartening.

We put the barres away, do a few center exercises, and move on to running through all the solos in Act I. Now there is no way of getting around it: Sasha and I have to look each other in the eyes, hold each other's hands, and dance together. We still haven't so much as said hello, but it's okay. "Hello" or even "how are you" is nothing more than a charade to us; it would feel unnecessary and even false. Whatever we need to say to each other, we can say much better through dance.

Vera Igorevna leads us through the staging differences in the Mariinsky production. Afterward we run through the entire act without stopping. In Act I, Giselle falls in love with Albrecht. She thinks she knows who he is, but in fact he's hiding his true identity. When this is discovered, she loses her mind and dies. At his servant's urging, distraught Albrecht runs away from the scene; the villagers mourn Giselle and the curtain lowers.

Sasha covers his face in his hands. Sveta drapes his cape around his shoulders and points yonder—"Flee, my lord!"—and he runs to the corner of the studio, where he stands breathing hard until the end of the music. I am still lying with my eyes closed in the middle of the studio floor, but I can feel him watching me intently, as if it's sunrise and I'm a ship that's just appeared on the horizon.

THE NEXT DAY, WE WORK out the details of Act II and finish with a run-through. We still haven't said a word to each other, which is made possible by the presence of our two voluble coaches.

Night has fallen in the forest. Sasha comes to visit me at my grave. He lays down an armful of lilies at the cross. Overcome with grief and guilt, he takes a knee and covers his face with one hand. I appear with two stems of lilies; he tries to catch me, but I slip between his fingers like smoke, leaving only lilies behind. He stands despairing. I float above and scatter more lilies over his head like rain. *I am now only a spirit, but here is the proof that I still love you.* He holds them over his heart, trembling with hope.

The Wilis arrive with their vengeful queen, Myrtha, who condemns Sasha to death. I rush out and stand between them, backing Sasha over to my grave. There, the power of the cross protects him and Myrtha's wand of asphodel is broken in two. To appease Myrtha, I dance in his stead—but that draws out Sasha from the sanctuary, and he begins to dance with me. The Wilis pull us apart. But escaping their clutches, we draw toward each other and embrace.

After our pas de deux, I dance my solo variation. It's the same choreography I've performed dozens of times. But something new pours out of me. There are times when you're not in control of art, art is in control of you. It's as though a faucet turns on suddenly and you are the cup that has to catch the water, but it's not just any water—it's the water of life—and every drop is precious; yet you know you are the perfect vessel for it and there is no other cup that was made for this purpose, so you are calm and you simply do everything to the best of your ability, which is exactly what is required, no more and no less.

After I run off stage, Sasha reappears for his variation. I've seen him dance this countless times, but now I see that he's changed it. There is a hand to his forehead that I don't recognize, new port de bras to the chassé pas de bourrée. Not only has he never danced Albrecht like this before, I've never seen anyone else do it. I realize why and my eyes cloud over.

The Wilis, however, remain implacable. Myrtha commands Sasha to dance until he collapses in exhaustion. I plead mercy but it's no use. Myrtha is about to end his life.

Then, the church bells toll in the distance.

The sun is rising.

The Wilis disappear like fog. Sasha rises and we dance our last pas de deux in the rosy light of dawn. It is time for my return to the grave. Sasha runs ahead of me and blocks my way, crossing his arms. *Don't go. Stay with me.* But I cannot remain any longer. Before I descend, I give him one last lily. *I forgive you.* Finding himself alone in the sunlit glade, he weeps and presses the lily to his lips.

When the music stops, Vera Igorevna leaves the room and Sveta turns her back to us, wiping her eyes. Sasha is crumpled in the center of the room and I am curled up by the wall, both of us crying and unable to comfort each other.

SASHA STANDS LINGERING FOR A few minutes while Vera Igorevna and Sveta gather their things and put on their coats. I peel off my pointe shoes slowly so that he doesn't have a choice but to leave with the teachers. Once the others' footsteps fade away, I fold over my legs and bury my face in my arms.

"Natasha," a man calls.

I raise my head thinking it's Sasha, but it's Dmitri.

"Can we talk?" he asks, but doesn't wait for my answer to walk inside. He picks up a chair, moves it by my side, and sits down with his habitual grace. Retirement hasn't diminished his abilities, and he is known to casually demonstrate the choreography without warming up.

"The rehearsals are going well with Sasha." Dmitri crosses his legs and interlaces his hands around the top knee. "I was watching from my office. The two of you—*do* something to each other."

I shrug, emptied as I am of any retorts or sarcasm.

"You know I just told you the truth. So listen to me." Dmitri leans in so closely that I can see his long black eyelashes, bright green irises, and the red vessels in the inner corners, feathery and tangled like mistletoe. I sit and listen to this man whose eyes are like a dark forest.

"You danced well today. But your best dancing days are over, Natasha. In every dancer's life there comes a point where you must accept that fact and still dance. It's not as though you can quit the minute you notice you're getting weaker. So you resist it; some days you may even think, 'actually I was mistaken, that was just an off day, I can get it back.' But eventually you realize the decline is real. From then on, you're hiding from yourself *and* the world that you're worsening. You're fighting for your life.

"Truthfully I thought you had more time left. I brought you back so you can work yourself up before you retire, but I made a mistake. At thirty-four, you won't dance Giselle as well as you did before, when you didn't have the knowledge of your own transience.

"It pains you to now think: How casually you spent your ability, how you didn't know! It's excruciating, I understand. Perhaps you won't believe me, since I've danced well or even extraordinarily countless times . . . But the truth is, there were only a few times in my life when I danced better than I could have humanly, as though I couldn't fail, as though I were a god. And after the last time that happened, I felt crazed. Days and months and years accumulated like grains of sand while I obsessively chased that transcendence just one more time.

"Maybe you're still willing to keep turning the pages. There is *Giselle* to look forward to, perhaps *Marguerite and Armand*, some contemporary works that you can dance with less strain. But I think you should stop while you're still ahead. This way you are a legend, not a failure. That's what I did."

I lick my dry lips and gaze at him beneath half-closed lids. "You forced me out of retirement and now you're pleading with me to retire. Are you for real?"

He chuckles. "Don't always be so suspicious. Besides, I have a proposition. I'm offering you the position of associate ballet director of Mariinsky Theatre. And who knows, if I were to move to another post in the next several years, you'd be poised to take my place. If that comes to pass, you will be one of the very few women artistic directors of a world-class ballet company. And, of course, the first one in Mariinsky history."

The first female director of Mariinsky Ballet. Even before the political fallout, I have never thought of returning permanently to Russia, let alone Mariinsky. I also can't deny that it feels like something I have to try—unless, of course, this is another of Dmitri's poison darts at me.

"Why should I believe you? We don't exactly get along." I shake my head. "I don't see why you want me to work with you."

"You want to know the truth?"

I nod.

"Well, firstly, you sometimes remind me of myself. Secondly and unfortunately, you are the most admired ballerina in the world.

Rightly so." He rises and stands on his long, strong legs that are like two towers of a citadel.

"Don't ever mention to anyone that I said this. Not even to me. See you at the stage run-through." With that, Dmitri turns on his heel and leaves.

THE DAY BEFORE THE PERFORMANCE is our first and only run-through onstage. From the get-go, being surrounded by other dancers throws me off. I haven't taken a company class since that first day, and all my rehearsals have been private, safe. Our Myrtha is Katia Reznikova, who was never cordial to me even by accident—no slippage of a hello when caught off guard or a muttered thanks. She still doesn't acknowledge my presence while we warm up side by side. I nearly feel respect for such consistency of character.

Adding to my malaise is Dmitri, sitting in the middle of the orchestra level with his ice-cream-cone microphone. Every time a villager or a Wili gets anything slightly wrong, he shouts corrections by name: "Front shoulder higher on that first arabesque, Masha. *Pozhaluysta!*" "Stretch that knee, Vlada. By god, stretch that foot all the way! *Pozhaluysta!*" He has a way of shouting *please* at the end of every command, which makes it actually sound worse, not better. And then there is the fact that this is the first time Dmitri, Sasha, and I are in the same room since the night he performed Mercutio. Sasha must realize this, and probably also Dmitri. I force myself to forget who I am and become Giselle.

When the rehearsal ends, I look toward Vera Igorevna and Sveta in the audience. They give me a nod and a smile—tentatively optimistic. So I haven't made a fool of myself, but it's not the best I've danced this role. Not by a long shot. I imagine the valves to my tear ducts closing; it seems to work, and my eyes stay dry while surrounded by company members.

In the safety of the soloist dressing room, I unlace my shoes, slither out of my costume, and put on the coat Nina lent me. By the time I leave the theater, the black night has fallen and all the streetlights have turned on, as if the city itself is a giant auditorium. It's uncommonly cold for autumn, and I tighten my coat collar around my neck. Then I feel a slight warmth nearby. The warmth grows until it stands next to me, holding me by the shoulder.

"Can we talk?" Sasha says. The light from a streetlamp falls across his face. I notice how fine lines have spread delicately and slowly, like fissures on a frozen lake, from the corners of his eyes, brows, and lips. Perhaps his golden hair also has a fair bit of silver in it.

"I— What is there to talk about?" I continue walking away.

"Look, I know you're still upset with me. But would you, please?" He points at a restaurant a block away. "Just give me half an hour."

I press my temples with my palms. "Fine," I say, and Sasha's face brightens.

The restaurant is no-frills. The fluorescent light hums quietly overhead, and the savory smell of fried onions is baked into the vinyl seats. We sit in a corner booth and I let Sasha order some vareniki, borscht, and salads. Once the waitress leaves, Sasha interlaces his hands on the table and gazes attentively at his own thumbs.

"I am truly sorry about what happened," he says.

"It really doesn't matter anymore. I don't care."

"But it does, and you do care. You haven't forgiven me."

"This is what it's about? You want my *forgiveness*?" I snort. "You are incorrigible. We are finished—that is the best that I can do for you. I need to save some kindness for myself, too."

"That's not what I meant! You don't have to forgive me. I just meant you're still hurting. And I'm still hurting." Sasha's nose becomes red and he looks out the window. "I didn't know how to be honest with you about all parts of myself. It was easier to pretend that this side didn't exist. As long as no one knew, it felt like it wasn't even real. And if you hadn't caught me, I'd still be hiding."

The waitress returns with our food, and Sasha clears his throat. He serves me first and puts some on his plate, and we both pretend to eat for a few minutes.

"Did I ever tell you about the bees?" he says, putting down his fork. I shake my head.

"Back in Donbas, my grandfather kept mason bees to help pollinate our fruit trees. These bees don't make honey, but they don't have stingers and are the gentlest little things. When I was young, I used to stand in front of their hive, watching them go in and out. Sometimes they go in with their head, other times with their rear—like backing a car into a parking space. At twilight, I would peer inside and see their sleeping heads or rear ends. They gathered their pollen for a few weeks, then laid their eggs, closed the entrance, and died. At the end of the season, my grandfather took the hive apart into dozens of wooden straws that contained the eggs. He put them in a jar in the shed for the winter.

"In early spring, he would crack open each straw and there would be four or five eggs inside, the shape and size of black beans. He would put the eggs out in the hive at a sunny corner of the garden, but not all of these would hatch on their own. After several days, he gathered these unhatched eggs in a bowl and brought them inside. Then he'd sit at the dining table, cutting a slight opening on the egg casing with a pair of small scissors, gently rolling the casing between his fingers, and setting these baby bees free. The baby bees always came out confused, disoriented. He put them in a different glass jar and they crawled around for a while in there, until he was ready to put them out in the garden.

"One night I was watching him do this and asked if I could help. I felt so happy when a baby bee came out between my fingers—it was like a miracle. Then I did another one, and another one. And then the next one didn't look right. It was as though it didn't have a body below the waist, and its wings were half the normal length. With horror I realized that when I was creating an opening in the casing, I'd accidentally cut the bee in half.

"The bee crawled, it was still clearly alive. I brought it outside to the garden and put it on a flower, hoping that it would be able to taste some nectar in the short life it had left. I cried, although mason bees never live longer than a few weeks at most—and although in the grand scheme of things, it was just a bee, not a dog or a cat or even a cow. Because, you know, I loved those bees. I loved and hurt them. I just keep thinking about that." Sasha presses a finger to the inner corners of his eyes. "I loved and hurt you. And I'm so, so sorry."

I can feel that he's been waiting to tell me this story for a long time. The image of Sasha as a child appears in my mind, and then all the subsequent Sashas—raw and explosive in adolescence, glorious in his twenties, passionate, gregarious, aloof, outrageous, faltering, defiant—overlay on top, and finally fade into the Sasha sitting across from me. He's waited two years and flown here at a moment's notice just to tell me this.

"It's okay," I say. "I understand. I forgive you."

Sasha reaches across the table and holds my hand.

"You are the only person I've ever loved," he says. When I don't say anything, he presses my hand to his lips. "I still love you."

"What about Théa?"

"She and I broke up a few months ago. Amicably. But it wasn't ever going to last." He squeezes my hand in both of his own. "Natasha, you and I were meant to be together. We are not people who meet easily and part easily, never to think of each other again. Later when we look back on these past two years, it will just feel like a blip. I haven't been happy. I can live a decent life without you but not anything that feels both extraordinary and true. Like a wonder, a miracle, a waking dream. You know what I mean. You agree with me."

I nod, and Sasha squeezes my hands tighter.

"I want to live the rest of my life with you. Have children with you. Do everything together," he continues, color rising to his cheeks.

"I miss you," I say, vision fogged by tears I'd been holding back all day. The life he speaks of blooms before my eyes—art, family, closeness like the pages of a book. I drop my chin and squeeze his hand. Without letting go, he half-rises from his seat to move over by my side. I want nothing more in the world than to feel his arms around me—so much so that my whole body aches.

Just then, the waitress returns to ask if we'd like dessert. Sasha sits back down. She clears the table, produces a check from her apron, and leaves with Sasha's credit card. And in that one minute, throughout which Sasha holds my hand with at least one of his own as if afraid of letting go, something shifts. He knows it, too, and the radiance that had warmed his face fades away.

"Does Théa know about Dmitri?" I ask, and he lowers his eyes. I pull away my hand to wipe the tears that are finally streaming down my cheeks, and he doesn't try to hold on.

"I can't, Sasha. I am sorry for you. I am sorry for us. I wish you the best, truly." Before I can lose my resolve, I rise and put on my coat. Sasha's eyes are red and wet, but he doesn't say anything more. We'd laid out all our cards, no one won, and now the game was finally over.

I GO THROUGH MY RITUAL for the night before a performance. I prepare my pointe shoes and pack my tights and warm-up gear. There's the hair and makeup kit, followed by stretches, a bath, and ointments. After everything is finished, I lie in bed with my headphones on, listening to tomorrow's music. I dream again of the black birds that swirl downward like a tornado, but I'm no longer afraid of them. When the morning comes, I open my eyes and see that it has flurried overnight, as if the birds from my dream have changed into snow.

IN THE LOBBY, I ASK for Igor Petrenko. The manager appears at the front desk, perfectly groomed in his three-piece suit at eight in the morning.

"How can I help you, Natalia Nikolaevna?" he asks, folding his hands over the marble counter. "And *merde* for tonight's performance."

"Oh, you know about it?"

"I have seen posters everywhere, Natalia Nikolaevna. And people are very excited. Petersburg hasn't seen you dance live in ten years, and you're the pride of this city." The manager smiles sheepishly. "After Ulanova, Makarova, Nureyev, Baryshnikov, Lopatkina . . . Now, Leonova."

"Well, Igor Vladimirovich, then you must come see me dance," I say, pulling out two tickets. "Friends and family sit in the Duke's box."

Igor Petrenko stares at the tickets in astonishment. "My daughter is eight. She's been taking ballet for a few years. She will pass out from joy."

"Then do be careful. She'll be seated next to Nina Berezina and Andrei Vasiliev, principal dancers of Mariinsky Theatre." I smile. The manager's jaw falls open, and he insists on bringing me breakfast to go and a tea with jam to soothe my nerves.

6:45 P.M. BEHIND THE LAYERS of drapery and a wooden screen painted to look like curtains, the stage hums with dancers breaking in their shoes. Stagehands wearing headsets weave in and out, testing the pulleys and dragging away props. The spotlight turns on with a clang, releasing the scent of celluloid and smoke. The air also smells of old velvet, rosin, string instruments, and powder.

I walk to the center of the stage and lie down. From here I can hear the musicians warming up on the other side of the curtains, the soft rustling of their scores. The strings tune their open E A D G C; the clarinets and the flutes run up and down their scales. The percussionist subtly strikes the timpani to check the pitch without surprising the spectators who are finding their seats. Their excited chatter fills the auditorium, which is bathed in the aureus glow of dozens of crystal chandeliers. Somewhere among them, I can almost hear those who came to see me: Nina and Andryusha, their children, Seryozha, Igor Petrenko and his daughter.

One by one, the dancers leave the stage and find their places in the wings. I am still lying at the center center, eyes shut. The stage manager passes me by whispering, "Curtains rise in five."

All the other dancers have walked off, but someone approaches and lies down next to me. I would recognize that particular shade of warmth anywhere. I open my eyes, and there he is. Somewhere between the boy whom I loved and the man whose path will lead farther and farther away from me, lies this person.

The conductor steps onto the podium and the audience hushes, so that I can hear the sound of his breathing as his chest rises and falls. We hold each other's gaze in that perfect silence.

The stage manager returns, imploring us to run off stage. The maestro bows, and the applause of the audience sets the evening on its course. By the time their clapping quiets down, Vera Igorevna can be heard hissing from the wings.

We squeeze each other's hand and smile, because of everything. All the beauty and tragedy of life can be found in the space between what could have been and what turns out to be. But mostly, I must tell you, it is beautiful.

There is the soft rustle of bows hovering in the air as the conductor lifts his baton for the overture. Moments before the curtains are raised, we spring up and run off to the wings, laughing like the children that we once were.

CURTAIN CALL

Plaudite, amici, comedia finita est.
Applaud, my friends, the comedy is over.

—Ludwig van Beethoven

WHEN I WAKE, HIS SIDE OF THE BED IS ALREADY EMPTY. I REACH OVER anyway and my hand falls on our cat, Finn. Strictly speaking, Finn belongs to Magnus, but the distinction was lost when they both moved into my apartment two years ago. Although Magnus raised him from kittenhood, Finn lost no time switching his allegiance over to me: when I so much as sit for a minute, the cat plops himself down somewhere on my body. I now start stroking his black fur, and he rolls over onto his back in pleasure. Then he jumps off the bed and points his head in the direction of the kitchen.

"Yes, yes. I know you're hungry," I mutter, slipping out of bed. I pad across the hallway to the living room and pull open the curtains. It is a soft, downy morning. The light is breaking through the fog to reflect on the river and then back on the sky, and that resonance seems like it could go on forever. This view is one of the reasons I picked this apartment on the Fontanka Embankment. And I love the parquet wooden floor and the original molding on the walls. But Magnus, who loves everything new and modern, wants to build us a house based on the idea of air and stone. He says he already has it all in his head. So far, client projects have taken precedence, and it's hard to find the right land or an old property in the middle of Petersburg. The wait will be worth it, Magnus assures me.

I feed Finn, eat a little breakfast, and head out for the day. It takes ten minutes of brisk walking to reach the theater. I arrive at my office to find that my assistant, Vika, has left a green juice on my desk. She is twenty-five, very pretty with pink cheeks and portobello-brown hair, and exceedingly smart: she can do things with my phone that I never thought was possible. Or even more basic functions. Once, I didn't know how to turn off and restart my latest iPhone, and was too proud to just look it up online. While Vika did it for me, I told her that she was resourceful beyond her years.

"But Natalia Nikolaevna, you were a prima ballerina at Bolshoi when you were my age." She laughed. "Also, what do you do when I'm not around?"

"I ask Magnus."

"And if he isn't around?" she asked. It's true that Magnus is often away for business, just like I am.

"I would chuck the phone into the river," I said.

While I'm sipping the green juice, Vika walks in with a clipboard. After the company class, there is a virtual meeting with a British arts trust, then a rehearsal for a Balanchine triple bill, a phone call with the Kennedy Center for our upcoming tour in December, then a stage run-through for a newly commissioned piece. Somewhere in the middle of all this, I am supposed to have a private meeting with a moody second soloist (promising although riddled with personal problems; find out what they are and determine action). Then it's time to attend the night's performance of *Don Quixote*.

"Save me with your magic powers, Vika," I grumble over the half-finished glass of juice.

"I'm sorry, Natalia Nikolaevna. Oh, and one more thing." Vika sets down the clipboard and fetches a package. "This came for you."

It's a heavy brown cardboard box, postmarked in Paris. There is a sender's address but no name. I reach for the box cutter, decide against it, and hand it back to her.

"Please drop it off at my apartment. I'll look at it later."

I DON'T TYPICALLY OVERSEE COMPANY class, but five new corps de ballet dancers are starting today. One of them is Elza Petrenko, the hotel manager Igor Petrenko's daughter. I didn't make the connection until after the auditions, since it's a common last name and she does not resemble her grandiloquent father. I scan the room and wave at Sveta, who starts giving the warm-up tendu combination without any introductory remarks—a power move that is sure to get noisy dancers to quiet down. I flash her a smile, and she returns a wink. Elza and her cohort scramble to find their spaces at the barre, the established members move a few inches with clear expressions of annoyance, and so nothing has changed in what Sveta used to call the fabric of tradition.

The rest of the day unfolds in a blur. The British arts trust had severed ties with Mariinsky upon Russia's full-scale invasion of Ukraine in 2022. This is our first meeting since the end of the war. Everyone is eager to work together again; they are hungry for Russian glamour, we are ready for British funding, and both sides want more trading of choreographic and performing talent. Then Vika whisks me away to rehearsal, handing me cookies along the way. The atmosphere in the studio is grim. The ballet master from the Balanchine Trust is very insistent on the straight, high arms, and our dancers with their rounded Vaganova arms stare at him when he shouts, "Higher! Yes! Just point at the ceiling!" More meetings, more rehearsals. I decide to give the recalcitrant second soloist a reprieve until the end of the week.

In the late afternoon, I sneak out of the theater for a walk. Vika has insisted that I take fresh air and eat the sandwich she bought for me, hours prior. When I have made it as far as the Bronze Horseman, my phone vibrates.

"Hello, Dmitri," I say, looking for a bench. Failing that, I take a seat on the grass lawn, where others are lying out in the sun and reading.

"Are you outside? Taking a leisurely stroll in the middle of work?" he says. "Must not be that busy there."

"I have literally just stepped away for a minute. It's as chaotic as ever. And how is New York?"

"Great. It's the *greatest city* in the world," he says in a faux-bright voice. "No, it's covered in filth, the subways are a horror, and the other night I saw two rats the size of cats fighting to death over a pizza crust. Don't get me started on the mattresses. Why are there so many abandoned, stained mattresses on the sidewalk? It's overly represented, even considering other forms of trash. It simply defies explanation."

"Sounds like you miss Petersburg. But I'm sorry, I'm not giving your old job back."

"Don't want it. Natasha, there are things money can't buy. But money can buy *me*."

"They chose the right artistic director, then." I take a bite out of the sandwich.

"Yes, we see very much eye to eye. Americans *love* money. It's always very validating when stereotypes turn out to be true." Dmitri sighs. "I watched a clip of the piece you choreographed for the Staatsballett Berlin. It was nicely done."

I stop chewing the sandwich and clear my throat. "Thank you, Dmitri."

"A pas de trois—two men, one woman," he says.

"I know, Dmitri, I created it," I say.

"I want my company to dance it in the summer season at the Met." Dmitri pauses and I can hear the snippets of his coffee order. "Come stage it. It would be good for you."

I take a big breath, my mind plunging into my 2030 calendar, already packed with breathtaking density. Next spring, the National Ballet of Ukraine and Mariinsky are performing in Asia with a joint touring company. This is what's taking all my energy, outside of our main program, but of course, Dmitri knows this—he is the one who masterminded the project, reaching deep into his contacts from the top of the ballet world. I wasn't far behind, waxing poetic on many stages and ten times as many Zoom meetings about art's sacred duty to unveil our humanity, heal our pain, and restore our conscience.

Sometimes my head spins with the frivolity of words; I don't really believe that our dancing together—or even the most transcendent art of any kind—can change a broken world. Art cannot feed the forgotten, protect the innocent, or bring back the dead. But more often—when I see something moving on stage, in a studio, on my way home—I can't help but believe there is a place where truth and beauty meet. I may not be able to reach this place or stay there very long. But I feel its nearness in the evening air, and that is enough.

"Your tour finishes mid-June. You can come to New York after that," Dmitri adds.

"What if I'm afraid of rats?"

"Don't be ridiculous. They only come out at night," he scoffs. "Hey, I have to go. Just think about it."

"I'll think about it."

It is almost midnight when I come home after the show. Finn greets me at the door; I pick him up with one arm and set the keys and the purse down with the other. There is a box on the dining room table, and I have to think for a moment before I realize that it's the package from earlier. I leave it there and head to my dressing room, peeling off layers of the day along the way. Magnus calls when I'm in my pajamas. He's just arrived in Niger to build climate-resilient housing complexes using indigenous methods and materials.

We met three years ago, standing in line at the airport in Amsterdam. He flustered me by asking me so many questions. I didn't know what this absurdly handsome and probably arrogant man in a well-tailored suit wanted from me. That he would voluntarily travel in such attire made him seem like a greedy corporate drone, not someone who eats vegan, develops green housing for underserved communities, or adopts a black cat specifically because "they're unadoptable." At first I was sharp and imperious, but somehow he softened me over the three-hour flight. By the time we landed in St. Petersburg, I'd agreed to dinner at his place the next night.

Although he was staying at an Airbnb, Magnus managed to cook a Lebanese feast of mujadara, hummus, and cucumber salad. He didn't like Norwegian food, he said. After we mopped up all the olive oil on our plates, we made love on the kitchen counter, the couch, the bed. He filled every part of me. It wasn't the kind of sex after which you wake hungry and sick with desire, but one that leaves you nourished, balanced, and content. And to his credit, spending time with Magnus has always had that effect on me. It's just that we don't spend enough time together. I suppose I should have been forewarned by meeting him at the airport.

I ask him about the project and the weather in Niger. His colleagues are wonderful, and it is intensely dry and hot.

"And how was your day?" he asks.

"Hmm. Very long," I reply. Early on, I realized that Magnus asked me about dance to be attentive, but he wasn't really that interested in it. He listened carefully and conscientiously, but with little comprehension and no joy. He enjoyed seeing a ballet like someone watching a movie in a foreign language. Eventually I stopped trying to share this side of me.

"It never ends," he says. "Hey, I have good news."

"Hmm?"

"I got a call from my friend about a property on Fontanka Embankment. It's not even on the market yet. It's not a historic building, so we can demolish it and rebuild from scratch. I think this is going to be our new home." He sounds happy, and I imagine him pacing the room in excitement.

"That's wonderful. Magnus, I'm tired and need to get to bed. I'll send you a photo of Finn."

We take turns saying I love you before hanging up. Finn jumps onto my lap and I stroke his fur for a while.

About five years ago, I visited Mama's old building one last time before it was torn down. Seryozha came with me; his parents had been one of the final families to vacate the *khrushchevka*. I'd feared the doors would be locked and barred, but all the entrances had been left open. In the several months since clearing out Mama's belongings, the *khrushchevka* had deteriorated further, as if its last remaining vitality had dissipated when the holdout residents left. Each time we spoke in the echoing hallway, the cracks in the wall seemed to spread. We walked through the rooms in Mama's apartment, saying goodbye in silence.

Then we went to Seryozha's old apartment across the courtyard. I could remember being there only a few times over the years. The floor plan was, of course, the same as our own. I put my head out the window. From this side of the building, I could see in the distance the warehouses and empty factories that would soon also be demolished and turned into new condos and offices. The twilight sky was streaked with ochre, purple, and the cawing of crows. They hung off the electric lines in a flock of hundreds. Then at an unknown cue, the birds took flight all at once. More joined them midair, so that the sky was black with thousands of crows flying wing to wing.

"Look, Seryozha!" I pointed, and he moved closer to me. The birds had created a massive sphere, and now they swirled down like a tornado. Just like in my dreams. "I've seen those crows before," I said, shivering.

"Ah, the rooks. Yes, they've been doing that since we were little. I used to watch them from right here. Didn't you have that view from your side?" Seryozha said, smiling. I shook my head.

"They roost in the smokestack of that abandoned factory. That's how they get inside." Seryozha nodded at the noisy formation in the sky, funneling into the chimney like black smoke going in the wrong direction. "These hawks come by every evening to hunt them. They typically take one or two rooks at least."

"Why don't they go somewhere else without the hawks?" I turned away, feeling sorry for the rooks. I didn't want to see any potential hawk dinnertime situation.

"Well, I guess because it's their home," Seryozha said, pulling the window shut. "Coming home is a very strong instinct. Even stronger than the fear of death."

Something clicked when I heard Seryozha speak.

"*Korit' ptits*," I said. "Pavel thought he said 'blame birds.' But it was *kormit' ptits*. 'Feed birds.'"

I renewed my search for Nikolai, but he was nowhere to be found. It's been years since anyone has seen or heard of him. One day though, I think he may be able to find his way home.

Is Magnus my home? I'm not sure, although I know who isn't my home. I have spoken with him a few times over the years since our last *Giselle.* If we happened to be in the same city at the same time, one of us would reach out. Over dinner, we would talk about our work—my choreography or directing, and his occasional gala performances and guesting; new art that we've seen or heard; and subtly about our partners, if we were in a relationship at the time. Like me, he remains unmarried, although I've passed the point of caring about that specific distinction.

What matters to us is that *Giselle* was the last time we both experienced a greater power take hold of us. We agree that this was the best day of both of our lives and that nothing can surpass it. When you share such a thing with someone, does it matter whether you're married to that person or to someone else, or in love with that person or someone else?

Finn nuzzles his nose in my palm, which is his way of demanding treats. I rise and go to the kitchen, and get distracted by the package from Paris that's still sitting on the dining room table. I wonder if it's from Sasha, although it isn't like him to send me surprise gifts. Ignoring Finn's pleas, I grab a box cutter and slice open the tape. From underneath a layer of bubble wrap, I pull out a photography book. The cover is sheathed in black fabric, and the title and author are etched in silver typeface:

Memento Vitae

Léon Mansouri

There is no note or signature anywhere. I keep turning the glossy pages, which are filled with black-and-white photographs of dancers: dressed in costume and waiting in the wings, rehearsing in Studio Lifar, warming up in the Foyer de la Danse. I recognize many of the dancers, although some are after my generation. My hands stop flipping at a double-page spread of Sasha in rehearsal, kicking his leg high, radiating joy even without a smile on his face. This must be when I brought Léon to our rehearsal one day; and on the very next page, there Sasha and I are together, our necks tenderly aligned and arms entwined, absorbed in our pas de deux. More familiar memories: Sasha holding court with Théa at the after-party, Dmitri smoking a cigarette by himself, me holding a cocktail and smiling into the camera in that "fuck you" Chanel dress. Me again, looking pensive and struck in front of *Le mur des je t'aime.*

Then on the very last page, there is my favorite photo he took of me in *Swan Lake.* Dressed as Odette, I am leaping high above the heads of the corps de ballet. When I close my eyes, I can still feel the hush of the auditorium as I took to the air, the soft gasp of disbelief, the moment of triumph, the years of sacrifice.

Next to the photo, Léon has scribbled in purple ink his only message to me:

Alis volat propriis (she flies with her own wings).

I close the book when Finn's cries of hunger become impossible to ignore. After feeding him treats, I put the memories away on my coffee table.

No matter how great a work of art is, it comes to an end. In fact, in order to be great, it *must* end.

But life never comes to an end. When one thread is knotted, even when another is broken, it continues weaving together to an everlasting music so that the whole of it can only be seen from the height of infinity.

AUTHOR'S NOTE

When I was an assistant in book publishing in the early 2010s, an editor cautioned against a fiction writer's abuse of acknowledgments, author's note, or bibliography, perhaps to "show off" one's depth of research. Personally, I think an author should feel free to explain as much (or as little) as she wants, but I understand the reasons for the editor's injunction. It would be ridiculous to see a bibliography of medieval Danish literature at the end of *Hamlet*. We're not reading it or seeing it onstage with the expectation that Shakespeare should cite his sources and defend the sufficiency of his research.

Nevertheless, I want to share a few of the literary inspirations behind this novel, because while writing it I felt in communion with other artists and works of art. And also, as a very occasional literary translator, I couldn't imagine not properly acknowledging the translators by name.

The first Anna Akhmatova epigraph is from "I haven't covered the little window" (1916) translated by Andrey Kneller. The second epigraph is from her "Fragment" (1959) translated by A. S. Kline. Act I opens with an epigraph from Nikolai Gogol's "Nevsky Prospekt" (1835), as translated by Richard Pevear and Larissa Volokhonsky. Also in Act I, the lines from Dante's *Inferno* are translated by John Ciardi. Act II epigraph is a version of Anton Chekhov's advice to fellow writers. I was unable to find its translator, but another version of it exists in *Chekhov Plays* (Wordsworth Editions, 2007) translated by Elisaveta Fen: "Let the things that happen on the stage be just as complex and yet just as simple as they are in life." The excerpt of "Habanera" from *Carmen* was translated from French by Lea F. Frey.

The source of Nijinsky's vatic epigraph is *The Diary of Vaslav Nijinsky: Unexpurgated Edition*, translated by Kyril Fitzlyon and edited by Joan Acocella. Finally, Ludwig van Beethoven is said to have uttered *Plaudite, amici, comedia finita est*—a phrase that can be traced to the end of plays in ancient Rome—on his deathbed.

City of Night Birds is an homage to artists who have inspired me for the better part of my life. Many of the composers, ballet dancers, and choreographers are already named in the text. On the literary side, I looked to the great Vasily Aksyonov. Most of all, I was deeply moved by the poetry and lives of Akhmatova and her fellow Acmeists. I am indebted to Nancy K. Anderson for *The Word That Causes Death's Defeat*, which comprises Akhmatova's "Requiem" and "Poem Without a Hero" in translation as well as a luminous biography of the poet.

ACKNOWLEDGMENTS

While working on *City of Night Birds*, so many readers of my first novel reached out to tell me they were waiting for my second. Without these readers around the world, I don't know if I would have kept writing. I'm grateful to each and every one of them, more than I can properly express.

Jody Kahn has been the most intelligent first reader, valiant champion, brilliant agent, and trusted confidante of mine in almost a decade of representing me. Thank you, Jody, and the rest of Brandt & Hochman, for your steadfast support. With patience, wisdom, and style (a combination found in the best editors), Sara Birmingham saw through the workings of this novel and asked it to become the best version it could ever be. (Any failure thereof is mine and mine alone.) I offer my deepest gratitude to Sara, Helen Atsma, Miriam Parker, Shelly Perron (who sagaciously copyedited both of my novels), TJ Calhoun, Deborah Ghim, and to everyone at Ecco. I am beyond thankful to the translators and international literary consultants of my first novel, who offered me their friendship and advice throughout the writing of my second novel. I was sustained by the sincerity, warmth, and ingenuity of Luis Girão, a professor at the University of São Paulo, Korean-Portuguese translator, and literary agent (he wrote the foreword to the Brazilian edition of *Beasts of a Little Land*). Kirill Batygin, who translated the Russian edition of *Beasts*, gave me invaluable insight about *City of Night Birds*, including its title and some Russian phrases.

Thank you also to my early readers, Mary Hood Luttrell, Bethany Hudson, Olivia Chen, Renee Rutledge, Kate Ristau, and Cassidy Klingman. I'm grateful to my ballet teachers who inspired a lifelong passion for this art, especially Ilana Suprun-Clyde at Princeton University and Xander Parish, international principal dancer and founder of Balletclass.com, whose gentle encouragement and beautiful classes became the silver lining during the challenging years of writing this book.

Since long before drafting *City of Night Birds*, I've been interested in the Horn of Africa. It is one of the regions most affected by the climate crisis, to which Africans themselves have contributed a negligible amount. Facing consecutive historic droughts, farmers and herders have been forced to give up their millennia-old traditions in search of water, food, and a path to survival. The war in Ukraine sent shock waves throughout the world and worsened the already-dire food insecurity in the Horn. I'm grateful to Caritas Internationalis and Caritas Somalia for the lifesaving work they do in one of the world's most neglected regions, and for allowing me to contribute a portion of my proceeds from *City of Night Birds* in hopes of peace and humanitarianism in Africa, as well as the rest of the world. I would also like to thank Regional Arts and Culture Council for supporting the writing of this book with a grant. I'll always be grateful that RACC gave me much-needed encouragement at crucial points of my literary career.

I try and continue to fail to write a book about a complete loner, because my friendships occupy too much space in my life to imagine otherwise: thank you, Renee Serell, for always uplifting and nurturing me; thank you, Elise Anderson, for reading my half-baked drafts with undeserved enthusiasm, ever since I was an unagented baby writer with big hopes and an even bigger, barely functioning laptop. Thank you, Dylan, for the decaf oat lattes, without which reviewing the proofs of this book would have been impossible. My parents have supported me with unconditional love and zeal throughout the writing of this book. Their belief in me makes me think the impossible is possible. Last but not least, my husband, David, and our ZOK family, whose love gives me strength and courage beyond my own limits. Green velvet couch, sunshine, Zeus and Ody piled on my lap—that's what I'll always remember about the writing of this book. To David, I offer a rose from my bouquet at the curtain call of *City of Night Birds*.